To Terry Wright, whose foresight and enterprise created the ISBSG

About the Editor

Peter Hill is the chief executive officer and a director of the International Software Benchmarking Standards Group (ISBSG). He has been in the information services industry for more than 40 years, with broad experience covering a number of industries working in both Australia and New Zealand.

For 12 years from 1982, Peter was the executive director and a major shareholder of an Australian software company.

Since selling his interest in the software company, Peter has headed up the ISBSG, a not-for-profit organization with a membership of 13 countries. Peter has been a speaker at conferences in Australia, Asia, Europe, and the USA. He has a number of published articles covering key aspects of the information services industry. He is a member of the China Software Process Improvement Network International Advisory Committee and was a past chairman, secretary, and fellow of the Australian Computer Society.

Peter has compiled and edited five books for the International Software Benchmarking Standards Group: *Software Project Estimation, The Benchmark Release 6, The Benchmark Release 8, Practical Project Estimation* (three editions), and *The Software Metrics Compendium.*

About the Technical Editor

David Cleary (david.cleary@charismatek.com) is a senior consultant with Charismatek Software Metrics in Melbourne, Australia. During his 20 years in the IT industry, he has worked in the areas of software development, software tool research, tertiary education, and software metrics and measurement.

At Charismatek, David provides consultancy and training services in Function Point Analysis, software project estimation, and benchmarking. He has major interests in the application of measurement to new and evolving software delivery technologies and in the effective use of software tools for software project estimation. He is also actively involved in the ongoing research into and development of Charismatek's Function Point WORKBENCH™ software tool.

Over many years David has been involved in the International Software Benchmarking Standards Group (ISBSG) as a member of its Technical and Product Advisory Committee. He has contributed to publications and to tool development including the *Practical Project Estimation* book editions and the *Comparative Estimating Tool.*

Practical Software Project Estimation: A Toolkit for Estimating Software Development Effort & Duration

International Software Benchmarking Standards Group
Compiled and edited by Peter R. Hill

New York Chicago San Francisco
Lisbon London Madrid Mexico City
Milan New Delhi San Juan
Seoul Singapore Sydney Toronto

The McGraw·Hill Companies

Library of Congress Cataloging-in-Publication Data

Practical software project estimation : a toolkit for estimating software development effort & duration / Compiled and edited by Peter R. Hill.
p. cm.
Includes bibliographical references and index.
ISBN 978-0-07-171791-5 (alk. paper)
1. Computer software—Development—Estimates. 2. Computer software—Development—Costs. I. Hill, Peter R.
QA76.76.D47P697 2011
005.1—dc22 2010030530

McGraw-Hill books are available at special quantity discounts to use as premiums and sales promotions, or for use in corporate training programs. To contact a representative, please e-mail us at bulksales@mcgraw-hill.com.

Practical Software Project Estimation: A Toolkit for Estimating Software Development Effort & Duration

1 2 3 4 5 6 7 8 9 0 DOC DOC 1 0 9 8 7 6 5 4 3 2 1 0

ISBN 978-0-07-171791-5
MHID 0-07-171791-9

Sponsoring Editor
Wendy Rinaldi

Editorial Supervisor
Janet Walden

Project Manager
Madhu Bhardwaj, Glyph International

Acquisitions Coordinator
Joya Anthony

Technical Editor
David Cleary

Copy Editor
Jan Jue

Proofreader
Claire Splan

Indexer
Claire Splan

Production Supervisor
Jean Bodeaux

Composition
Glyph International

Illustration
Glyph International

Art Director, Cover
Jeff Weeks

Cover Designer
Jeff Weeks

Contents at a Glance

Contents

Foreword

The 1982 initial estimate for the Central Artery/Tunnel project in Boston, MA, was $2.2 billion. Congress approved funding in 1987 and construction began in 1991. Aptly nicknamed the "Big Dig," the project was plagued with serious miscalculations and the budget and time schedule escalated considerably. By 1994, the project estimate inflated to almost $10 billion, according to financial reports released by the Commonwealth of Massachusetts assessors and the Federal General Accounting Office. By early 2000, it became publicly known that the project would be well over and above the $10 billion limit. While there was much political upheaval and firings, the project went on. In the end, the original estimate of $2.2 billion ballooned to a final cost exceeding $22 billion, the project lasted 13 years, and the finished product was characterized by fewer features than had been planned, of poorer quality, and at the cost of a life.

In 1996, soon after the first CHAOS University event, we decided to run three special focus groups in Boston, Chicago, and San Francisco. In these groups, we invited four Fortune 500–type organizations. Each organization brought a team of senior IT, financial, and software development executives. We asked each team to choose a project and to write down on a card their resolution using our triple constraint standard. Then we polled each team in turn. One of the team answers was most memorable. In this team, the project manager's card read "successful," the CIO's card read, "challenged," and the CFO's card read, "failed."

In a follow-up round, we asked the PM why he thought the project was successful. He replied that although the project was a little late, over budget, and missing some functions, "We got it done." The now visibly irritated CIO said, "I don't think a million dollars over budget and a year late is *little*." The CFO replied, "Yes, it cost twice as much and took twice as long, but none of that really matters; we are just not using the product." We then went around the table to the other organizations to talk about their projects.

In the next round of questions, we came back to the PM to ask if he had changed his mind. He had; he considered what the CFO said and now felt it was a failed project because it did not deliver a useful product. The CFO then said she thought that the PM and the development organization did their jobs but that it was a failure of the organization, so she would now call the project a success because it had been completed. The CIO was looking very perplexed and bewildered. Shaking his head he said, "I just don't know, it is not a success, but is it a failure? I just don't know! I am undecided."

Here we had one project, three people, and six different answers. We went through two more rounds of projects, for a total of 36 projects in the three focus group sessions. Everyone struggled with defining their results. Of the 36 projects tested, there were several that all three agreed on, but only one project that all three people said was a success.

Having an accurate project budget is a key component of measuring success. You might consider accurate estimates an oxymoron, like jumbo shrimp or military intelligence, because the definition of each component contradicts the other. *Accuracy* means conforming closely to some standard. It is being precise or having just a very small error of any kind. An *estimate* is calculating approximately the amount, extent, magnitude, position, or value of a project. It is an opinion or a rough guess about the cost, time, and scope of a project. Therefore, an accurate estimate means to have a close guess. With project estimates, as in the game of horseshoes, closeness counts. And also like horseshoes, accurate estimates require skill, experience, information, and luck for a good outcome.

Yogi Berra once said, "It's tough to make predictions, especially about the future." Let's face it, creating accurate predictions for a software project is hard. The delta between expectations and reality is often disappointment. In developing a more systematic approach toward project estimating, you need to face a bit of realism. Truly reliable estimates are rare. Profiling one project against others to isolate costs is tricky and difficult at best, but this approach is much better than many of the alternatives. Having multiple estimation techniques is even better. Accurate estimates require good tools, lots of historical data, experienced people, and a good to very good understanding of the scope of the project.

The Standish Group research shows that only 4 percent of IT executives believe their organization is highly skilled at estimating software projects. Another 28 percent think they are at least skilled, but over two thirds believe this is an area of much needed improvement. In this regard, most IT executives believe that there has only been slight or no improvement in skills for accurately estimating software projects over the last few years. Therefore, our conclusion is that not only are we bad at estimating project costs and schedules, we are not getting any better.

We often joke that there are two types of estimates, lucky and lousy. Fortunately, this book, *Practical Software Project Estimation*, can help you and your organization improve your software estimates and thereby improve your project delivery. Having this great source of project cost data provides additional luck, and using this resource can make your estimates less lousy.

Jim Johnson, Chairman
The Standish Group

Acknowledgments

A special thanks to the following companies and individuals who contributed to the production of this book:

- David Cleary of Charismatek Software Metrics, who was the technical editor for the content and was responsible for Chapter 13 with the excellent estimating examples and case studies and for Chapter 14. David also provided all manner of support during compilation and editing.
- Pam Morris of Total Metrics for content in Chapters 5 and 6, for Chapter 15 on estimating cost, and for reviewing other chapters.
- Pekka Forselius of 4SUM Partners, Finland, who acted as a content planner and reviewer as well as providing valuable content, particularly for the chapter on software size estimation.
- Charles Symons for the COSMIC FSM content and for providing a host of valuable suggestions.
- Carol Dekkers of Quality Plus Technologies Inc., who provided valuable input with content for Chapter 1 plus the complete Chapters 18 and 19.
- Dr. Chris Lokan of the University of NSW—Australian Defence Force Academy (and the principal ISBSG analyst) for the estimation analysis, project delivery rate tables, and content of Chapter 3.
- Luca Santillo of Agile Metrics and Luigi Buglione of the Italian Software Metrics Association (ISMA-GUFPI) for content for Chapters 5, 10, and 12.
- Michael Stringer for his revision work on Chapters 11 and 16.
- Rob Thomsett of The Thomsett Company for allowing the use of material from his book *Third Wave Project Management*.

- George Ansell, the ISBSG Repository Manager, for his reviews, input, and advice.

The following organizations are sponsors of the ISBSG:

- Software Productivity Research
- Agile Metrics
- Charismatek Software Metrics
- Quality Plus Technologies
- Total Metrics
- 4SUM Partners
- The Victorian State Government—Australia

ISBSG Member contact details can be found in Appendix F.

Introduction

The Problem

The results reported in the Standish Group's report "CHAOS Summary 2009" showed a marked decrease in project success rates, with only 32 percent of projects succeeding; that is, they are delivered on time, on budget, with required features and functionality. Forty-four percent were "challenged," meaning they were late, over budget, and/or had less than the required features and functionality. Twenty-four percent failed; that is, they were canceled prior to completion, or delivered and never used.

This report showed a decrease in the success rates from the previous study, as well as a significant increase in the number of failures. They were the worst in the last five study periods, with the highest failure rate in over a decade.

The Standish reports have identified formal parametric-based estimating as one of the key requirements for project success. Capers Jones[1] reported similar results, identifying formal cost-estimating as the leading factor preventing project failures; those projects estimated using formal tools and methodologies were twice as likely to succeed compared with the projects estimated using informal methods.

NOTE *Projects estimated using formal tools and methodologies are twice as likely to succeed compared with projects estimated using informal methods.*

Software development is a risky, complex, and costly process. The complexity of the task means that it is difficult to predict development effort and schedules.

Where a fee is being charged for the development of software, the impact on the business of poor estimates of software development effort, schedules, and associated costs is easy to appreciate. Depending upon the method of charging, either the IT service provider or the client will experience direct, unscheduled, and unexpected financial losses.

[1] Capers Jones, Chief Scientist Emeritus SPR, www.SPR.com.

Less obvious is the impact in organizations where no "real" money is paid for IT services. However, even in these organizations, poor prediction of software costs and other project outcomes will impact the business bottom line in a number of ways:

- Missed delivery dates can mean lost business.
- Resources allocated to a "failing" project can mean lost opportunity to progress with other projects.
- A canceled project usually means money spent for no delivered business value.
- Cost overruns, whether against budget or expectations, can mean that the business case for IT investment in the project is no longer valid.

Consequently, it is important to any business to ensure that software development estimates are as accurate as they can be, using the information available at the time of estimation. Estimates need to be preceded by a thorough risk analysis and then be based on measured or quantified experience. The method of derivation should be verifiable and defensible. It is also critical—both for the organization and the project team—that the effort estimates and associated scheduled delivery dates for the software project are achievable.

The Solution

Software project estimation is not a black art. There are well-defined estimating techniques, project history repositories, and reliable estimating equations available. In this book our intention is to provide information and practical estimating techniques—primarily based on the International Software Benchmarking Standards Group (ISBSG) software project history data—that will assist project managers with the task of estimating the three key variables that follow the establishment of software project requirements, namely: Size, Effort, and Duration.

A large part of the content of this book is based on the utilization of the project data collected by the ISBSG to produce accurate software estimates. At the time of writing, the Development & Enhancement Repository contains data from more than 5,000 completed projects from around the world.

The complete ISBSG data set is available on the "Estimating, Benchmarking & Research Suite," which can be licensed from www.isbsg.org.

This book has been developed for those professionals who recognize the need for sound project estimates but who need the information and tools to achieve that objective.

Readers are not expected to be knowledgeable of, or proficient in, the use of functional size measurement. For those who are interested, chapters provide simple explanations and examples of how to use a functional size measure. It is important to reference the Glossary to gain a clear understanding of the key terms used in this book, for example, "project delivery rate," "speed of delivery," "functional size," and so on.

All project managers, professional system developers, and lecturers in information technology should find a wealth of useful information in this book.

A Map of This Book

The following table helps to quickly identify which chapters to focus on to obtain answers to a number of commonly asked questions about project estimation, listed in the first column. The second column indicates the first chapter to focus upon to obtain answers to the question in the first column. The third column indicates any chapters that further expand upon the issues described in the chapter referenced in the second column.

Question	Chapter	For Additional Information
How accurate have estimates been for completed projects?	Chapter 3	Appendix D
How can I get an early estimate of software size?	Chapter 5	Chapters 17 to 22
Are there multiple ways of estimating? What are they?	Chapter 1	Chapters 6, 7, 8, 9, and 10
I know the effort required, but can I meet the deadline?	Chapter 7	Appendix C
What if my project contains quite different components?	Chapter 11	
How can I standardize and formalize my estimating?	Chapter 16	Appendix B
Are there existing formulas that I can use for my estimates?	Appendix C	Chapter 7
Are Agile projects different?	Chapter 14	
Is there a way that I can check the completeness of requirements?	Chapter 6	
What is in the ISBSG Repository of project data?	Appendix A	Glossary

Whether you are looking for a quick indicative estimate for a feasibility report; a detailed estimate for a quotation or capital expenditure request; or a way to standardize and formalize your quoting, this book provides what you need.

This publication has been developed for those professionals who face the day-to-day challenge of coming up with credible estimates for effort and duration of software projects. Readers are not expected to be knowledgeable of, or proficient in the use of, functional size measurement. For those who are interested, there are chapters that provide simple explanations and examples of how to measure software size using a functional size measure.

As well as the professionals who produce estimates, other system developers, project managers, students, and lecturers should find a wealth of useful information here.

CHAPTER 1

Project Estimation: Background, Concepts, and Approaches

In this chapter we explain the typical and distinct types of requirements that make up a software development or enhancement project; the various effort estimation approaches that are covered in this book; what is involved in producing a detailed estimate; and the use of functional size[1] measurement in effort estimation.

Throughout this book we concentrate on estimating the effort and duration involved in a software project. Effort and duration estimation normally leads to the estimation of cost, so we have provided an introduction to cost estimation in Chapter 15.

Types of Project Requirements

Before we delve into the different estimation approaches, it is important to understand the different types of requirements that make up a project and to be aware of what is, and is not, included in the estimation approaches in this book.

The project estimation approaches explained in this book rely on the functional size of the software as a key input variable and are

[1] *Functional size* is the size of the software to be developed. It is expressed in units such as *function points*. The units may vary depending on the chosen functional size measurement method (FSMM). Functional size measurement can be compared to the measurement of a building being expressed in square meters or square feet.

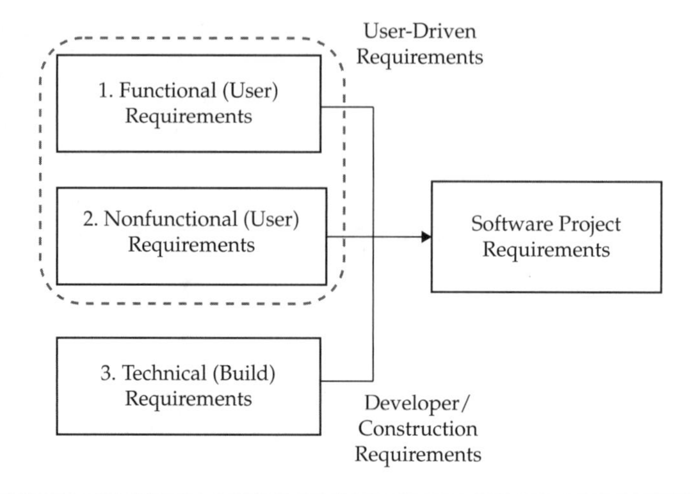

FIGURE 1-1 Types of software development project requirements

applicable to projects where software is developed or enhanced. This will be explained further after the discussion on types of requirements, since not every project that involves software or systems is suitable for functional size measurement. Functional size measurement pertains specifically to projects where software is developed, modified, or enhanced.

To make sense of functional size measurement and where it fits with estimating, it is useful to discuss the three types of software project requirements. Figure 1-1 shows the different types of software project requirements. Elsewhere in this book we will discuss a number of ways to establish the functional size of a piece of software without needing detailed knowledge of functional sizing.

NOTE *The word "user" in the context of functional size measurement means any person or thing that interacts with the software at any time (such as other pieces of software, hardware, end users, and administrators) that has a requirement for data or services supported by the software being developed.[2] This is an important concept because functional size measurement can be used to size software that has no human users. For example, the software interacts with other software or hardware. It may be useful to think of a "user" as analogous to an actor in the Use Case methodology. (For other definitions, refer to the Glossary.)*

As depicted in Figure 1-1, project requirements can be categorized into three distinct types (this breakdown also increases understanding

[2] For a definition of "user" in the context of functional size, refer to ISO/IEC 14143-1:2007 as (ISO, 2007) standard.

between the users and the project team). The three types of requirements are as follows:

- **Functional requirements** These represent WHAT functions will be included in the software. Functional requirements are the business processes performed by or supported by the software (for example, record and store ambient temperature) and include the functions that the software must perform. The size of functional requirements is expressed in function points.
- **Nonfunctional requirements** This is the second type of software requirement and represents HOW the software must perform. Nonfunctional requirements describe how the software must operate and are not included in functional size. Sometimes known as "quality requirements," the nonfunctional requirements include *suitability, accuracy, interoperability, compliance, security, reliability, efficiency, maintainability, portability,* and *quality in use,* as described by the ISO (International Organization for Standardization) standard ISO/IEC (International Electrotechnical Commission) 9126 series, plus a range of performance requirements. While these requirements should also be defined by the system's users/customers, they are often not articulated separately (or at all), but rather are sprinkled throughout requirements documents.

  The nonfunctional requirements are the contracted specifications for the software and include requirements for security (for example, data encryption), performance (for example, response time and reliability), accuracy (for example, governmental approvals required), and other specifications of how the software must perform.
- **Technical (build) requirements** These requirements address how the software will be developed or "built" and include tools, methods, type of project, resource skill levels, and so on. These requirements are where architectural design, configuration management methods, development methodology, use of packages, and use of CASE (Computer Aided Software Engineering) tools, for example, come into play. The technical requirements include hardware and software requirements, infrastructure requirements, database type, and so on.

All three types of project requirements are necessary to produce a realistic estimate of the total software project effort.

Functional Size

Knowing the functional size of the software to be developed is essential for macro estimation. Chapter 18 provides an introduction to functional sizing.

Functional size represents the size of the functional requirements. Functional size is an important input in software estimation, but it is only one of a number of required variables. For a new development project, functional size is the size of all of the delivered or installed functionality (analogous to a building's floor plan). For an enhancement project, functional size is the total size of all functional requirements that are new, renovated (changed), or removed (deleted) from the software.

Nonfunctional requirements fall outside functional size. The value adjustment factor (VAF)—which is an optional step in the IFPUG (International Function Point Users Group) function point method—is intended to address a portion of nonfunctional requirements.[3] According to industry experts including Barry Boehm (COCOMO II), Watts Humphrey (Software Engineering Institute), and Bill Perry (Quality Assurance Institute), the impact of nonfunctional requirements can double the effort required to develop software depending on the exact constraints involved.

NOTE *Functional size measurement pertains only to the size of the software's functional user requirements.*

Software Estimation Approaches

There are two major software estimation approaches: *macro* (for example, top-down; parametric) and *micro* (for example, bottom-up; task based), although some estimation approaches combine typical aspects of both macro and micro techniques. Within each approach are several estimating techniques, as shown in Table 1-1.

Note that the estimating techniques listed in Table 1-1 are the techniques presented in this book, not a definitive or exhaustive list of estimating techniques. Any of the techniques could be used at any point in the life cycle. However, the more accurate our estimate of the project's size, the more precise our effort and duration estimates can be. The relative precision of our resultant estimates will match the precision of our inputs.

Table 1-2 outlines some of the strengths and weaknesses of each estimation technique.

Note that all the macro techniques have problems with small projects as a result of the greater variation in the ratios of size to effort and duration typically seen in smaller projects.

---

[3] Note that the VAF may be phased out in the future and replaced by an alternative option.

Approach	Estimation Technique	When Applicable
Macro-Estimation	**Equation Use** In this method, the size of the project is applied to an appropriate equation that has been derived from project data. The result is a useful indicative, or "ballpark" estimate of effort and duration. Includes Program Evaluation and Review Technique (PERT) equations.	Useful when little information is known or when requirements are incomplete. High-level estimate.
	Comparison Essentially, this involves finding a group of completed projects with project attributes similar to those of the proposed project, and using the data from those projects to provide a guide for the estimate of the effort and duration for your new project.	Useful when enough project attributes and a range for the functional size are known. This allows the estimator to adequately gauge that the comparison projects are similar.
	Analogy This method is based on being able to find a completed project that is a very good match to your proposed project based on its major attributes. The project delivery rate and speed of delivery from the analog are then used to guide the estimate of the effort and duration for your new project.	Useful when even more information is known about the project being estimated. Best accomplished after requirements are complete.
Micro-Estimation	**Work Breakdown** In this method, the effort and duration associated with each component or activity of the software project is separately estimated and the results aggregated to produce an estimate of the whole job. This is a bottom-up technique.	Useful when the project scope is well defined and an accurate work breakdown structure can be defined. Typically, experienced project team members estimate their project tasks based on historical completed similar tasks, and the overall estimate is the aggregated sum of all work breakdown structure task estimates.

TABLE 1-1 Estimation Approaches and Techniques

Technique	Strengths	Weaknesses
Equation Use	Based on a depth of historical data. Ideal for an indicative estimate early in the life of a project.	Too imprecise for accurate estimation. You need to be confident that the equation being used is relevant to your project. The equation always provides an estimate, even if your project is unusual or exceptional. Not very useful for small project estimation.[4]
Comparison	Based on representative experience. Objective, repeatable, verifiable, defensible. Efficient and if used correctly, provides a good guide to the likely effort your project will consume.	Based on representative *past* experience that may no longer be relevant. For best results, the technique needs to be aligned to your environment/organization. Cannot be used when no past experience is available.
Analogy	Based on representative experience. Objective, repeatable, verifiable, defensible.	Based on a *past* experience that may no longer be relevant. Difficult to find suitable analog projects. For best results, needs to be closely aligned to your environment or organization.
Work Breakdown	Detailed and specific to this project.	Subjective, can be optimistic. Requires detailed knowledge of the proposed project's structure and individual components. Requires extensive knowledge of the organization and development environment. May overlook items or activities.

Table 1-2 Estimation Techniques Strengths and Weaknesses

[4] Although there is no *specified* size as to what constitutes a small project, for a project measured in function points, most software metrics consultants agree on a lower limit of around 30 function points.

Other Techniques

Techniques from artificial intelligence research have also been applied to develop software effort estimation models. For example, artificial neural networks and decision trees have been used to estimate effort. These methods do not require the user to propose an explicit functional form for the model, only the input and output metrics. These techniques are beyond the scope of this book.

Estimate Ranges

Remember that the earlier an estimate (or if there is little known data, a "guesstimate") is performed, the less accurate it will be. For this reason, when relaying an estimate to your customer, you should always provide a plus/minus range to accompany the estimate to indicate the degree of confidence in the estimate. Your original estimate is the most likely estimate, while upper and lower figures are generally the optimistic and pessimistic estimates. The Project Management Institute's Project Management Body of Knowledge (PMBOK® version 4) provides useful guidance on estimate ranges.

A number of equation approaches can be used to present a weighted average of the estimate (examples include PERT, CPM, Monte Carlo). The following example uses the Program Evaluation and Review Technique (PERT) approach to estimate likely effort for individual project activities:

$$Te = \frac{To + 4\,Tm + Tp}{6}$$

where

Te = expected effort
To = most optimistic estimate
Tm = most likely estimate
Tp = most pessimistic estimate

Rather than giving the customer a fixed, single number of effort hours, it is far more helpful to state: "Our estimate is 250 hours, plus or minus 50 hours, based on what we know about the project at this stage."

Timing of Estimates

Figure 1-2 shows you the impact that your increasing knowledge of the system requirements will have on the accuracy of your estimates.

Figure 1-3[5] is provided to assist you in deciding when particular estimating methods are most appropriate in the life cycle of your project.

[5] Figure 1-3 is supplied by Charles Symons of Software Measurement Services Ltd.

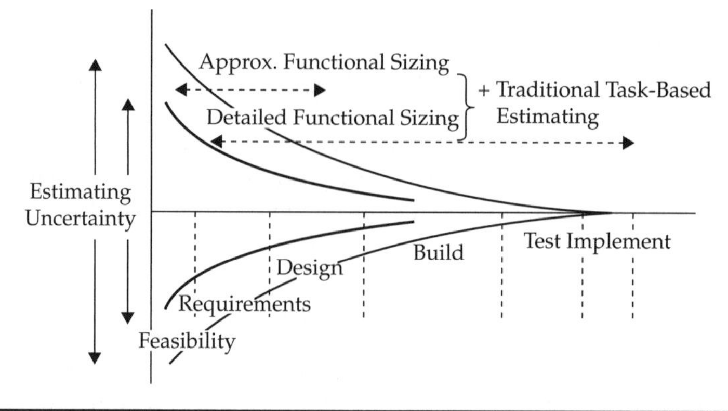

FIGURE 1-2 The cone of uncertainty

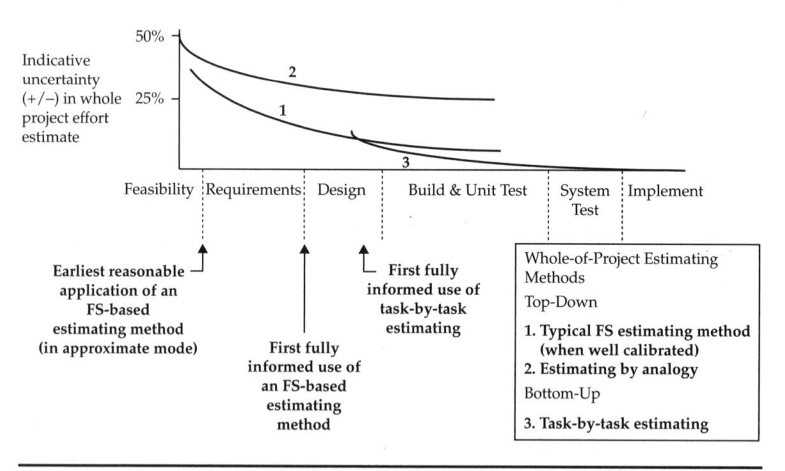

FIGURE 1-3 Estimating methods in the project life cycle

All of the macro-estimation techniques presented in this book can be applied with both approximate and detailed functional sizing. However, as the graph shows, the precision of the resultant estimates will improve as the precision of the functional sizing improves.

Producing a Detailed Estimate

To produce a detailed estimate—as opposed to an initial ballpark or indicative estimate for feasibility consideration—typically a micro-estimating technique (for example, work breakdown) will be used to develop the effort estimate. A macro-estimating technique can then be used to *validate* the micro-estimate.

NOTE *Where the macro- and micro-estimates vary by more than 10 to 15 percent, you should identify why and rework your estimates.*

Estimates are best derived from an organization's own experience database. You can build your own experience database by entering your project data in the ISBSG Repository.[6]

If you have not yet established your own "experience" database, you can use the ISBSG Repository as your source for macro-estimations.

NOTE *If you have entered data from your projects into the ISBSG Repository, you have the best of both worlds. You can extract your projects to derive the project delivery rate (expressed in hours per function point) to be used. Then you can extract similar projects from other organizations for comparison. The project data from other organizations will be particularly useful where you are estimating a project that includes a variable that you have no previous experience of, for example: a platform or language that you have not used previously.*

Functional size[7] is only one of the many variables known to influence effort, but it is recognized as a key driver. As the functional size increases, so does associated effort.

In its simplest form, this relationship is expressed as:

Effort = Size * Project Delivery Rate

where Project Delivery Rate is expressed as *Hours per Functional Point* and *hours* are effort hours.

If you are using comparison or analog macro-estimation methods,[8] the information shown in Table 1-3 should be included in your set of attributes for selecting similar projects.

Use your common sense when matching projects and/or adjusting project delivery rates. For example:

- If the only similar project identified was negatively impacted by the learning associated with the introduction of a new technology, but the skills acquired will be utilized by this project, then the project delivery rate (PDR) can be expected to be better (that is, have a lower PDR) than the similar project.
- If this project is similar to a previous project, with the exception that you have to provide additional deliverables (for example, a user manual), then the project delivery rate can be expected to be less productive (that is, higher).

---

[6] Refer to the appendixes for a detailed description of the data in the ISBSG Repository. Go to www.isbsg.org for information on how to submit projects for inclusion in the Repository.

[7] For the estimating examples in this book, the functional size measure used is units of function points according to the IFPUG method (FP). Note that all of the IFPUG releases use the same units of measure: IFPUG function points. At this printing, the most recent IFPUG release is IFPUG 4.3 (published in September 2009). For further information visit www.ifpug.org.

[8] Both these approaches are covered in detail in Chapter 13 in this book.

Project type	Development, Enhancement, or Redevelopment (on a new platform).
Size	Functional size measurement.
Project goals	In terms of quality, cost, schedule, and constraints (that is, priority of each). Note that *cost, scope* (functionality and quality), and *time* (effort) are the famous "triple constraint" of project management.
Development platform	Mainframe, midrange, PC, or multiplatform.
Language	Programming language or language level.
Task selection	Similar project profile in terms of activities and deliverables from those activities. (Phases and work activities included.)

TABLE 1-3 Attributes for Estimation by Comparison and Analogy

A commercial estimating tool can be used for estimating using industry data or your organization's experience or knowledge database. Be aware that you need to know the basics of software project estimating and how your organization supports estimation *before* shopping for an estimating tool.

Use of Function Point Sizing (Functional Size Measurement) in Effort Estimation

Functional requirements are sized in function points and are measured using a functional size measurement method such as COSMIC (Common Software Measurement International Consortium), FiSMA (Finnish Software Measurement Association), IFPUG, or NESMA (Netherlands Software Metrics Association). Each of these ISO/IEC standardized functional size measurement methods has its own units of measure and approach to determining functional size. A tutorial on functional size measurement can be found in Chapter 18. Simple case studies that illustrate the counting of function points are also provided.

Functional size has a role to play in both the macro- and micro-estimating approaches, as shown in Table 1-4.

Approach	Use of Functional Sizing
Macro-estimating	Functional size is a key input to most estimating equations and project comparisons.
Micro-estimating	The functional size allows you to calculate the "expected" project delivery rate for comparison with past projects.

TABLE 1-4 Use of Functional Size Approximation in Estimation Approaches

Summary

In this book we explain the three macro-estimation techniques in detail and define the data and tools that you need to appropriately use these techniques. We also provide an overview of micro-estimation.

Any technique is only as good as the data and information on which it is based. You cannot expect any technique to compensate for lack of definition, understanding, or agreement on the scope of the software job to be done. Just as a chain is only as strong as its weakest link, estimates of effort are only as reliable as the least reliable input variable.

And finally: *Never rely on a single estimation method for a project.* The more cross-checks and sanity checks you can employ, the better.

CHAPTER 2

Factors That Influence Productivity

Throughout this book we talk about project delivery rate (PDR) and refer to project attributes or characteristics that might influence the PDR that you use for your estimate. (PDR is the expression in hours per function point of how long it takes to deliver/develop functionality.) For the purposes of this book, two groups of project attributes will influence your estimates:

- Those that the ISBSG has identified and analyzed from its project repository data
- Those project-specific characteristics that are not recorded in a metrics repository

The first group impacts the various estimation techniques covered in this book; the latter group—project-specific characteristics—impacts the *adjustment* of the estimate you obtain from using the techniques in this book, to allow for the peculiarities of your organization, environment, and project.

This book does not cover risk analysis, but a detailed risk analysis should be undertaken prior to any project estimation. The risk analysis may highlight the factors that will influence the adjustment that you make to your estimates and the factors that might negatively impact the chances of project success.

NOTE *Formal risk assessment is an essential prerequisite for project estimation.*

Project Attributes That Influence Project Delivery Rate

The ISBSG has performed a detailed statistical analysis of the project data contained in its repository to identify the project attributes that influence productivity, and hence, estimates of effort and duration.

So what are the main factors that can have an impact on PDR? Only a few attributes seem to be consistently related to PDR.

Language and team size have been shown to impact PDR. Readers will be interested in platform (which reflects the development environment) and in the rates achieved by the different organization types and the business areas within organizations. These have been analyzed and a summary of the findings follows.

NOTE *Low project delivery rate means better productivity, fewer hours per function point.*

Are Some Languages Better Than Others?

A valuable breakdown considers project delivery rate for individual languages. The choice of languages tends to be governed by the choice of platform (PC, midrange, mainframe, or multiplatform). Detailed analysis showed that most languages are concentrated on a single type of platform; Java is the only language that is well represented on all platforms.

NOTE *ISBSG research has shown that the primary programming language is one of the two factors that have the greatest ability to explain variations in project delivery rate (team size[1] is the other).*

The observations in Tables 2-1 to 2-4 are based on an analysis of 1,681 projects from the repository (details on how these projects were selected are presented in Appendix B).

The project groups analyzed for midrange computers are generally smaller, so take care before you jump to a conclusion. The main 3GLs are COBOL, C, and Java.

PC projects now include quite a wide range of 3GLs and 4GLs.

For those languages that appear on more than one platform, some clear trends can be seen. Mainframe PDR values tend to be 15 hours or more per function point. On other platforms, PDR tends to be 8 to 12 hours per function point. PDR in multiplatform environments is generally close to PDR in PC environments, except with traditional 3GLs such as COBOL and PL/I. These observations probably reflect the better tools and interactive development environments available on non-mainframe platforms, especially for newer languages.

---

[1] The ISBSG collects data on and reports on Maximum Team Size (refer to the Glossary).

Language	Findings
Visual Basic	Visual Basic projects are spread across a wide range of project delivery rates. There are two main groups: about a quarter fall into the range from 1 to 5 hours per function point, and half into the range from 25 to 32 hours per function point. The mean is 25 and the median is 27 hours per function point.
Java	Java projects range evenly from 3 to 30 hours per function point, with half in the range from 11 to 27 hours per function point. The median and mean are both about 18 hours per function point.
COBOL	COBOL projects display a very wide distribution of PDR values: the full range from 1 to 80 hours per function point is represented. The distribution is skewed, though, with smaller values more common. The median is 17 hours per function point, and the mean is 23 hours per function point.
C/C++	Half of the C projects have PDR values between 8 and 16 hours per function point. A smaller group ranges from 22 to 30 hours per function point, and a few are over 50 hours per function point. The median is 16, and the mean is 22 hours per function point. C++ appears worse, with no clear pattern and "averages" over 30 hours per function point (median 32, mean 34).
Oracle	Oracle projects have quite a broad spread, but most PDR values are small. Over half are below 7 hours per function point; smaller groups are at around 20 and 30 hours per function point. The median is 7 hours per function point, and the mean is 12 hours per function point.
PL/I	Like COBOL projects, PL/I projects have a skewed distribution of PDR values, with smaller values more common. Almost half lie in the range from 1 to 10 hours per function point. Over one-third lie in the range from 13 to 25 hours per function point. The rest are scattered between 25 and 55 hours per function point. Mean and median project delivery rates are both about 14 hours per function point, but few projects are actually close to that value.
Scripting languages	Most projects that use scripting languages have PDR values below 15 hours per function point, but a few have much higher values. The median is 13 hours per function point, and the mean is 18 hours per function point.

TABLE 2-1 Languages – Mainframe Development Environments

Language	Findings
C/C++	Midrange C projects are similar to C projects on mainframe projects, with slightly better PDR in general. The median is 15 hours per function point, and the mean is 18 hours per function point. Unlike mainframe projects, on this platform C++ is better than C, with half in the range from 5 to 9 hours per function point and few above 20 hours per function point; the median is 8 hours per function point.
Java	Though the full range is from 4 to over 70 hours per function point, most Java projects lie in the range from 4 to 9 hours per function point; 9 hours is the median.
Oracle	Oracle projects range from 2 to 29 hours per function point. Most lie between 2 and 10 hours per function point, with median 9 and mean 11 hours per function point.
SQL	SQL projects vary greatly in range from 4 to 54 hours per function point, but most are below 20 hours per function point. The median is 13 hours per function point.

Table 2-2 Languages – Midrange Development Environments

Language	Findings
ASP	ASP projects range from 2 to 14 hours per function point. Median and mean are both 6 hours per function point.
Oracle	Oracle projects are spread fairly evenly from 1 to 33 hours per function point. The median is 9 and the mean is 10 hours per function point.
SQL	SQL ranges from 3 to 12 hours per function point, with an average of 5 hours per function point and a median of 4.
C/C++	Again, C projects appear to have better PDR rates than C++ projects, but the sample of C projects is small, so this conclusion is risky. Treating them as a single combined group, nearly all are between 3 and 15 hours per function point. The median is 10 hours per function point, and the mean is 14 hours per function point.
COBOL	COBOL ranges widely, from 3 to over 30 hours per function point. Almost half are below 6 hours per function point. The rest are scattered from 9 to 35 hours per function point. The median is 10 hours per function point, and the mean is 13 hours per function point.
Visual Basic	Visual Basic projects range from 1 to 24 hours per function point, but nearly all are below 12 hours per function point. The mean and median are both 7 hours per function point.
Java	Nearly all Java projects are between 2 and 12 hours per function point. The median is 8 hours per function point, and the mean is 9 hours per function point.

Table 2-3 Languages – PC Development Environments

Language	Findings
ABAP	ABAP projects have a spike (i.e., a most common value) at about 8 hours per function point; three-quarters are below 15 hours per function point. The median is 10 and the mean is 12 hours per function point.
C/C++	Most projects lie in the range from 2 to 13 hours per function point. The median is 5, and the mean is 10 hours per function point. In this environment, C and C++ projects appear indistinguishable in terms of PDR (though it must be noted that the sample sizes are small).
C#	PDR is notably poorer than for C or C++, in this data set. The range is 2 to 49 hours per function point, with most projects falling between 6 and 26 hours per function point. The mean is 17 and the median is 14 hours per function point.
COBOL	COBOL projects on multiplatforms resemble PC and midrange COBOL projects in their spread of PDR values, which is 3 to 30 hours per function point. This time, though, the values tend much more toward the higher end of the range. In terms of PDR, multiplatform COBOL projects most closely resemble mainframe COBOL projects. The mean is 23 and the median is 20 hours per function point.
Java	Nearly all Java projects fall between 4 and 10 hours per function point. The mean is 7 and the median is 6 hours per function point. This is similar to Java projects on midrange and PC platforms.
Lotus Notes	These projects are spread from 2 to 12 hours per function point, with most at 5 hours or fewer per function point. The median is 4 and the mean is 5 hours per function point.
PL/I	The range of project delivery rates is wide, from 8 to 62 hours per function point. Most are between 10 and 25 hours per function point; the median is 21 and the mean is 25 hours per function point.
Visual Basic	The range of project delivery rates is wide, from 1 to 61 hours per function point. Most are between 3 and 15 hours per function point; the median is 8 and the mean is 14 hours per function point.

TABLE 2-4 Languages – Multiplatform Development Environments

What Is the Impact of Team Size?

Maximum team size is known to be one of the most important factors that affects PDR. The ISBSG collects data on maximum team size. In Appendix B we provide a table that can be used to adjust PDR to allow for team size.

Once a team size exceeds five people, productivity decreases. Projects with maximum team sizes of five or more have significantly higher (worse) project delivery rates than projects with smaller teams. If the team size on your project will exceed five, allow for a greater range of error in the estimate.

What Other Project Attributes Are Interesting?

In addition to the two project attributes that have the most significant impact on PDR, some others are worth considering. Project attributes like business area, development platform, and so on, have been analyzed to see whether they appear to be associated with variations in project delivery rate. The analysis was done for each attribute separately. They all indicate factors that might be relevant in understanding delivery rates. You can do further analysis by using the ISBSG "Estimating, Benchmarking & Research Suite" to identify other factors that might be relevant to your organization and project.

Does the Platform Make a Difference?

To date, *development platform* has been the best indicator of the *environment* in which the project is being developed. So the term more correctly refers to the whole environment/process, not specifically to the hardware platform.

NOTE Development platform *actually indicates development process and environment.*

We split platforms into four types: PC, midrange, mainframe, and multiplatform. Mainframes have a broad range of project delivery rates. PCs show a narrower range of project delivery rate values, which reflects good predictability. PC-based projects also show a generally lower project delivery rate (that is, fewer hours per function point, which should reduce cost and project length). Coincidentally, midrange platforms are also midrange in their PDRs, not as good as PCs, but better and more predictable than mainframes.

There are two likely reasons for the major differences in productivity between PC, midrange, and mainframe development projects:

- The differences in the development process, such as how the software was specified, designed, tested, and documented
- The differences in the business environment, such as the number of business stakeholders and number of users

The ISBSG performed a detailed analysis of the differences between the PC, midrange, and mainframe projects. This analysis showed, as one might expect, that mainframe projects had more business units involved, and supported a larger numbers of concurrent users. Such factors would result in poorer (higher) hours per function point values, because of the additional effort required to communicate with and obtain input from a larger number of people.

Methodologies

The ISBSG's analysis revealed that mainframe projects make more frequent use of methodologies. The methodologies used on mainframe projects are likely to be purchased but then applied with some customization. In contrast, PC projects make infrequent use of methodologies, and the methodologies that are used on PC projects are likely to be written in-house.

Purchased methodologies are almost always comprehensive and detailed. Projects that follow them tend to produce a wide range of documents, such as specifications, designs, plans, change and issue lists, and test cases. In contrast, in-house methodologies tend to focus only on key parts of a software project's life cycle. Projects that follow in-house methodologies, or no methodology at all, tend to produce fewer documents. A software project that produces fewer documents is likely to have a better (lower) hours per function point value than a project that produces many documents.

Of course, software projects produce documents in order to communicate with multiple business units and to avoid the cost of rework resulting from poor specification, design, and planning. So there is likely to be a trade-off between project delivery rate and defects delivered.[2]

Development Platform Summary

The PC environment shows the best (that is, lowest) project delivery rates of the three platforms. Mainframe environments have the highest project delivery rates. Multiplatform environments have similar project delivery rates to PCs. If you use the regression equations provided in the appendixes, ensure that you choose the equations appropriate for the platform/environment that you are developing on.

Development Type

Project delivery rates for new developments are significantly different from those for enhancements. New developments average 8 to 12 hours per function point, and enhancements average 12 to 16 hours per function point. The difference is probably due to factors other than the development type; for example, a much greater proportion of enhancements were mainframe projects, whereas new developments include more PC projects.

Language Type

4GLs as a whole have significantly better (lower) project delivery rates than 3GLs.

Application Type

Management information systems (MISs) show better (that is, lower) project development rates than do transaction/production systems.

[2] Refer to the ISBSG Special Report: *Techniques and Tools – Special Report II.*

Application Architecture

PDR tends to be best for multitier systems and worst for client-server systems, with stand-alone systems falling somewhere in between. The difference is probably due to factors other than the architecture; in particular, in the projects studied here the maximum team size happens to be greatest for client-server projects and smallest for multitier systems.

Other Project-Specific Characteristics Known to Influence PDR

The list of project-specific characteristics known to influence software development productivity (and hence total effort) that have not been the subject of the ISBSG statistical analysis includes

- Intrinsic team skills
- Staff experience levels with the technology
- Level of technical innovation
- Use of contractors/part-time resources
- Product performance
- Quality attributes required
- Budget constraints
- Developers' environment
- Stability of requirements

These are some of the project-specific characteristics not included directly in the common estimation techniques, but which you must take into account when calculating the final total project effort or cost estimate.

Several different estimation methods are available that include these project-specific characteristics:

- COCOMO II: 23 productivity factors
- IFPUG value adjusted factor (VAF): 14 factors[3]
- FiSMA ND21 situation analysis for new development: 21 factors

All these methods ask the user to select from a list of the project-specific characteristics applicable to their project. Based on the selected values, the method gives a coefficient figure, which is a multiplier for the preliminary effort estimate counted from the software size and delivery rate. Table 2-5 shows the lists of productivity

[3] Note that the VAF is likely to be phased out in the future.

COCOMO II	VAF	FiSMA ND21
Project scale factor attributes:	**General system characteristics:**	**Project organizational factors:**
1. Precedentedness	1. Data communications	1. Involvement of the customer representatives
2. Development flexibility	2. Distributed data processing	2. Performance and availability of the development environment
3. Architecture/risk resolution	3. Performance	3. Availability of IT staff
4. Team cohesion	4. Heavily used configuration	4. Number of stakeholders
5. Process maturity	5. Transaction rate	5. Pressure on schedule
6. Required software reliability	6. Online data entry	**Process factors:**
7. Database size	7. End-user efficiency	6. Impact of standards
8. Product complexity	8. Online update	7. Impact of methods
9. Develop for reuse	9. Complex processing	8. Impact of tools
10. Documentation match to life-cycle needs	10. Reusability	9. Level of change management
11. Execution time constraint	11. Installation ease	10. Maturity of software development process
12. Main storage constraint	12. Operational ease	**Product quality factors:**
13. Platform volatility	13. Multiple sites	11. Functionality requirements
14. Analysis personnel capability	14. Facilitate change	12. Reliability requirements
15. Programmer personnel capability		13. Usability requirements
16. Personnel continuity		14. Efficiency requirements
17. Applications experience		15. Maintainability requirements
18. Personnel platform experience		16. Portability requirements
19. Language and tool experience		**People factors:**
20. Use of software tools		17. Analysis skills of staff
21. Multisite development		18. Application knowledge of staff
22. Required development schedule		19. Tool skills of staff
23. Other		20. Experience of project management
		21. Team skills of the project team

TABLE 2-5 Comparison of Popular Productivity Analysis Methods (*continued*)

COCOMO II	VAF	FiSMA ND21
Ratings: VL/L/N/H/VH/XH The meaning of each choice per factor is explained in Barry Boehm's book.[4]	**Ratings:** 0 = Not present, or no influence 1 = Incidental influence 2 = Moderate influence 3 = Average influence 4 = Significant influence 5 = Strong influence throughout The guidelines on how to determine degree of influence are explained in the IFPUG "Counting Practices" manuals.[5]	**Ratings:** -- = Circumstances much worse than in average – = Worse than in average +/– = Normal situation + = Circumstances better than in average ++ = Much better than in average The meaning of each choice per factor is explained in the FiSMA method definition document.[6]
Coefficient: The exact value of each choice per factor shall be calibrated by the user. The variance of coefficient depends on the calibration.	**Coefficient:** 0.65–1.35	**Coefficient:** 0.5–2.5 in practice, but theoretically between 0.1 and 15. Exact values of each choice per factor vary between 0.88 and 1.14, based on experience database.

Table 2-5 Comparison of Popular Productivity Analysis Methods

[4] *Software Cost Estimation with COCOMO II*, Barry Boehm et al (Prentice Hall).

[5] ISO/IEC 20926: Information Technology – Function Point Counting Practices Manual, ISO/IEC, 2003.

[6] Finnish Software Measurement Association, FiSMA ry, FiSMA Specification for ND21 available at: www.fisma.fi/in-english/methods.

factors for three commonly used methods. Note that COCOMO II is an effort/duration estimation technique where size along with many other factors is a key input, whereas IFPUG and FiSMA are sizing techniques that provide methods that adjust the counted size, not the likely productivity.

Some of the methods that analyze project-specific productivity factors cover the impact of code reuse with a single question. If the impact of reuse is a key issue for your projects, then you should evaluate which methods best address the inclusion of reuse.

Summary

Two project characteristics have the most impact on PDR: programming language and team size. Other project characteristics that can have an impact include development platform/environment, development type, application type, and application architecture. Having established a PDR for your estimate using the ISBSG data, you should then adjust it to reflect your specific environment.

CHAPTER 3

Software Estimates: How Accurate Are They?

Using the data from completed projects[1], this chapter will provide you with an idea of how people have gone about estimating their projects and how well they did it. Use the findings of this analysis to guide your approach to estimating and the allowances that you make to your estimate for the factors specific to your project. Use both macro- and micro-estimating techniques to obtain the most reliable estimate.

Submitters of project data to the ISBSG provide details of the estimation techniques they use in their projects, as well as both estimated and actual project statistics. Values for the four key project attributes are sought: project effort, duration, cost, and size.

The ISBSG Data Repository now has over 850 projects for which estimation data is available. Of those, 691 provide estimated and actual project statistics for one or more of the attributes of effort, cost, duration, and size; 661 provide data about estimation techniques used; and 632 projects provide data about statistics and methods.

This chapter presents an analysis of those projects. It summarizes the estimation techniques used, the accuracy of the estimates, and the relationships between estimates.

In most respects these projects are typical of the full set of projects in the ISBSG Data Repository. So the value of the findings presented here is the same as the value of the ISBSG Data Repository as a whole. The ISBSG believes that the repository represents the best part of the software industry. This is because projects in the repository are complete (and therefore more successful than many projects) and

[1] Refer to Appendix D for details of the project demographics of the data used for the analysis in this chapter.

come from organizations with sufficient process maturity to include a software metrics program.

NOTE *When using the ISBSG equations and data, be aware that they probably reflect the best 25 percent of the industry.*

The findings presented here pertain to this particular collection of projects. It is possible that some findings are not generally applicable. Nevertheless, most observations are in accordance with intuition. This analysis provides a picture of the state of estimation in good software projects.

What Does "Accurate" Mean?

Whether an estimate is judged to be "accurate" or not depends on how much variation is acceptable between the estimated and actual value.

Two different thresholds are used in this analysis: 10 percent (that is, an estimate is considered to be accurate if the actual value is between 90 percent and 110 percent of the estimated value) and 20 percent (that is, an estimate is considered to be accurate if the actual value is between 80 percent and 120 percent of the estimated value). For effort, which is both the most important measure and the one with the greatest variation in accuracy, a threshold of 50 percent is also considered (that is, an estimate is considered to be accurate if the actual value is between 50 percent and 150 percent of the estimated value).

The choice of threshold clearly influences the percentages of estimates that are considered to be accurate. Readers should bear this in mind when quoting percentages from this chapter.

The Project Details

Release 11 of the ISBSG Repository has 861 projects for which some form of data about estimation is available. These projects represent a broad cross-section of the software industry.

The profile of these projects is similar to the total collection of projects in the ISBSG Data Repository. This is important, because it means you can expect that the results from this chapter apply just as well to the whole repository.

A General Picture

Effort is the worst estimated of the four key project attributes (effort, cost, duration, and size). For the other three, at least half of the projects are estimated accurately. For effort only, about one-third of projects are estimated accurately.

The two most important estimates are project effort and duration (cost is dominated by effort, and size is mainly relevant as an input to the other estimates).

From the 449 projects for which we know both the estimated and actual effort plus estimated and actual project delivery date, we can make the following observations:

With a threshold of 10 percent for accuracy:

- 25 percent met both estimates to within 10 percent.
- 23 percent underestimated effort and were delivered late.
- 22 percent underestimated effort, but estimated the delivery date accurately.
- 13 percent overestimated effort, but estimated the delivery date accurately.
- 8 percent estimated effort accurately, but were delivered late.
- Only 1 percent of projects came in more than 10 percent below the estimate for both effort and delivery date (that is, overestimated).
- The remaining combinations only account for 1 or 2 percent each.

With a threshold of 20 percent for accuracy:

- 44 percent met both estimates to within 20 percent.
- 15 percent underestimated effort and were delivered late.
- 19 percent underestimated effort, but estimated the delivery date accurately.
- 9 percent overestimated effort, but estimated the delivery date accurately.
- 8 percent estimated effort accurately, but were delivered late.
- Only one project came in more than 20 percent below the estimate for both effort and delivery date (that is, overestimated).
- The remaining combinations only account for 1 or 2 percent each.

Errors in estimating effort correspond closely to errors in estimating cost, in both the size of the error and whether it is an overestimate or underestimate. It is clear that cost and effort are strongly related. This supports the intuition that cost is determined mainly by effort, since the major resource consumed by a software project is human effort.

Errors in size estimates also correspond to errors in effort estimates, although the association is not as strong as that between effort and cost. If size is estimated accurately, effort is usually estimated accurately (about half of projects) or is underestimated (about one-third of projects). If size is underestimated, effort usually is, too (about 60 percent of projects).

- With a 10 percent threshold and size estimated accurately: effort is accurate in 44 percent of cases and underestimated in 39 percent.
- With a 20 percent threshold and size estimated accurately: effort is accurate in 59 percent of cases and underestimated in 28 percent.
- With a 10 percent threshold and size underestimated: effort is underestimated in 62 percent.
- With a 20 percent threshold and size underestimated: effort is underestimated in 57 percent.

Interestingly, no relationship exists at all between actual project delivery rate and the accuracy of the estimates. You might expect that projects delivered ahead of schedule, or with less effort than estimated, would have low (that is, good) PDR, but there is no indication of this. Projects delivered in line with their estimates had a wide range of PDRs.

NOTE *There is no relationship between actual project delivery rate (productivity) and the accuracy of the estimate.*

Estimation Techniques

Size estimates are usually based on a data model, often involving a CASE tool, a functional specification, analogy with a previous project, or on a Use Case model.

For delivery date, effort, and cost:

- About one-third of the projects use only work breakdown estimation.
- 10 to 15 percent of the projects base the estimate only on a functional specification.
- 15 to 30 percent of the projects use both.
- 18 percent of the projects use neither; instead they use life-cycle models or tools.
- "Fixed cost" determines the cost estimate in 15 percent of the projects.
- The delivery date is imposed externally in 30 percent of projects ("Management directive," 22 percent; "legal requirement," 6 percent; and "End user business goals" or similar, 2 percent).

- If a size estimate is available, it is usually used to help estimate delivery date, effort, and/or cost. If no size estimate is available, work breakdown estimation or management directive generally determines the estimate delivery date, effort, and cost.

There is no association between other project attributes (organization type, development type, and so on) and the estimation techniques used.

In most cases, there is little relationship between which estimating techniques are used and how accurate the estimates are. What evidence there is suggests that estimates based on a functional specification slightly outperform work breakdown techniques.

NOTE *"Management directive" predetermines the delivery date in 22 percent of the projects.*

Individual Estimates

In this section, we analyze each of the four types of estimate: how often projects are underestimated and overestimated, what overruns or underruns are typical, what types of projects are likely to be overestimated or underestimated, and so on.

The samples analyzed here are smaller than the full set of 850 projects. Some projects contained information on the estimation techniques used, but did not give the estimates themselves. Of the remaining projects that provide at least one estimate, few give all four estimates.

Effort Estimates

Data is available for 581 projects. Effort is usually underestimated:

- 19 percent overestimated effort by at least 10 percent; 11 percent overestimated effort by at least 20 percent; 3 percent overestimated effort by at least 50 percent.
- 36 percent estimated effort to within 10 percent of the actual value; 56 percent estimated effort to within 20 percent of the actual value; 78 percent estimated effort to within 50 percent of the actual value.
- 45 percent underestimated effort by at least 10 percent (median error is 40 percent); 33 percent underestimated effort by at least 20 percent (median error is 67 percent); 19 percent underestimated effort by at least 50 percent (median error is 98 percent).

Across the whole 581 projects, the mean error is an underestimate of 50 percent. The median is an underestimate of 6 percent. The largest error saw effort underestimated by a factor of over 80 times.

NOTE *Forty-five percent of the projects underestimated effort by at least 10 percent.*

The overestimates occurred in small projects, only about half the size of the repository average. Actual effort for these projects averaged 70 percent of estimated effort.

Underestimates occurred in a wide range of projects. There is a weak trend toward larger projects, with larger development teams and longer durations, being more often underestimated. There are no other patterns in terms of which types of projects are estimated better or worse than other types.

For the projects with effort underestimated, on average the actual error is 67 to 100 percent; in other words, the actual effort approaches double the estimate.

NOTE *For the projects with effort underestimated, on average the actual effort approaches double the estimate.*

For the most part, large errors in estimated effort are accompanied by similarly large errors in estimated cost.

Effort Estimation Techniques

The two main techniques for estimating effort are task-based work-breakdown methods, and estimation based on an estimate of functional size. Task-based methods are more common (63 percent of projects compared to 31 percent, including 20 percent of projects that used both techniques).

Task-based methods are more likely to underestimate effort. Using a 10 percent margin for accuracy, task-based methods estimate effort accurately (to within 10 percent) in 32 percent of projects, and underestimate effort by at least 10 percent in 49 percent of projects. For function point–based methods the corresponding percentages are 40 percent accurate and 35 percent underestimated. Using a 20 percent tolerance for accuracy, the gap is smaller: 54 percent accurate and 35 percent underestimated with task-based methods, 53 percent accurate and 29 percent underestimated with function point–based methods.

On the other hand, median errors are smaller with task-based methods. The median underestimate with task-based methods is 41 percent using a 10 percent threshold for accuracy, and 66 percent using a 20 percent threshold for accuracy. With function point–based methods the corresponding median underestimates are 72 percent and 86 percent respectively.

It appears that task-based estimates of effort are more likely to be wrong, but less likely to be badly wrong, than estimates based on functional size.

Delivery Date (Project Duration)

Estimated and actual delivery date and project duration are known for 538 projects.

Across the whole data set the mean actual duration is 9.8 months, and the median is 7.6 months. The mean estimated duration is 8 months and the median is 6.6 months.

Delivery date is estimated relatively well. Around 70 percent of the projects were delivered early or on time, including 37.5 percent that were delivered as scheduled:

- 5 percent of projects were delivered more than 10 percent ahead of schedule (that is, actual duration was less than 90 percent of the estimated duration), including 3 percent delivered more than 20 percent ahead of schedule.
- 60 percent of projects were delivered with an actual duration within 10 percent of their estimated duration, and 70 percent were delivered with an actual duration within 20 percent of their estimated duration. These numbers include 37.5 percent of projects that were delivered as scheduled.
- 35 percent of projects were delivered more than 10 percent late, including 27 percent delivered more than 20 percent late.

The projects delivered early are below average in actual duration (mean and median both around 7.5 months) and above average in estimated duration (mean and median both around 12 months). Lower durations and higher estimates could both contribute to the estimates of duration being too low in these projects. The median error was an underrun of 22 percent.

The projects delivered on time showed a wide spread of durations, sizes, and other project characteristics. No patterns can be seen.

Of the projects delivered more than 10 percent late, 19 percent were up to 1 month late, 25 percent were 1 to 2 months late, 22 percent were 2 to 3 months late, 17 percent were 3 to 6 months late, and 15 percent were more than 6 months late. Three percent were a year or more late, with the worst overrun being 33 months. Late projects averaged 98 percent mean overrun and 40 percent median overrun in duration.

NOTE *Late projects have a median overrun of 40 percent in duration.*

The accuracy of the estimates varies according to how long the project was estimated to take in the first place.

- Projects that were estimated to take a year or more were generally delivered on time. For 65 percent of projects the actual duration was within 10 percent of the estimate, and

20 percent underestimated duration by at least 10 percent. Only 5 percent were late by more than 3 months. The median overrun was 13 percent, or about 2 months.

- Projects that were estimated to take 6 to 12 months did less well. The actual duration was within 10 percent of the estimate in 61 percent of them. Thirty-five percent of the projects underestimated duration by over 10 percent. Thirteen percent were late by more than 3 months. The median overrun was 2.5 months, or 30 percent.
- Estimates were about as accurate for projects that were estimated to take 3 to 6 months as for projects estimated to take 6 to 12 months. However, the worst underestimates came from this group (five of the six projects delivered more than a year late were in this group). Again, 61 percent of the projects estimated duration to within 10 percent of the actual duration, and 36 percent underestimated duration by more than 10 percent. Eleven percent underestimated duration by more than 3 months. The median overrun was 2.1 months, or 45 percent. (The percentage is bigger, even though the number of months is smaller, because the average duration is shorter.)
- Projects that were estimated to take up to 3 months have the biggest errors in percentage terms (because the planned duration is shortest—for example, a project that was planned to take 1 month and was delivered 3 months late has a 300 percent error), but the actual values are not so bad. Forty-five percent of the projects estimated duration to within 10 percent of the actual duration, and 42 percent underestimated duration by over 10 percent. Fifteen percent underestimated duration by more than 3 months. The median overrun was 2.3 months, or 127 percent.

When expressed as percentages, the errors are smaller for projects with large estimated durations and larger for projects with small estimated durations. This is just a consequence of dividing by small or large numbers when calculating percentage errors. It is more relevant to note that across all ranges of estimated duration, if duration was underestimated, the delay was about 2 months; delays of more than 3 months are more common in shorter projects than in projects that were estimated to take a year or more.

Duration Estimation Techniques

If a size estimate is available, it is generally used as an input for estimating duration, either directly, or as an input to an estimating tool. If no size estimate is available, duration is normally determined by management directive or by work breakdown techniques.

The estimating techniques have some impact on the accuracy of the estimated duration. Work breakdown techniques are accurate 24 percent of the time; the mean error is a 32 percent underestimate, and the median error is a 4 percent underestimate. FP-based estimates are either very good or very bad: just under half are accurate, but 21 percent are wrong by 50 percent or more; the mean error is a 30 percent underestimate, and the median is a 10 percent underestimate. In projects whose delivery date was determined by management directive, most were delivered on time or 1 month late; only 10 percent were delivered more than 2 months late. Projects whose delivery date is determined by legal requirements or client directive do best, with an average error of only about 10 percent.

In summary, duration tends to be estimated fairly well, particularly for projects planned to take 12 months or more. If duration is overestimated, it is probably by about 20 percent. If duration is underestimated, the average overrun is about 2 to 3 months.

Cost Estimates

Cost tends to be estimated more accurately than effort. Although underestimates are again more common and larger than overestimates, really bad errors are rare, and most errors are smaller than is seen with effort.

Estimated and actual costs can be analyzed for 117 projects:

- 21 percent overestimated cost by at least 10 percent (median overestimate is 28 percent). Eleven percent overestimated cost by at least 20 percent (median overestimate is 46 percent).
- 44 percent estimated cost accurately to within 10 percent, and 64 percent estimated cost accurately to within 20 percent.
- 35 percent underestimated cost by at least 10 percent (median underestimate is 44 percent). Twenty-five percent of projects underestimated cost by at least 20 percent (median underestimate is 67 percent).

The proportional size of these groups is about 1 (overestimate) to 6 (accurate) to 2 (underestimate) for accuracy within 20 percent, and 2 (overestimate) to 4 (accurate) to 3 (underestimate) for accuracy within 10 percent.

These statistics should be treated with some caution. Ten percent of projects report their actual cost as being exactly the same as the estimated cost. Considering that some of these involve six-figure costs that are quoted to the nearest $10, this seems unrealistic.

Most of the projects in which cost is overestimated are small, of fewer than 200 FP; the median is 125 FP. Not surprisingly at this size range, enhancement projects dominate. No other patterns are evident.

When cost is underestimated, for six projects the errors are huge (300 percent to 900 percent), another five exceed 100 percent, and a further seven exceed 50 percent. When the six huge errors are excluded, the mean error is an underestimate of 46 percent; the overall median error is an underestimate of 44 percent.

NOTE *For projects with cost underestimated, the median error is an underestimate of about 45 percent.*

A clear trend can be seen when estimation techniques are considered: FP-based techniques are more accurate more of the time. For projects using just work breakdown techniques, 42 percent are accurate to within 10 percent; a further 12 percent are accurate to within 20 percent; nearly half misestimate cost by 20 percent or more; underestimates are twice as common as overestimates, and tend to be worse; and the median underestimate is around 50 percent. For projects using functional size–based techniques, 61 percent are accurate to within 10 percent; a further 30 percent are accurate to within 20 percent; and only 9 percent misestimate cost by 20 percent or more; the median underestimate is 14 percent.

NOTE *When functional size–based techniques are used for a cost estimate, the estimate is within 20 percent of the actual cost 90 percent of the time.*

The overestimated projects are all small; the largest is 286 FP, the median size is 127 FP, and the mean size is 145 FP. No other patterns can be seen between project characteristics and the accuracy of cost estimates.

When both cost and effort are known, the association between them is strong. If the projects are ranked in order of effort error (biggest underestimate down to the biggest overestimate) and then ranked in order of cost error, the correlation between the ranks is very high at 0.79. Big errors in estimating effort go with big errors in estimating cost.

In summary, for around half of the projects the cost estimate is accurate. Of the rest, underestimates are about twice as likely to occur as overestimates, and the error is likely to be greater. Estimates produced using functional size–based techniques are more accurate than estimates produced from a task breakdown and are within 20 percent of the actual cost 90 percent of the time.

Summary

A collection of over 850 projects has been analyzed to see how, and how well, people estimated their software projects.

Although the findings summarized below pertain to this particular collection of projects, the ISBSG believes that they provide a good picture of the state of estimates in good software projects.

Size approximation techniques:

- When a size approximation is available, it is usually used to help estimate delivery date, effort, and/or cost. If a size approximation is not available, work breakdown techniques are used. Functional size–based techniques generally produce slightly more accurate estimates.

Accuracy of different types of estimate:

- Delivery date is often estimated well. Over half of the projects were delivered early or on time, and 70 percent were delivered no later than 1 month late. Once a project is more than a month late, the median error is about 2.5 months overrun. Projects planned to run for a year or more are delivered on time; the worst errors occur in projects planned to run for about 4 to 6 months.
- Effort is estimated worst. Over half of projects underestimate effort by at least 10 percent. Some enormous errors occur, with actual effort up to 80 times the estimate. On average, effort is underestimated by about 50 percent. There are no patterns to explain which types of projects are estimated better or worse than other types.
- Errors in cost estimates are closely related to errors in effort estimates, supporting the intuition that effort largely determines cost. But cost estimates are not generally as inaccurate as effort estimates. This may be because extra effort recorded against a project is unpaid.
- There is no relationship between project delivery rate and the accuracy of estimates.
- For everything except effort, half or more of the projects are estimated accurately; for effort, that drops to a third of the projects.

Overestimates and underestimates:

- A late project averages an overrun of 2 to 3 months.
- If effort is underestimated, the average overrun is 67 to 100 percent. The average across all projects is to underestimate effort by 50 percent.
- If cost is underestimated, the average overrun is 25 to 30 percent.
- Overestimates are rare, usually small, and occur in small projects. When anything is overestimated, it is probably by about 20 percent.

Factors influencing accuracy:

- As a general guide, smaller projects are more likely to be estimated accurately or overestimated. Larger and, more particularly, longer projects are more likely to be underestimated.
- Estimates appear to be less accurate for projects involving newer technologies, and for those with a large and varied user base.

Use the information provided in this chapter to guide both your approach to preparing estimates for a project, and the allowances that you make to your estimate for factors specific to your project. Use both macro- and micro-estimating techniques to obtain the most reliable estimate.

CHAPTER 4

Sizing Software and Size-Approximation Accuracy

This chapter introduces the concept that functional size measurement of software can be performed at different levels of accuracy to suit different purposes. It will introduce the concept of *approximating* size rather than measuring it. *Approximating size* techniques can be used when there is insufficient opportunity, time, or perhaps information to perform a detailed size measurement.

Functional size measurement (FSM)[1] is the most accepted approach to measuring the size of a software project. Standard functional size measurement methods[2] are often unsuitable to be used early in the life of a project[3] because they require some kind of structured analysis before identifying and classifying functions, counting elementary components, and performing numerical transformations, in line with their specific counting rules.

Although simple in concept, functional size measurement is not a trivial task. However, there are several simple but effective ways of roughly determining the functional size of a project without doing a detailed functional size measurement. The resulting "approximated" size is much less accurate than the measured size, but the error range

[1] ISO/IEC 14143-1:2007 – Software Engineering – Software measurement – Functional size measurement – Definition of concepts.

[2] ISO14143-6 – Information technology – Software measurement – Functional size measurement – Part 6: Guide for use of ISO/IEC 14143 series and related international standards.

[3] This chapter assumes the functional size of the software system being developed as the main cost driver of the project. Physical dimensions (for example, LOC) are excluded as estimating factors, due to the higher difficulty in estimating those dimensions in the initial phases of the project when nothing has been produced or even designed.

may be acceptable for the purpose for which the size will be used, that is, early project estimation.

Size approximation techniques can also be used by those practitioners who do not currently measure functional size but need a method of mapping the lessons of this book back to their environment.

Sizing Accuracy Levels

The advantages of approximating size are offset by the unavoidable lack of precision of the results. It is important to distinguish each measure as either an *exact measure* (that is, performing a functional size measurement as per the ISO standard guidelines) or an *approximation.*

A measurement can be conducted at a number of *accuracy levels*[4], based on the

- Purpose of the measurement
- Quality of documentation/information available
- Amount of time available to complete the measurement

The different levels of sizing accuracy range from Level 1 to Level 6, from the most accurate to least accurate.

Level 1 is the most accurate size measurement, follows formal measurement guidelines, and involves detailed cataloging, classifying, weighting, and cross-referencing of each of the functional components.

In contrast, at the other end of the accuracy scale, Level 6 functional size is not a measurement as such, but an approximation of the size. Rather than identifying, classifying, and sizing each functional component, Level 6 predicts the size based on a number of easily identified attributes of the software. It provides a "ballpark" size for the project.

Each level of sizing is classified based on the listed tasks being performed.

Measuring as per the following guidelines, the precision experienced for each level is

- Level 6 = ±20% to ±200%
- Level 5 = ±15% to ±20%
- Level 4 = ±15%
- Levels 3 to 1 = ±10%

[4] "Levels of Function Point Counting," by Pam Morris (Total Metrics) – Version 1.3 2004 (www.Totalmetrics.com).

Level 6: Size Approximation

Functional size is approximated without identifying exact functions. It is based on project characteristics that have historically shown some correlation to the total size (for example, number of reports, number of third normal form tables, and so on). The "most likely" size of the project is then derived by statistically evaluating the results predicted by the various project characteristics. Typically, between 10 and 40 characteristics are assessed. Assumptions should be documented and the size should always be notated, highlighting that it is an approximation, not a measured size.

The accuracy range of Level 6 approximations depends on such things as the algorithms used, the *functional fit* of the project to that of the history data from which the algorithms were derived, the number of characteristics used for the calculation, and the accuracy of the measurement of the characteristics.

Level 5: Rough Size Measure

- Software is functionally decomposed, but only to functional areas or functional groups, not to Base Functional Component[5] (BFC) level (that is, not to elementary process level).
- For each functional area, the number of Base Functional Components is roughly tallied using information from menus, file lists, screen lists, and report lists.
- Weightings for the groups of BFCs are assigned using industry defaults.
- Diagrams and system interface documentation is used.

Level 4: Default Complexity Measure

- Software to be built by the project is functionally decomposed to BFC level (processes and data groups are individually identified).
- All BFCs are uniquely identified and classified according to type.
- Default weightings for size are assigned to the individual BFC based on either industry default complexity ratings (for example, IFPUG files: Low and IFPUG Processes = Average) or defaults derived locally within the organization for software of this type.

[5] Base Functional Component (BFC) is an elementary unit of Functional User Requirements defined by and used by an FSM method for measurement purposes (ISO/IEC 14143-1 :2006). For example, BFCs correspond to an *elementary process* or a *logical file* in the IFPUG FSM method and a *functional process* in the COSMIC method.

Level 3: Detailed Measure

- As for Level 4, except complexity is individually assessed, and weightings are assigned to each BFC (for example, for IFPUG FSM, DETs and FTRs are identified using the IFPUG complexity matrices where possible).
- Explanatory notes are attached to BFCs where necessary.

Level 2: Detailed Linked Measure

- As for Level 3, except all relationships between BFCs are formally documented (that is, relationships between processes and the data they access are individually identified and documented. This is often referred to as *linking* processes and data.)
- Exact numbers of *subcomponents* of BFCs are identified; for example, in IFPUG FSM, that is the number of DETs and FTRs; for COSMIC FSM, that is the uniquely named *subprocesses* identified.

Level 1: Detailed Linked and Labelled Measure

- As for Level 2, but more comprehensive supporting documentation for the sizing. For example:
  - Cross-referencing between physical and logical artifacts of the software. For example, between physical files and logical data groups and between specified use cases and logical processes.
  - Keywords (also referred to as labels or attributes) are attached to relevant BFCs (for selective reporting).

NOTE *Choose the level of sizing based on the documentation and time available plus the use of the resultant size.*

Table 4-1 lists the basic attributes of each of the sizing levels to help you choose the one most suited to your need.

If the size has been *measured* using Level 5 or 4 guidelines, then to have more confidence in the number, the size measurement should be revisited and performed more accurately as more information becomes available.

If the size has been *approximated* using Level 6 methods, then it is recommended that this size be recalculated during the development as more information is collected for the project.[6] Ideally, once the project is approved, a more detailed measurement should be

[6] Refer to Figures 1-2 and 1-3.

Level	Size Measure	Best Suited For	Issues	Prerequisites
1	Very detailed Easily auditable Accurate Very well documented Easily maintained	Benchmarking projects Detailed estimates Project tracking Detailed baseline model Metrics reporting for strategic level	Very time intensive Requires very skilled counters Expensive for large systems	High-quality documentation Data model Full access to system experts
2	Very detailed Easily auditable Accurate Very well documented Easily maintained	Benchmarking projects Detailed estimates Project tracking Detailed baseline model	Time intensive Expensive for large systems	Good/high quality documentation Data model Full access to system experts
3	Detailed Auditable Accurate Well documented Very maintainable	Benchmarking projects Detailed estimates Baseline application measurement for portfolio sizing Detailed baseline model	Time intensive Reasonably cost-effective for large systems	Good quality documentation Data model (if available) Access to system experts

TABLE 4-1 Basic Attributes of Sizing Levels (*continued*)

Level	Size Measure	Best Suited For	Issues	Prerequisites
4	Less detailed Auditable Reasonably accurate Documented Maintainable	Portfolio baseline assessment Benchmarking development or support ratios Quality metrics High-level estimates Baseline model	Efficient Cost-effective for large systems	Average quality documentation Data model (if possible) Access to system experts
5	Low detail Less accurate Documented (issues and assumptions) "Skeleton" (base for more refined measurement)	Portfolio baseline assessment Benchmarking support ratios Baseline model	Very efficient Cost-effective for large systems with little enhancement	Summarized system documentation Access to system experts (for the duration of measurement)
6	Very little detail—size results only Accuracy historically has been demonstrated to be within +/– 20% Not documented Not maintainable	Portfolio baseline assessment Software asset valuation Project scoping Estimating count durations Benchmarking support ratios	Very efficient Very cost-effective for large systems with very little enhancement	Accurate completion of a questionnaire Access to system experts (short interview)

TABLE 4-1 Basic Attributes of Sizing Levels

performed and the size updated as functionality changes, particularly if the size values are used to:

- Adjust the effort, cost, and time estimates
- Control the scope creep and record change requests

NOTE *As the project progresses, the size estimate should be validated and refined (eventually moving from low-accuracy to high-accuracy techniques).*

It is recommended that every size approximation should be expressed as three values: minimum, most likely, and maximum estimated size, where the most likely is not necessarily the average between the extreme values. Alternatively, the size approximation should express a confidence interval, or accuracy percentage, to help understand how close the estimate is likely to be to the actual size of the software being analyzed. It is up to the person using the result to decide whether to use each value, or to use only one of the values in the approximation interval, as a basis for further estimations of effort, cost, or duration.

Classifying Size Approximation Techniques

Basically, any approximation technique comprises some input, calculation, and output, where the input variables are some kind of information about the software project being sized, and the basic output is the approximated size. Size approximations may use a *direct* or *derived* approach:

- **Direct size approximation** ("expert opinion") predicts the size based on analogical reasoning and intuition, typically using past experience; the size result is achieved directly without a formal step-by-step, structured process. Direct estimation may be improved by means of Delphi iterations[7] or some kind of analogy with known projects.
- **Derived size approximation** ("algorithmic method") involves a defined algorithmic or structured approach, based on theoretical or statistical models.

Size Approximation Accuracy

Here we look at the accuracy of the sizing approximations provided in the projects submitted to the ISBSG repository when compared with the counted size of the software delivered.

[7] Refer to Chapter 10.

In Chapter 3 we saw that 30 to 40 percent of projects used functional size techniques as part of estimating duration, effort, or cost. They may have used an approximation of size, or a size value counted carefully from the project specification; the latter is perhaps most likely.

This section considers a different question: if size in function points was approximated early in a project, how does the approximation compare with the final "properly counted" size?

Errors can arise from several sources: inaccuracies that are inevitable when an approximation is produced from incomplete information; inaccuracies that might be caused by using a poor technique to do the approximation; and *scope creep,* when the final system contains functionality that was not part of the initial specification.

Three main techniques are used for approximating size:

- 40 percent approximate size from a data model.
- 20 percent approximate size from the functional specification or use case model.
- 16 percent approximate size by analogy with previous projects.

Generally, size is approximated well. Perhaps this is to be expected in a database of projects primarily submitted by organizations that establish size by some form of functional sizing method.

Size approximations are provided for 322 projects:

- 12 percent over-approximated size by at least 10 percent; 8 percent over-approximated size by at least 20 percent.
- 53 percent were approximated accurately to within 10 percent (16 percent were exact); 65 percent were estimated accurately to within 20 percent.
- 35 percent under-approximated size by at least 10 percent; 27 percent underestimated size by at least 20 percent.

The proportional size of these groups is about 1 (over-approximate) to 6 (accurate) to 3 (under-approximate). There is a slight indication that errors are larger when approximation is based on a data model rather than on the functional specification or use case model, but really the pattern varies little whichever methods are used.

When size is over-approximated, the average error is about 30 percent. When it is under-approximated by 10 percent or more, the median under-approximation is 30 percent; among projects where the under-approximation is 20 percent or more, the median under-approximation is 60 percent. The largest error is nearly 400 percent, meaning the actual size was almost five times the approximation.

In summary, for over half of the projects the size approximation is accurate. Of the rest, under-approximations are about three times as likely to occur as over-approximations, and the error is likely to be two or more times as bad. Approximations produced from the functional specification are slightly more likely to be more accurate than those produced from a data model.

Summary

In this chapter we have introduced the concept that functional size measurement of software can be performed at different levels of accuracy to suit different purposes, and we have provided a six-level accuracy hierarchy. We have also introduced the concept of "approximating" size rather than measuring size and have looked at the accuracy of the approximations submitted to the ISBSG Repository.

CHAPTER 5

Some Practical Software Size Approximation Techniques

In the startup phase of a software development project, the project sponsor (that is, the customer) wants to know how much the software will cost and how long it will take to develop. The developer (in-house or external) needs to establish the approximate size of the software to be developed in order to estimate the effort, cost, and time for planning purposes. To satisfy these needs, the size of the software needs to be established, but as it is early in the life cycle of the proposed project, a full function point count is not practical or economically sensible.

In this chapter we will provide examples of quick sizing techniques for each of the three functional size measurement (FSM) methods most represented in the ISBSG Repository, namely: IFPUG, FiSMA, and COSMIC. These are simple but effective ways of roughly determining the functional size of a project.

NOTE *In this chapter you will find some simple but effective ways of roughly determining the functional size of a project even when a function point count has not been completed.*

Many software size approximation techniques are available in the literature and industry practice. The following are just a few examples. A number of commercial software metrics consulting companies also provide products and services to assist in size approximation, and some useful sizing tools are now available.

ID	Size Class	Range (FP)	ID	Size Class	Range (FP)
DEV_{XS}	Very Small	0–150	ENH_{XS}	Very Small	0–60
DEV_{S}	Small	150–300	ENH_{S}	Small	60–120
DEV_{M}	Medium	300–600	ENH_{M}	Medium	120–240
DEV_{L}	Large	600–1,200	ENH_{L}	Large	240–480
DEV_{XL}	Very Large	1,200–5,000	ENH_{XL}	Very Large	480–2,000
DEV_{XXL}	Extremely Large	>5,000	ENH_{XXL}	Extremely Large	>2,000

Table 5-1 Direct Size Approximation

Direct Size Approximation

This method uses statistical distribution of total functional size, both for new development and for enhancement projects.

An analysis of size distribution of the ISBSG database leads to the size classes reported in Table 5-1 for development ("DEV") and for enhancement ("ENH") projects.

Example: Direct Size Approximation

Consider the analogy between your team's last five development projects and the planned development project:

- Projects 1 and 2 fell into size class DEV_S (Small), that is, between 150 and 300 FP.
- Projects 3 and 4 fell into size class DEV_M (Medium), that is, 300 to 600 FP.
- Project 5 fell into size class DEV_L (Large), or 600 to 1,200 FP.

Interview the project sponsor and analysts from the planned and past projects, and then compare the projects for relative functionality delivered. If it is decided that the planned project will have about the same amount of required functionality of projects 3 and 4 (that is, "much more than projects 1 and 2" and "no more than half of project 5"), then the most likely size range of the new project will be in the range of projects 3 and 4 (Medium), that is, 300 to 600 FP.

This analogy-based approach provides only a ballpark project size.

Derived Size Approximation

There are a number of ways of deriving an approximate size for a proposed piece of software. Here we provide details on three techniques to derive IFPUG, COSMIC and FiSMA sizes. We also provide some examples of extrapolative approaches.

Early Approximation of Functional Size Using ISBSG Data

In the example that follows, we use the known ratios of the IFPUG functional size components from the ISBSG repository data.[1] It is possible to derive similar functional type relationship patterns for all five FSM methods.

NOTE *Function point internal logical files closely resemble a count of logical entities.*

Often the functional component that you will have the most knowledge of is the *internal logical files* (ILFs). These closely resemble a count of the entities in a logical data model, modeled to second normal form. If a high-level data model has been developed as part of the requirements analysis, this can be used to approximate the number of internal logical files.

An IFPUG function point count identifies all occurrences of the following five base functional component types, (BFC types):

- **Internal logical files (ILF)** Data maintained by processes within the software
- **External interface files (EIF)** Data referenced by processes within the software
- **External inputs (EI)** Processes that enter data to be stored within the software
- **External outputs (EO)** Processes that extract derived data to be provided to the user
- **External queries (EQ)** Processes that retrieve stored data to be provided to the user

From the ISBSG analysis of its history data, it has been observed that the relationships between these five component types remains relatively constant for new development projects and for complete applications; that is, each component type contributes a consistent percentage of function points to the overall total size of the application.

Investigation into the rationale for the relationships shows good reasons why this consistency exists. For any complete application that operates as a software system, the data entered would be expected to be processed and stored for later retrieval. It therefore follows that we would expect a strong relationship between *input* functions (data

---

[1] Note that this method relies on a single algorithm (most of the commercial products that approximate size rely on between 10 and 40 algorithms). The more relationships that can be analyzed and that can contribute to an approximated size, the more accurate the size estimate will be.

entered) and the *logical files* (internal data storage) and the *output* and *query* functions that retrieve data stored from the internal stores and the external stores, *interface files.*

Note that these relationships have only been found to be relevant to software that operates as a self-contained system, that is, a cohesive set of functionality that is loosely coupled with other applications. Therefore, it may not be advisable to use approximation-sizing techniques to predict the size of any enhancement project that has a mix of added, changed, and deleted functionality scattered over several functional areas within an application.

Figure 5-1 shows the relationships between the five components of the IFPUG functional size method from new development project data in the ISBSG Repository. These relationships can be used to estimate the size of a project. For projects sized by the IFPUG functional sizing method, versions 4.*x*, and with an ISBSG quality rating of "A" or "B," the relative contribution of each component type to the total count is depicted in Figure 5-1.

Use these relationships to approximate the size of a software development project:

Example 1: Internal Logical Files

If the high-level logical data model had 40 logical tables, it may be reasonably assumed that these relate to approximately 40 internal *logical files.* Analysis of the ISBSG Repository also shows that most internal *logical files* in applications are rated as being low to medium in complexity. The mean score attributed to them across all projects is 8.6 function points.

Based upon the preceding, it can be assumed that the total score for the internal *logical files* component of the function point count will be

40 (ILFs) × 8.6 (mean score for internal *logical files*) = 344 FPs

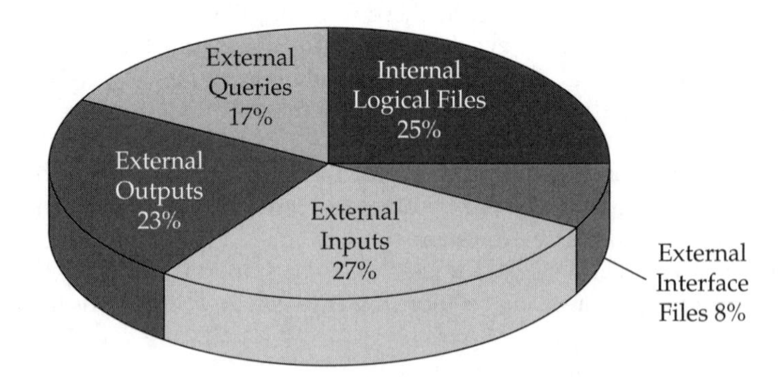

FIGURE 5-1 Function point mix – new developments (Source: Estimating, Benchmarking & Research Suite Release 11)

From the preceding pie chart it can be seen that the internal *logical files* component of the function point count is typically around 25 percent. Based on this, the total functional size of the required application is predicted to be around:

$$344 \text{ FPs} \times 100/25 = 1{,}376 \text{ FPs}$$

It would be sensible to notify the customer that the size is ≈1,400 FP (with an allowance of plus or minus 25 percent).

Example 2: External Outputs

In a situation where the planned project is a redevelopment of an existing application, the number of unique reports and extract files output from the existing application can be assumed to be equivalent to the external *output* components in the new project.

Analysis of the ISBSG Repository shows that most external *outputs* are rated as being medium in complexity. The mean score attributed to them across all projects in the repository is 5.4 function points. If the existing application has 47 different reports and 3 different extract files, then the total number of external *outputs* can be assumed to be 50. (Note: ensure that you exclude any obsolete, unused reports from your calculations.)

Based upon the preceding, it can be assumed that the total score for the external *outputs* component of the functional size measure will be

$$50 \text{ (EOs)} \times 5.4 \text{ (mean score for external } \textit{outputs}\text{)} = 270 \text{ FPs}$$

From the pie chart in Figure 5-1, it can be seen that the external *outputs* component of the functional size measure is typically around 23 percent. On this basis the total functional size for the required application is predicted to be around:

$$270 \text{ FPs} \times 100/23 = 1{,}174 \text{ FPs}$$

It would be sensible to notify the customer that the size is ≈1,200 FP (with an allowance of plus or minus 25 percent).

KISS Quick Software Size Estimation Technique

KISS (Keep It Simple Stupid) Quick is a size estimation approach that was developed together with the FiSMA functional size measurement method. It is most accurate with FiSMA function points, but can be used also with IFPUG and NESMA function points.

The KISS Quick approach starts with a questionnaire consisting of 28 questions. For each question, the answer is the number of occurrences of the particular functional component type. Each type has a specific multiplier for each measurement method (only IFPUG & FiSMA are shown in Table 5-2; values of the multipliers are derived from history data, and they equal zero where the method does not

	Number of Navigation and Query Functions (No Update)	Number (e.g.)	IFPUG Multipl.	FiSMA Multipl.
1	Number of starting icons?		0	1.0
2	Number of login and logout screens?	(1)	3	1.8
3	Number of different menus?		0	1.8
4	Number of parameter selection lists (drop-down lists)?		3	1.0
5	Number of inquiry screens (db retrieving, on screen)?	(3)	4	3.4
6	Number of browsing list screens (occurrences of same type data)?		4	2.3
7	Number of screens for starting report generation?		3	3.4
	User Input Functions (Update)			
8	Number of 3-functional (create, update, and delete) user input screens?		21	16.8
9	Number of 2-functional (create and/or update and/or delete) screens?	(2)	15	11.2
10	Number of 1-functional (create or update or delete) screens?		9	5.6
	Noninteractive User Output Functions			
11	Number of output forms (fixed layout)?		5	4.9
12	Number of reports?		7	6.5
13	Number of text messages or e-mails?		4	3.0
14	Number of monitor screen outputs?		7	6.5
	Interface Services Between This and Other Applications			
15	Number of messages sent to other applications?	(6)	5	3.6
16	Number of messages received from other applications?	(6)	5	5.5
17	Number of signals sent to a device?		5	1.4
18	Number of signals received from a device?		5	2.0
19	Number of batch records sent to another application?		5	3.6
20	Number of batch records received from other applications?		5	5.5

TABLE 5-2 KISS Quick Estimation Multiplier Table (*continued*)

	Number of Navigation and Query Functions (No Update)	Number (e.g.)	IFPUG Multipl.	FiSMA Multipl.
	Persistent Data Storage Functions			
21	Number of entity types?		7	3.9
22	Number of other logical record types?		7	3.9
	Independent Algorithmic Functions			
23	Number of independent calculation routines?		0	5.1
24	Number of independent simulation routines?		0	5.1
25	Number of independent formatting routines?		0	5.1
26	Number of independent database cleaning routines?		0	5.1
27	Number of independent security routines?		0	5.1
28	Number of other independent algorithmic routines?		0	5.1

TABLE 5-2 KISS Quick Estimation Multiplier Table

count that functionality type). The number of occurrences is then multiplied with the multipliers, and next the total sum of function points is calculated. This estimation method is rated as a "rough size measure."

Example: Basic KISS Quick Approach

Let's assume that you are developing a user interface application, which will be part of a three-tier information system. You know that there will be one login screen, three different inquiry screens, and two different two-function input screens. These are the services that the user can easily identify. Because of the three-tier system architecture, you know that your user interface application must communicate with the business logic application. The logical requirement is to send six different messages (one for each screen; the data elements on each screen are different) and also to receive six different messages. You also know that there will be no local data storage or customer-specified algorithmic services in the user interface application.

- If you want to know the application size in IFPUG function points, you use the multipliers from the IFPUG column and get the size estimate:

  $1 \times 3 + 3 \times 4 + 2 \times 15 + 6 \times 5 + 6 \times 5 = 105$ FP

- If you want to know the application size in FiSMA function points, you use the multipliers from the FiSMA column and get the size estimate:

  $1 \times 1.8 + 3 \times 3.4 + 2 \times 11.2 + 6 \times 3.6 + 6 \times 5.5 = 89$ FP

As we see from the example, the size of the user interface application will be approximately 100 function points with each of these measurement methods.

Moving from Basic KISS Quick Approach to Other Accuracy Levels

As mentioned earlier, the basic KISS Quick approach is rated as a "rough size measurement" method. When using FiSMA function points, the approach and measurement can be easily modified to gain more accuracy. If we need a ballpark estimate of the size in a very early phase of the development life cycle, we can use Table 5-3.

The basic KISS Quick approach just mentioned would give us a ballpark size estimate of $2 \times 12 + 4 \times 6 + 6 \times 5 + 6 \times 5 = 108$ FiSMA function points. It is slightly larger than the outcome from the basic KISS Quick, but still roughly 100 FP, providing a reasonably accurate size estimate.

With the basic KISS Quick questionnaire, you have found the numbers of occurrences of each functional type (28 FiSMA Base Functional Component [BFC] types). You can reach the next accuracy level by giving names to all those occurrences. For example, when you answered that you will have three different inquiry screens, each representing 3.4 function points, your estimate can be upgraded to the "default complexity measure" level by naming the screens but keeping the size default values. Moving to higher levels of accuracy requires additional information (for example, related numbers of data elements and reading references).

Questions	Number	Multipl.	FP
How many input screens?	(2)	× 12 =	
How many other screens?	(4)	× 6 =	
How many report and output form types?		× 6 =	
How many interface record types to other systems?	(6)	× 5 =	
How many interface record types from other systems?	(6)	× 5 =	
How many entity types?		× 4 =	
How many algorithmic business rules?		× 5 =	

TABLE 5-3 KISS Quick Estimation for FiSMA

Early & Quick Software Size Estimation Technique

The Early & Quick (E&Q) technique[2] combines different approaches in order to provide better size estimates. It uses both analogical and analytical classification of functional components at different levels of detail for different branches of the system (aggregations and multilevel approach). The overall uncertainty level in the estimate (expressed as a range of *minimum, likely*, and *maximum* values) is the weighted sum of the individual components' uncertainty levels. This technique provides a table of statistically validated values, derived from the ISBSG and other sources. Due to its multilevel/mixed approach, the sizing level for E&Q depends on how many details the measurer has and can explore:

- **Level 5** For higher hierarchical components (macro processes, general processes, and multiple and generic logical data groups)
- **Level 4** For lower hierarchical components (typical processes and base functional processes, and internal and external logical data groups with generic complexity)
- **Level 3** For functions where the low/average/high complexity is determined

The starting point of this technique is the product breakdown structure of the system being studied, the basic elements of which are the following software objects:

- Logical data groups (files)
- Elementary (functional) processes

Further aggregations are provided:

- Logical data groups (files) can be grouped in multiple data groups.
- Elementary (functional) processes can be grouped in small, medium, or large "typical" and "general" software processes.
- General processes can be grouped in small, medium, or large "macro" software processes.

Table 5-4 shows the descriptions for all the software objects and their aggregates.

The following section provides Early & Quick hints, levels, and ranges for COSMIC FSM methods. The Early & Quick technique can also be used for IFPUG. This technique provides results within ±25 percent of the actual size of the project or application being approximated.

[2] Refer to References.

Name	Description	Brief Definition
LDG	Logical data group	A group of logical attributes—a conceptual entity that is functionally significant as a whole for the user. An internal logical file or external interface file (ILF, EIF in IFPUG), or permanent objects of interest (OOI in COSMIC).
MDG	Multiple data group	A set of two or more logical data groups. Its size is evaluated based on the (estimated) amount of included logical data groups.
BFP	Base functional process	The smallest software process with autonomy and significant characteristics, allowing the user to achieve a unitary business objective. It corresponds to an external input, external output, or external query (IFPUG), or to any functional process (COSMIC).
TFP	Typical functional process	A particular case of a general process: a set of most frequent transactions on a logical data group (or a small set of LDGs). Usually denoted as "Management of [LDG/OOI]." It can be of three "flavors": CRUD (create, retrieve, update, and delete), CRUDL (CRUD + elementary list), or CRUDL + Report (totals or other derived data).
GFP	General functional process	A set of two or more average FPs. It can be likened to an operational subsystem, which provides an organized whole response to a specific application goal. Its size is evaluated based on the (estimated) quantity of included FPs.
MFP	Macro functional process	A set of two or more average general processes. It can be likened to a relevant subsystem, or even to a bounded application, of an overall information system. Its size is evaluated based on the (estimated) quantity of included general processes.

TABLE 5-4 Early & Quick Software Objects

Early & Quick for COSMIC Function Point Size

In the COSMIC method[3], objects of interest are identified, but not assigned any numerical values.

COSMIC Transactional Functions

Base functional processes correspond to the functional processes of the standard COSMIC method. Typical functional processes and

[3] Refer to Chapter 20.

higher-level aggregations (general and macro functional processes) are also defined.

COSMIC Ranges and Numerical Assignments

Each E&QC FFP (full function point) element is assigned three estimated values, that is, minimum, likely, and maximum COSMIC function points. Tables 5-5 and 5-6 show component ranges and numerical assignments for the "business application software" case (for example, MIS [management information system]) and the real-time case.

Type	Level/Complexity	E_{min}	E_{likely}	E_{max}
BFP	Low (2–5 DM)	2.0	3.6	5.0
	Average (5–8 DM)	5.0	6.3	8.0
	High (8–14 DM)	8.0	10.5	14.0
	Very High (14+ DM)	14.0	18.0	25.0
TFP	Low CRUD/L	14.4	18.0	25.2
	Average CRUD/L	25.2	30.0	42.0
	High CRUD/L	42.0	50.0	65.0
GFP	Low (6–10 BFPs)	20.0	50.0	100.0
	Average (10–15 BFPs)	40.0	80.0	160.0
	High (15–20 BFPs)	55.0	110.0	210.0

TABLE 5-5 Early & Quick COSMIC Ranges for Business Application Software

Type	Level / Complexity	E_{min}	E_{likely}	E_{max}
BFP	Low (2–3 DM)	2.0	2.5	3.0
	Average (3–5 DM)	3.0	4.0	5.0
	High (5–10 DM)	5.0	7.5	10.0
	Very High (10+ DM)	10.0	15.0	20.0
GFP	Low (6–10 BFPs)	15.0	32.0	75.0
	Average (10–15 BFPs)	25.0	38.0	110.0
	High (15–20 BFPs)	38.0	70.0	150.0

TABLE 5-6 Early & Quick COSMIC Ranges for Real-Time Software

Some Other Examples of Extrapolative Approaches to Size Approximation

Other examples of extrapolative approaches to size approximation are

- **FP Prognosis** FP = 7.3 × #Inputs + Outputs + 56
- **NESMA Indicative FP** FP = 35 × ILFs + 15 × EIFs
- **Lite or Quick & Early FP** FP = 4 × EIs + 5 × EOs + 4 × EQs + 10 × ILFs + 7 × EIFs
- **Weighted Averages** FP = 4.3 × EIs + 5.4 × EOs + 3.8 × EQs + 7.4 × ILFs + 5.5 × EIFs
- **Thirties Rule of Thumb** One logical file equals "thirty something" unadjusted FPs. So for an application that has about 40 logical files, a very rough size can be obtained as follows: 40 × 35 = 1,400 FP. This sort of rough estimate should have an allowance of plus or minus 30 percent or more.

Using Functional Size to Estimate Project Effort and Duration

If functional size is being used to estimate the effort and duration of a development or enhancement project, try and get the most accurate size that you can within the limitations of information and resources available. Use several size approximation techniques to refine the result before using its values in the project estimation exercise, since an error in the size compounds the errors in the estimates of effort and duration.

NOTE *When using approximated sizes for project estimation purposes, be aware of the need to validate, refine, and eventually translate your size estimates into exact measures, in order to avoid spreading uncertainty from the size approximation to the effort and duration estimates.*

Once you have established your project's software functional size expressed as a number of functional size measurement method units (for example, function points) you can use the ISBSG data to estimate the likely project effort and duration. The following chapters present estimating techniques that allow you to do this.

NOTE *Remember that approximating (or measuring) functional size only results in an approximate (or measured) software size. This is a measure of the amount of software product to be delivered; it is not an estimate of project effort, duration, or cost.*

The Need for Caution

Whether size is approximated or measured for use as an early cost indicator for the project, a contingency of 20 percent to 30 percent should be added to allow for functionality not apparent early in the life cycle. Historical data indicates that this scope creep typically occurs as a result of additional functionality being identified as user requirements evolve in subsequent development phases.

The approximation techniques discussed earlier are only valid if your application or development project is loosely coupled with other applications and generically fits the profile of projects currently in the ISBSG Repository.

Summary

In this chapter we provided examples of just some of the approximating size techniques that can be used when there is insufficient opportunity, time, or perhaps information to perform a detailed size measurement.

CHAPTER 6

The Problem of Missing Functionality

One of the major factors contributing to "blowouts" in software project costs and schedules is scope creep. *Scope creep* is the introduction of additional functionality that either was not specifically defined or was not identified at the time of estimation. Undefined functionality will be missing from the functional size; consequently, the project will be underestimated.

Identifying Missing Functionality

By comparing the different types of functionality delivered by completed software projects, you can gain an insight into what may be missing from your project's early specifications. Functional sizing of the requirements of an application quantifies the different types of functionality to be delivered by the application. As detailed in the previous chapter, industry figures available from the ISBSG Repository for projects—measured with IFPUG function points—indicate that complete applications tend to have consistent and predictable ratios of function points contributed by each of the function types. This profile of functionality delivered by each of the function types for your planned application can be compared with that of the profile of typical completed and implemented applications. Such a comparison will highlight potential areas where the project specifications are incomplete or where there are anomalies.

Note that that this approach for identifying missing functionality is unlikely to work for enhancement projects, simply because a particular enhancement can be focused upon for only certain types of functionality, for example, reporting. In such a case its function type profile will reflect that focus, and it will not align with the overall application profile.

In addition to considering the average profile determined from the ISBSG data, it is important to consider the nature of the application in question. For example, if the application were for end-of-month reporting, you would expect it to have a quite different function type profile than if it were an online contact management system. You would expect the end-of-month reporting application to have a higher percentage of its functionality associated with external outputs and external queries than the online contact management system.

Figure 6-1 illustrates a case where the project manager for a new development of a financial application performs a detailed function point count of the planned project and then compares the percentage contribution of each type of functionality against the ISBSG Repository values. The inner chart in Figure 6-1 represents ISBSG Development Project Data, where n = 798. The outer chart shows the example financial application. This quantitative comparison shows the disparity between the planned project and the typical ISBSG profile. (A comparison with the ISBSG typical profile is appropriate here because the financial application being developed is expected to have a function type profile that would align with the profile for an average application.)

The project manager noted that the reporting requirements ("External Outputs" function points) had the largest percentage discrepancy, being much lower than expected (10 percent compared against the expected 22 percent of the total function points). The user subsequently confirmed that the first release of the software was expected to deliver all reporting requirements but that not all reports had been specified. As a result, the project manager increased the original functional size to allow for the extra percent of reports

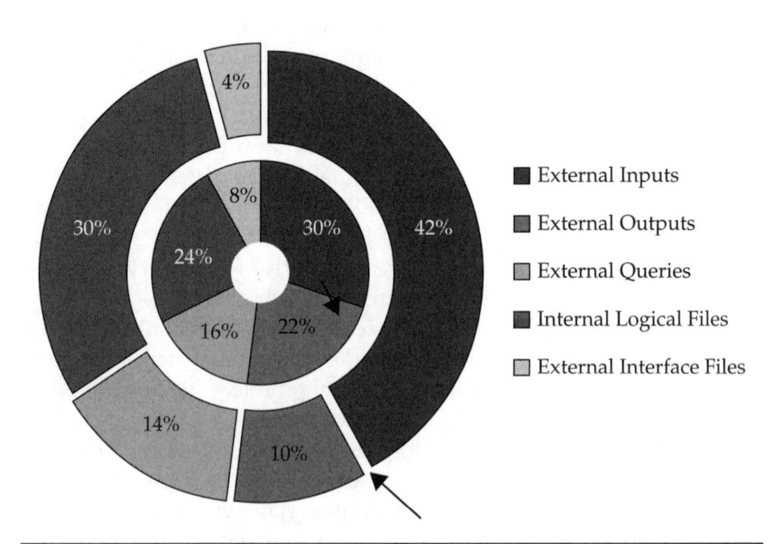

Figure 6-1 Checking the completeness of project requirements using ISBSG Release 11 industry data

predicted by the ISBSG figures. The project manager calculated the early project estimates using this higher functional size figure, which was more likely to reflect the finished product. The ISBSG comparison enabled the project manager to quantify the functionality that was potentially missing and to justify the higher estimate.

Managing Changes and Additions to Functionality

The method just offered is useful for projects that attempt to define all functional requirements before moving to the build stage of the project (this also suggests a waterfall approach to the development). Many projects adopt an approach that does not demand that all the functional requirements are known prior to programming work commencing. A number of techniques that include significant user involvement during the life cycle of the project, and that allow for incremental development, have been identified as offering significant improvements in project delivery rate, speed of delivery, and quality (a lower number of defects delivered). These are reported in the ISBSG's "Techniques & Tools – Special Report II," which covers techniques like Prototyping, JAD, and Agile.

Scope Management

The scope management approach has also been employed in Europe, Japan, and Australia to manage changes and additions to functionality. Two approaches are used: southernSCOPE (Victorian Government, Australia) or northernSCOPE™ (FiSMA, Finland). Both techniques use the ISBSG history data to help verify quotations provided by software vendors. Both are based on three major principles:

- Use of functional size measurement
- Use of unit pricing $/FP
- Use of an independent scope manager

As with the incremental techniques, both these approaches are designed to achieve improved communication between the developers and their customers and users. More information about these concepts is available at the web sites of the owner organizations.

Summary

The typical ISBSG profile of new development projects can be used to compare against the profile of a proposed project as a check that all the requirements are likely to have been included in the functional specification and the functional size.

CHAPTER 7

Estimating Using Equations

One technique for software project estimation involves the use of regression equations. These equations allow you to calculate an estimate for a particular project metric, such as effort and duration, by simply inserting the calculated size[1] of your project into the appropriate equation. This estimation technique is commonly used to produce indicative or ballpark project estimates early in the life of a project. The method is not sufficiently accurate to produce an estimate that could be relied on for quoting or business case requirements, but is useful for an early indication of whether a project idea is feasible, or when you are short of time and information. In these situations the equation technique can meet your needs.

NOTE *The equation technique for estimation is commonly used to produce an initial, indicative project estimate.*

ISBSG Regression Equation Tables

A set of regression equations has been produced from the data in the ISBSG Repository. These equations are available in the tables in Appendix C. You can use these equations to calculate the following project metrics:

- Project delivery rates (productivity, expressed as hours per function point[2])

[1] Historically, regression equations used KLOC (thousands of lines of code) as their units of measure for software size; however, all regression equations in this book use IFPUG 4.*x* function points to measure functional size.

[2] "Function point" means unadjusted function point (UFP).

- Effort (person hours—for the development team only)
- Duration (elapsed months)
- Speed of delivery (function points delivered per elapsed month) for the project as a whole
- Speed of delivery per person (function points delivered per elapsed month per development team member)

Two groups of equations are provided with the following independent variables:

- Equations that utilize size (in unadjusted function points) and maximum team size
- Equations that utilize size only

Within these groups, equations are provided by:

- Platform (mainframe, midrange, PC, and multiplatform)
- Language type (3GL, 4GL, and application generator)
- Development type (enhancement and new development)
- Combinations of platforms, language type, and development type

You must have an estimate or calculation of project size for these estimates. If team size is known or estimated as well, so much the better, but it makes no sense to attempt to produce estimates based on team size alone without knowing the project size.

An example of how to use the basic equations to produce a ballpark estimate based on language level is provided at the end of this chapter.

Using the ISBSG Regression Equations

Use of the ISBSG equations is straightforward. Having selected the appropriate equation from the tables provided, to produce your estimate, you insert the calculated functional size of your project and (if available) the maximum team size.

For example, suppose you want to produce estimates for an enhancement project that is being developed for a *multiplatform*[3] environment, and the project has a functional size of 260 function points, with a planned maximum team size of 4. Using Tables C-1.0,

[3] Refer to Appendix C for the equation tables.

C-1.1, C-1.3, and C-1.4 from Appendix C, you would come up with the following estimates:

Project Delivery Rate	$PDR_{RE} = 38.97 \times Size^{-0.566} \times TeamSize^{0.951}$	$= 38.97 \times 260^{-0.566} \times 4^{0.951}$	≈ 6.3 hours per function point
Project Work Effort	$PWE_{RE} = 38.97 \times Size^{0.434} \times TeamSize^{0.951}$	$= 38.97 \times 260^{0.434} \times 4^{0.951}$	≈ 1,627 hours
Speed of Delivery (whole project)	$SD_{RE} = 0.44 \times Size^{0.852} \times TeamSize^{-0.228}$	$= 0.44 \times 260^{0.852} \times 4^{-0.228}$	≈ 37 function points per month
Speed of Delivery (per developer)	$SD_{RE} = 0.44 \times Size^{0.852} \times TeamSize^{-1.228}$	$= 0.44 \times 260^{0.852} \times 4^{-1.228}$	≈ 9.2 function points per month per developer

The following is an example of how to perform these equations using an MS Excel formula:

```
=(38.97*(260^-0.566)*(4^0.951))
```

(For ^ press SHIFT-6.)

Duration cannot be estimated directly from size and team size (no useful equations can be presented in Table C-1.2). Using the third row of Table C-2.2 leads to an estimated duration of 5.3 months. The general equation relating effort to duration (see item 2.b after Table C-2.2) gives an estimate of 4.2 months. Dividing 260 FP by 37 FP per month (from the table immediately preceding this text) gives an estimate of 7.1 months.

So the estimates for this project indicate that it will consume around 1,600 hours of effort and have an elapsed time of approximately 5 to 7 calendar months.

NOTE *It is very important to treat estimates obtained from the regression equations as ballpark figures only.*

Creating Graphs from the Equations

You can use the equations in Appendix C to create estimation charts for your environment. For example, using the equation in Table C-2.1, "Project Work Effort, estimated from software size only," for midrange platform & 4GL, you can create a simple MS Excel table, as shown next, for 50 through 1,000 function points, and then create a useful graph, as shown in Figure 7-1.

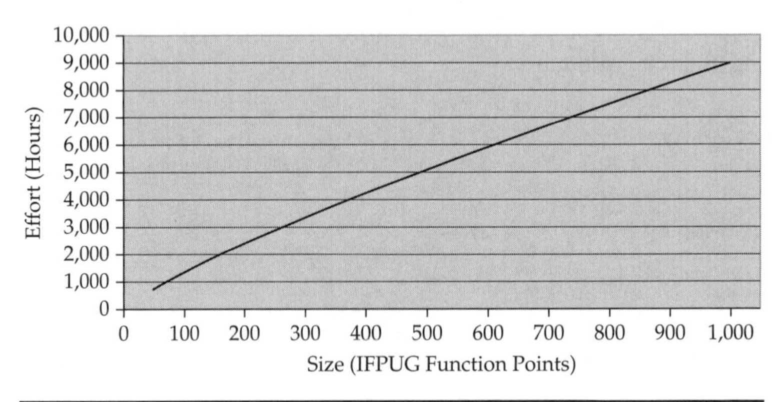

FIGURE 7-1 Example Effort Estimation Chart, MR & 4GL

Class	C	E	N	R2 (Adj)	Median MRE
MF & 3GL	**51.34**	**0.730**	365	0.37	0.56
MF & 4GL	**18.39**	**0.838**	41	0.44	0.51
MR & 3GL	**43.17**	**0.742**	71	0.53	0.45
MR & 4GL	**29.07**	**0.830**	47	0.65	0.40
PC & 3GL	**13.83**	**0.889**	140	0.56	0.51
PC & 4GL	**31.05**	**0.710**	50	0.36	0.57

NOTE *Effort includes project management, administration, and the software team.*

Example Effort Estimate Using the Equations

Using Table C-2.1 in Appendix C, the effort equations derived from the ISBSG's data for the different combinations of platform and development show the following ballpark effort estimates for a project of 500 function points:

Platform and Language	Effort Equation	Estimated Effort for 500 FP Project
MF & 3GL	$Effort = 51.34*FPSize^{0.730}$	4,794 person hours
MF & 4GL	$Effort = 18.39*FPSize^{0.838}$	3,360 person hours
MR & 3GL	$Effort = 43.17*FPSize^{0.742}$	4,343 person hours
MR & 4GL	$Effort = 29.07*FPSize^{0.830}$	5,053 person hours
PC & 3GL	$Effort = 13.83*FPSize^{0.889}$	3,469 person hours
PC & 4GL	$Effort = 31.05*FPSize^{0.710}$	2,561 person hours
Multi & 3GL	$Effort = 23.96*FPSize^{0.831}$	4,191 person hours
Multi & 4GL	$Effort = 15.86*FPSize^{0.867}$	3,470 person hours

NOTE *The effort predicted by the ISBSG equations includes all effort across all phases of the life cycle from project initiation to project completion for software developers, project managers, and project administration.*

The following results using the equations that utilize software size and maximum team size offer an interesting comparison. Because only those equations are presented in which size and team size both have a significant impact, the set of platform and language combinations excludes some that occurred in the equivalent set based upon software size alone, in the previous example.

Platform and Language	Effort Equation Utilizing Software Size and Maximum Team Size	Estimated Effort for 500 FP Project with a Max Team Size of 5
MR & 3GL	$Effort = 42.94 * FPSize^{0.395} * MxTeam^{0.994}$	2,475 person hours
MR & 4GL	$Effort = 56.86 * FPSize^{0.336} * MxTeam^{0.967}$	2,175 person hours
PC & 3GL	$Effort = 28.66 * FPSize^{0.501} * MxTeam^{0.780}$	2,263 person hours
Multi & 3GL	$Effort = 36.44 * FPSize^{0.509} * MxTeam^{0.833}$	3,293 person hours
Multi & 4GL	$Effort = 9.35 * FPSize^{0.718} * MxTeam^{0.801}$	2,941 person hours

Of course, these estimates are just indicative and need to be adjusted to allow for other factors that impact productivity and are specific to your project and environment. You should present any estimates as a range, or plus/minus ≈30 percent.

The obvious limitation of this equation-based technique for project estimation is that the equations cannot address the specific attributes of a particular project. The equations model an average project derived from the ISBSG Repository.

It is very important to treat estimates obtained from the regression equations as ballpark figures only. More accurate estimates will be obtained by using an estimation technique that considers the particular attributes of a planned project.

Summary

The use of the regression equation estimation technique is useful to produce indicative or ballpark project estimates early in the life of a project.

CHAPTER 8

Estimating Using Comparison

In the previous chapter, we described the use of the ISBSG regression equations to produce indicative project estimates. The limitations of this equation-based technique are detailed in that chapter. To achieve more detailed estimates—aligned more specifically to the attributes of the project being planned, rather than being based on those of the average project in the ISBSG Repository—we need to use another estimation technique.

In this chapter we describe an estimation technique based on comparison of the target project with a number of projects in the ISBSG Repository that have similar attributes to the target project.

Comparison-based estimation differs from the analogy-based estimation (which is covered in the next chapter) in that comparison-based estimation uses the median values for effort, duration, and so on, from a group of projects that are similar to the target project. Analogy operates with one or perhaps two past projects selected on the basis of their close similarity to the target project.

NOTE *Comparison-based estimation involves selecting a group of completed projects that share the characteristics of your target project, then using the average of the median effort and duration values.*

Using the Comparison Technique

The comparison technique uses the attributes of the target project and compares them with projects in the ISBSG Repository, to produce an estimate of project delivery rate and speed of delivery, and hence project effort and duration.

The steps are as follows:

1. Establish the size of the software to be delivered by the target project.
2. Determine the development type and platform applicable to the target project.
3. Select the appropriate subset[1] of ISBSG Repository[2] data.
4. Define the other attributes of the target project (for example, Programming Language, Application Type, Maximum Team Size, Tools, and so on). You should define attributes that are likely to influence the target project's project delivery rate or speed of delivery.
5. Search the selected subset of ISBSG data for projects with the same values for the defined attributes as the target project.
6. For all the matching projects found by your search, for each of the defined attributes, calculate the median[3] project delivery rate and speed of delivery.
7. Determine the average of the medians of the project delivery rates and speeds of delivery, and use those averages in conjunction with the software's functional size to calculate the target project effort and duration estimates.

Because the resulting values determined by this technique are aligned to the specific attributes and values of the target project, they should be better estimates of that project's project delivery rate and speed of delivery—and hence effort and duration—than the values obtained from the equations that reflected the average project in the repository.

The following is an example of using comparison-based estimation against the ISBSG Repository to determine effort and duration estimates for a planned small-sized, that is, 250 FP, new development project being undertaken on a PC platform. Table 8-1 shows project selection attributes and values, and Table 8-2 displays project estimation attributes and values. Only those projects matching these attribute values will be used in the estimation calculation.

---

[1] Because the performance achieved on projects of different sizes and development types and using different development platforms varies significantly, it is recommended that you select only projects of a similar size and having the same development type and platform as the target project.

[2] The complete ISBSG project data is available on the "ISBSG Estimating, Benchmarking & Research Suite" that can be licensed from www.isbsg.org or from ISBSG member organizations.

[3] The median is used instead of the mean to determine average project delivery rate and speed of delivery, so as to reduce the effect of outlying data points.

Attribute	**Value**
Size Range	*0 to 500 function points*
Development Type	*New Development*
Development Platform	*PC*

Table 8-1 Project Selection Attributes and Values

Attribute	**Target Project Value**	**ISBSG Median Project Delivery Rate** *(hours per function point)*	**ISBSG Median Speed of Delivery** *(function points per month)*
Primary Programming Language	Visual Basic	*6.5*	*51.0*
Organization Type	Banking	*5.3*	*44.4*
Application Type	Management Information System	*9.1*	*31.3*
Maximum Team Size	3 to 4	*9.0*	*33.4*
Used JAD	Yes	*8.9*	*27.0*
Web Development	Yes	*5.9*	*52.2*
	Average:	$PDR_{AC} = 7.4$	$SD_{AC} = 39.9$

Table 8-2 Project Estimation Attributes and Values

First, determine the project delivery rate (PDR_{AC}) and speed of delivery (SD_{AC}) estimates.

Next, use the project delivery rate and speed of delivery estimates in conjunction with the project's functional size to calculate the project work effort (PWE_{AC}) and project duration (PD_{AC}) estimates, as shown in Table 8-3.

In this example, comparison-based estimation indicates that completing the target project to deliver the new software will require around *1,850 hours of work* and take *6.3 months.* These are likely estimates and should be presented as part of a range also showing conservative and optimistic estimates. The ISBSG Comparative Estimation Tool[4] provides such a range.

[4] ISBSG provides a "Comparative Estimating Tool" that can be licensed from www.isbsg.org or from ISBSG member organizations.

Software Size	Size = functional size of delivered project		*= 250 function points*
Project Delivery Rate	PDR_{AC} = average of category median project delivery rates		*= 7.4 hours per function point*
Project Work Effort	$PWE_{AC} = PDR_{AC} \times$ Functional Size	*= 7.4 × 250*	*= 1,850 hours*
Speed of Delivery	SD_{AC} = average of category median speeds of delivery		*= 39.9 function points per month*
Project Duration	$PD_{AC} = Size/SD_{AC}$	*= 250/39.9*	*= 6.3 months*

TABLE 8-3 Project Work Effort and Duration Estimates

NOTE *You must always make allowances and adjustments for factors peculiar to your project.*

Summary

Comparison-based estimation is useful and is likely to produce a more accurate estimate than one based on the regression equations. By introducing a direct comparison of attribute values that are specific to the target project with projects in the ISBSG Repository, the resulting estimates should prove to be more reliable. You must, of course, always make further allowances and adjustments for factors that you perceive to be peculiar to your project.

CHAPTER 9

Estimating Using Analogy

Analogy-based estimation is another technique for early life-cycle macro-estimation. Analogy-based estimation involves selecting one or two completed projects that closely match the characteristics of the target project. The chosen project(s), or *analog(s),* are then used as the base for your new estimate. Tools are available to search your chosen project history database for a suitable analog.[1]

NOTE *Analogy-based estimation involves selecting one or two completed projects that closely match the characteristics of the target project.*

Analogy-based estimation differs from the comparison-based estimation covered in the previous chapter, in that comparison-based estimation uses the averages and medians from a *group* of similar projects. Analogy operates with *one,* or perhaps *two,* past projects, selected on the basis of their close similarity to the target project. Comparing a target project to a past project is commonly used in an informal way when "guesstimating"; consequently, it is a familiar technique to the practitioner.

In this chapter we describe the formal analogical estimation technique, its implementation, and its advantages and drawbacks. In Chapter 13 you will find an example of how to do an estimate using the analogical technique with the ISBSG data.

[1] For example, "Angel" (**AN**alo**G**y softwar**E** too**L**). Refer to http://dec.bournemouth.ac.uk/ESERG/ANGEL/ESCOM96.html.

Background: Reasoning by Analogy

An analogy expresses the similarity of different things. The word "analogy" is derived from the Greek words expressing geometric proportions or symmetries, *ana logos,* which can be translated as "according to a ratio." An analogy between different things depends on the presence of the same or similar attributes in the things being compared.

When we reason by analogy, we compare two things: a "target" and a "source" analog. The target analog is the thing about which we wish to make a conclusion or a prediction. The source analog is the thing whose similar attributes are used to make the conclusion or prediction. For example, we might predict the likely duration of a journey based on a past journey that has very similar characteristics to the one being planned.

Estimating by Analogy

Estimating software project effort by analogy simply involves finding one or two past projects that have similar significant attributes to the target project that you wish to estimate. An estimate of the effort to complete a new software project is made by comparison with one or more previously completed projects.

Estimating software project effort by analogy usually involves a number of steps:

1. Establishing the attributes of the target project, and then measuring or estimating the values of those project attributes. Analysis of the ISBSG data has revealed attributes that have an impact on project delivery rate. Table 9-1 is a guide to the attributes that you should consider.[2]
2. Searching a repository of completed projects for a project that closely matches the target project as a source analog to compare against.
3. Using the known effort that was used in developing the source analog as an initial estimate for the target project.
4. Comparing the chosen attributes (for example, size, platform, and so on) for the target and source projects.
5. Establishing or adjusting the initial effort estimate in light of the differences between the target and source projects.

[2] This list of attributes reflects those that the ISBSG data has revealed have a significant impact on project delivery rate. If, however, you think that other attributes included in the ISBSG Repository, or in another repository that you are using, are relevant for your own project, then you should also consider those additional attributes in your estimation analysis.

Software Size	Application Type
Development Platform	Maximum Team Size
Development Type	Use of Prototyping
Primary Programming Language	Use of JAD
Organization Type	Web Development

TABLE 9-1 Attributes That Impact Project Delivery

It is very important that you use your judgment to exclude inappropriate analogs and not be tempted to adopt a "likely" analog without due care

It is not clear how best to judge the appropriateness of a potential analog for a target project. Analogical tools can assist in the selection process by ranking past projects according to how well they match the target. Once an analog has been selected, you are faced with the question of how best to use it to derive an estimate for the target project. It is probable that the analog differs from the target project in some respects that influence effort. You need to think about what adjustments should be made to the effort value of the analog to reflect these differences.

NOTE *It is very important that you use your judgment to exclude inappropriate analogs and not be tempted to adopt a "likely" analog without due care.*

Advantages of Estimating by Analogy

The accuracy of estimates from experiments with analogy tools demonstrates that software effort estimation by analogy is a viable estimation method. Analogy-based estimation also offers some advantages:

- *It is easy to understand the basis for an estimate.* Analogy-based estimation is quite different from the input-output models, as estimates are based on concrete past examples. People are used to seeking out an analogy to help them estimate everyday tasks. (We regularly estimate the likely duration of a planned journey based on previous experiences.) This familiarity may explain why people are comfortable estimating in this manner.
- *It is useful where the domain is difficult to model.* We know that many factors influence the effort needed to complete a software project. We know less about how these factors interact with each other, or how best to model the range of factors via software

metrics. Estimation by analogy can be used successfully without having a clear model of how effort is related to other project factors. It relies primarily on selecting a past project that is a close match to the target project, rather than assuming a general relationship between effort and other project characteristics that applies to all projects.

- *It can be used with partial knowledge of the target project.* Analogy-based estimation allows people to use whatever information they have available to search for and select an analog, rather than prescribing particular inputs.
- *It can avoid the inaccuracies of equation-based model use.* Analogy-based estimation has the potential to provide accurate estimates even using another organization's data, provided an appropriate analog for the target project is found within the data set used for estimation. An analog is appropriate if effort and associated factors are related in a similar way for both the target project and analog.
- *It has the potential to mitigate problems with outliers.*[3] Analogy-based estimation does not rely on calibrating a single model to suit all projects. If the target project is typical of a data set, it is likely that one or more appropriate analog projects will be found to base the estimate on. Outliers in the data set have no influence on the estimate at all. If the target project is itself an outlier, at least the lack of a similar project to compare against may make this apparent to the estimator. When using an equation-based model, an estimator may be lulled into a false sense of security because the model will generate an estimate even for the outlier.

NOTE *If the target project is unusual, at least the lack of a similar project to compare against may highlight this to the estimator.*

- *It offers the chance to learn from past experience.* When estimating by analogy, it is convenient to select a potential comparable project via scrutiny of available metric values, because this information is concise and easily compared. Ideally, analogy-based estimation would be applied within an organization with access to other information associated with past projects, not just project metrics. Information such as project debriefing reports could help managers identify risks that the new project faces and avoid mistakes that have been made in the past.

[3] An *outlier* in this context is a project with metrics that differ markedly from the sample group.

The Drawbacks of Estimating by Analogy

Naturally, some difficulties with analogy-based estimation offset its advantages. Its accuracy relies on three factors:

- The availability of an appropriate analog
- The soundness of the strategy for selecting the analog
- The manner in which differences between the analog and target are allowed for when deriving an estimate

There may be no appropriate analog project within an available data set for the project that you want to estimate. One danger is that an analog may be selected and used regardless of its appropriateness. An old project could be selected as an analog because it appears similar to the target project, even though factors affecting effort have changed over time.

Summary

Analogical estimation offers another macro-estimating alternative. It relies heavily on the availability of an appropriate analog. This in turn relies on your ability to define the attributes of the target project to a level of granularity that will result in any identified analog being a true match with the proposed project. That said, if a suitable analog is available, this method of estimation offers another viable estimating option.

In Chapter 13 you will find an example of how to perform an estimate using the analogical technique utilizing the ISBSG data.

CHAPTER 10

Estimating Using Work Breakdown Structure

Throughout this book we have stressed the importance of not relying on one method of estimation. We advise you to use different techniques to provide "sanity checks" for your preferred estimation approach. While the emphasis in this book has been on techniques for macro-estimation, particularly utilizing the project history available in the ISBSG Repository, it is important to at least make reference to the essential micro-estimation technique, commonly known as a work breakdown structure (WBS). As there are many publications available that provide detailed material on work breakdown structures, this chapter provides only a basic introduction.

Work Breakdown Structure: Introduction

For work breakdown estimates, the main development phases are broken down into tasks and then into subtasks. PMBOK refers to this as "bottom-up estimates." To reduce the possibility of failing to include all the tasks, the project team members and stakeholders should be involved in the process of task identification and recording. This process then provides a base for a bottom-up estimate.

The team-based technique of *Wide-Band Delphi* estimation (developed by the Rand Corporation in 1948) is now widely used for software project WBS-based estimates. The technique is also taught in many universities and software organizations. After researching estimation techniques used by software organizations, the University of West Florida discovered that a number of software organizations utilize the technique, without referring to it by its name. So, even though few organizations claim to use the Delphi technique by name, the methodology is widely used.

NOTE *Formal risk assessment is an essential project estimation prerequisite.*

The following approach to work breakdown software estimation—based on the Delphi technique—can be used:

1. Provide team members with the relevant information regarding the project (business case, quality requirements, and so on).
2. Conduct a formal risk assessment.
3. Develop task lists.
4. Each person in the development team individually estimates each task using sensitivity analysis[1] to provide a best case, likely, and worst case estimate.
5. All estimates are then written on a white board, grouped in the three ranges.
6. Each person discusses the various assumptions and issues they considered when developing their estimates.
7. If appropriate, the various estimates are adjusted based on the team discussion.
8. Each range is averaged with outliers being discarded.
9. The resultant ranges are used as the basis for the effort and duration estimates.

The team discussions incorporated into this technique are very important because they allow the team members and stakeholders to learn about the various assumptions that were made during the estimation process.

NOTE *ISBSG research indicates that better project estimates are obtained by using a combination of work breakdown and macro-estimating techniques.*

As micro-estimation is a vital part of any project estimation effort, we recommend that you acquaint yourself with the work breakdown estimation technique and use it in addition to macro-estimation techniques.

---

[1] This technique involves making estimates ranged into three figures: optimistic, realistic (most likely), and pessimistic.

Using Process Models for Micro-Estimation

Another alternative for the breakdown of macro-activities into operational tasks is to use software life-cycle macro-phases[2] and to map these with the process model adopted in your own quality management system, or to use an external standard process model such as CMMI-DEV, SPICE (ISO/IEC 15504-5), or ISO/IEC 12207. Use of one of these will provide a framework to ensure that all standard and repeated activities are included. As your projects will then share the same definitions, ambiguities will be minimized, and this will also allow the comparison of projects. The result will be a three-tier WBS:

- Macro-Software Life-Cycle Phase (for example, "Design")
- Process (according to the chosen process model, for example, "Architectural Design")
- Task (according to the chosen process model, for example, "Review Architectural Design Specification")

Depending upon the process model chosen, it is possible to have a different number of process groups (or categories, depending upon the terminology used). For instance:

- CMMI-DEV has distributed its 22 process areas into four process *categories* (Project Management, Process Management, Support, and Engineering).
- ISO/IEC 15504-5 distributed its 48 processes into three main blocks of *processes* (Primary, Organizational, Support) for a total of nine process *groups* (**Primary**: Acquisition, Supply, Engineering, Operation; **Organizational**: Management, Process Improvement, Resource and Infrastructure, Reuse; **Support:** Support).

Figure 10-1 compares the two models' contents against those categories.

Two main questions arise from such classification into process categories:

- *What is the impact of the number of process categories on the WBS?* From a practical viewpoint, some useful information can be gained from a Gantt chart structured using these classifications. For instance, it would allow the following:
  - Easier matching of activity types to the related personnel skills required. This would provide a more granular classification of a generic "analysis" process, which would lead to different allocations (and related costs) for functional/business analysts and for technical analysts.

[2] Refer to "Project effort breakdown" in the Glossary.

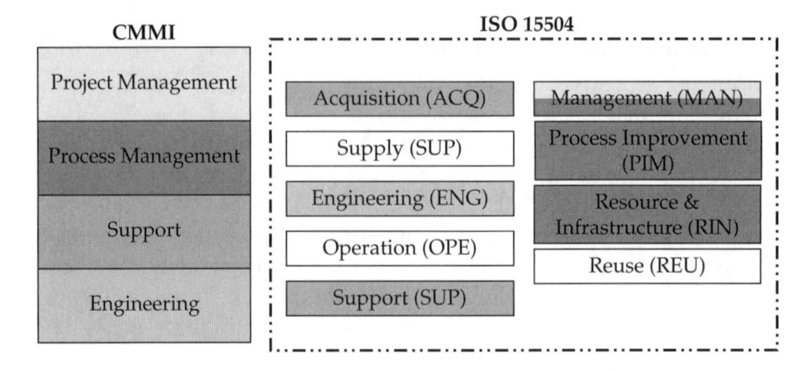

FIGURE 10-1 Process categories in CMMI and ISO 15504[3]

- Knowledge of the balance between categories and their alignment to expected thresholds for a certain kind/group of projects. This will allow you to more accurately assess the effort breakdown for the various project tasks (for example, business analysis).
- More accurate estimation and planning through an appropriate balance of activities in the project.

- *Why choose one reference model over another?*
  - Business viewpoint: this could be a case of requiring compliance with a model because it is a de facto standard and will allow for benchmarking (for example, CMMI-DEV).
  - Technical viewpoint—two alternatives:
    - *Choose a single model.* Usually, the larger the number of process groups, the broader the coverage of possible processes and related tasks performed in an organization. The choice of a specific model (and related number of process categories and processes) should be done in line with the organization's Quality Management Standard purpose and scope.
    - *Combine models.* Another option is to merge two models, integrating their best aspects into a single, customized model. For instance, CMMI-DEV has a reduced presence of processes related to reuse practices, while ISO 15504 has a devoted process. Or if you require more detail for testing or measurement, you could use specific "vertical" maturity models from those domains.

[3] The aim of this figure is to provide a snapshot of comparable groups by processes and related activities, marked with shades. Please note that categories that cannot be mapped (for example, Reuse) are shown with a white background.

Summary

Work breakdown structures are an important tool in software project estimation. They provide a micro-approach to estimating, thereby allowing a cross-check between the results achieved from micro and macro techniques. A sound approach to estimating a software development project is to use both a macro-estimation technique and a work breakdown micro-estimate.

CHAPTER 11

How Do I Estimate a Project Comprising Varying Components?

Some projects are characterized by subsets of functionality where different project delivery rates apply. For these projects it may be useful to apply macro-estimating methods to each subset and to aggregate the results. This chapter provides some examples of situations where you may wish to estimate project subsets.

Subsets Implemented Utilizing Different Technologies

It is common for systems to use mixed technologies in the software solution. For example, a 4GL or a report generator may be used to build reports, while the rest of the system may be developed in a lower-level language. Each technology subset should be independently sized, and then its effort should be estimated.

Code and Reference Tables

Many information systems are characterized by code and reference tables used to ensure the validity, consistency, and integrity of other data and to enable data selection. In data warehousing systems, the contribution of code and reference tables to the functional size has been observed to be as high as 60 percent, but in normal MIS systems is often around 30 to 40 percent.

The method used for building maintenance functionality for these tables varies among organizations and among technologies used. But as a general observation, where the data element format for each table is the same or similar (for example, a code, name, and maybe a short description), a generic technique for the software construction is common. This approach develops a generalized set of maintenance functions for code and reference tables. Indeed, some technology platforms will readily generate this functionality. A faster project delivery rate can be expected for this approach.

Subsets Characterized by Technical or Other Complexities

Many software development projects have functionality subsets that will be challenging to design and/or build because of technical or other complexities. The project delivery rate (hours per function point) you might expect to achieve in these areas may be significantly worse than for other functionality in the project.

Reused Code

Not all software will be built from scratch. Some of the software solution functionality may be acquired from systems previously built, or may be bought.

Some common examples of this type of functionality are the following:

- Security
- Utility software for backup/recovery/retrieval
- Utility software for searching, for example, by wildcard or phonetic matches
- Drawing tools
- Event/audit log browsing and searching

The project delivery rate you choose when you are reusing code will depend upon the amount of customization or modification needed, but normally you can expect to achieve a rate better than would be achieved if you had to write the code from scratch.

Summary

A software project can be made up of components that can be expected to have significantly different project delivery rates. You need to be aware of this, identify the components of your proposed project, estimate each component based on its individual characteristics, and then sum the totals to achieve a realistic estimate for the total software component of your project.

CHAPTER 12

Using Project History Databases

Software project history data can come from two sources: from an organization's own history of completed projects, and from databases of industry software project history.

Use of an Organization's Own Experience Data

The project delivery rate used for estimation (expressed in hours per function point) is best derived from an organization's own "experience" database. This experience database holds information about the organization's internal project history. Different organizations have their own characteristics that influence their processes and their productivity. Many of these characteristics are difficult to identify, let alone quantify. They will include variables like the impact of the working environment, staff mindset and staff morale, work mix (development/support), management, organization structure, and the relationship with clients/users.

When data is collected on in-house projects, the impact of these types of variables is embedded in the data. The biggest difficulty when building your in-house experience database is deciding what to collect. One of the prime goals of the ISBSG initiative is to provide a common language that can be used by IT practitioners in measuring their productivity and comparing themselves. You can build your own experience database by entering your project data in the ISBSG Repository.[1] From the project identification codes supplied to you when you submit data on projects, you will be able to extract your organization's projects from the ISBSG Data Release.

[1] Refer to Appendix E on the benefits of submitting projects to the ISBSG Repository. Also refer to http://www.isbsg.org/submitdata, Project data | Submit a project.

If you do enter your project data into the ISBSG Repository, you have the best of both worlds. You can extract your projects to derive the project delivery rates you have achieved, and you can extract similar projects from other organizations for comparison.

Use of the ISBSG Data

Industry data such as the ISBSG data is useful in estimating, in particular when you have no relevant experience data from your own organization to draw upon, or when you are planning a project that has characteristics unlike any of your previous projects. At the very least, industry data will give you some indication of the reasonableness of your own figures.

The ISBSG Repository

The data in the ISBSG Repository is not random project data, but is more likely to be representative of projects with higher than average productivity.

The key reason for higher than average productivity being represented lies in the method of ISBSG Repository collection. Many corporate repositories have been compiled by consultancy companies that were invited into organizations to benchmark them against the industry. This is often the result of serious concerns about the efficiency of the IT division. As such, these corporate repositories tend to reflect a random sample of industry projects. The source of the ISBSG Repository has been different in that the project data has been submitted voluntarily, by software practitioners who have a genuine interest in maximizing their productivity. These practitioners could reasonably be regarded as "mature" in their measurement philosophy and practices, and have proactively sought to benchmark their projects against the world. Other significant differentiating attributes of the ISBSG data include:

- Some organizations simply cannot contribute to the repository. The criteria for including a project in the repository generally exclude organizations that do not use functional size measurement.[2] They also exclude projects for which work effort (in person-hours) is not available.
- Only organizations that collect the necessary metrics can contribute to the repository. Organizations with software metrics programs are likely to be among the more mature software development organizations.

[2] Although the repository does accept projects that have been sized using methods other than functional units (for example, LOC and use case points), the ISBSG does not perform validation on these size measures; it simply records them for general information.

- Organizations also choose which of their projects they submit. They might choose typical projects, but they might choose only their best projects.
- The majority of the projects in the repository are less than 500 function points in size. There are few really big projects.

In determining which data to collect, the ISBSG philosophy has been that a minimum set of data will be collected that is meaningful, readily available, and *objective*. As such, much of the "soft" (subjective) data, which is important to estimating, is not collected. ISBSG does collect some data on "people factors" and "product and process quality," but not currently in areas like the general novelty of the project (has this type of system been built before?), the complexity of the problem being addressed, the stability of user requirements, and project constraints.

These considerations do not lessen the value of the data in the repository. The focus of the repository is as much on understanding best practice in the IT industry as on overall averages. However, the key metrics have been studied and tested. The results of this work demonstrate that the sample represented by the repository is self-contained, internally consistent, and contains no apparent anomalies. The repository is therefore a very valuable collection of data for estimation.

Guidelines for Use of the ISBSG Data

As the ISBSG project history data is readily available to IT practitioners and researchers, it is important that its users have a sound knowledge of the data—are aware of its strengths, limitations, and positioning—prior to analyzing or using it. It is important to give careful thought to the project data that you will include in any data set that you plan to use. You need to think about the meaning of the data, and not just treat it as numbers to be used without selectivity. What project types can be legitimately compared or analyzed together?

Here are some examples:

- **Project Rating** The ISBSG considers that projects with a data quality rating of A or B are suitable for statistical analysis. Projects rated C or D may still provide valuable data, but uncertainty about some of their size or effort values means that it is best not to include them in your estimation data sets.
- **Normalized Effort**[3] For effort, consider what risk and gain is involved in using normalized effort. *The Summary Work*

[3] Refer to Appendix A.

Effort shown in the data is the total effort for the project. What is counted within that total varies, because different projects record effort at different levels of detail (see the *Resource Level* and *Recording Method* fields).

A resource level of *1* means that only the effort of the development team is recorded; *2* means that support team effort is also recorded; *3* adds computer operations; and *4* adds effort expended by the end user or client.

You can do two things to make sure you compare effort appropriately:

- It is best to select only those projects that record the same effort detail as you do.
- You don't have to ignore every other project—you can use rules of thumb to translate approximately between different levels of effort.

Previous analysis of projects in the ISBSG Repository shows that level 2 effort is about 10–12 percent more than level 1, level 3 adds about another 1 or 2 percent, and level 4 is about 20–25 percent more than level 1.

NOTE *If you use approximations like this, you add uncertainty to your data and add risk to any conclusions that you draw.*

- **Functional Size Measurement Methods (FSMM)** It will be optimal for size comparisons if all the selected projects have been measured using the same (or compatible) FSMM and version. If you mix methods, you need to know their characteristics. For example, you shouldn't mix projects sized using pre-IFPUG 4 with those sized using IFPUG 4.*x*[4] (the sizing changed with that release). New development projects sized using the NESMA standard can be included with IFPUG 4.x projects. Use the *Count Approach* field in the data (and perhaps also the *FP Standards* and *Reference Table Approach* fields), to select projects that use the same sizing method that you use.
- **Other Criteria** Other criteria that may be important are organization type, business area type, application type, user base, and development techniques.

  You will want to select projects that are similar to yours in important project attributes.

---

[4] "IFPUG 4.*x*" refers to the IFPUG 4 series of releases (4, 4.1, 4.2, and so on).

The ISBSG suggests that the most important criteria for selecting projects are as follows:

- *Size* (if yours is a really large project, there is not much value to you in studying small ones, and vice versa)
- *Development type* (new development, enhancement, or redevelopment)
- *Primary programming language* or *language type* (for example, 3GL, 4GL)
- *Development platform* (mainframe, midrange, or PC)

Bear in mind that as you add more selection criteria, the number of projects selected inevitably gets smaller. You can end up with small groups of projects, or perhaps even no projects that satisfy all criteria. How important the group size is will depend on what you want to do with the data.

In summary it is important that any data subset that you use has integrity. The key points are to choose only appropriately rated data, to ensure that measurements are defined the same way (that is, FSM releases are compatible and effort measures are consistent), and that the measurements apply to the same thing (that is, effort normalization and effort levels).

Presentation of Statistics

Appendix B provides an explanation of the ISBSG's presentation of statistics and a brief guide to using the statistics and the various tables provided in the appendixes.

Using Several Estimation Approaches

Means, medians, and regression lines should be used with caution, especially where sample sizes are small, and variances or standard deviations are high. You should not rely on a single estimation method, especially since the macro-estimation methods described in this book are based on broad averages.

We suggest that you derive your estimates from a relevant subset of the projects in the ISBSG data set, and that you use your traditional estimating methods as a reasonableness check.

Summary

The ISBSG project history data is a very valuable resource for estimation, but it must be used carefully and with an understanding of what it does and does not represent.

CHAPTER 13

Project Estimation Using the ISBSG Repository

This chapter provides a practical introduction to using the macro-estimating techniques described in this book. We present a software development case study and then describe three different macro-estimating techniques that utilize data from the ISBSG Repository to estimate project work effort and duration for the target project outlined in the case study. The macro-estimating techniques described are the following:

- Estimating using regression equations
- Estimating using comparison
- Estimating using analogy

Step-by-step examples of how each of these estimating techniques can be applied to the case study project are presented, and the benefits and limitations of each technique are discussed.

The examples utilize project data taken from the "ISBSG Estimating, Benchmarking & Research Suite Release 11" (ISBSG Repository).[1]

Case Study: A Student and Staff Records Management System (SSRM)

Overview

The Supersoft software company will soon begin developing a student and staff records management system to be called SSRM.

[1] The "ISBSG Estimating, Benchmarking & Research Suite Release 11" contains data on over 5,000 projects. It can be licensed from www.isbsg.org or from ISBSG member organizations.

SSRM is a management information system to be developed for a local college. SSRM will allow college administrators to enter, maintain, and report on a range of information including:

- Students' personal, course, and results information
- Staff members' personal, course, and employment history information

SSRM will also allow individual students and staff members to obtain summaries of their own information. To facilitate ease of use, SSRM must allow access from any location via a standard web browser interface.

SSRM will be developed to operate on a midrange UNIX platform. Users will be able to remotely access SSRM via any standard web browser, but all the system's processing will be performed on the UNIX platform.

Even though SSRM will replace several existing systems, its requirements are sufficiently different from those systems that it is considered a new development, not as a redevelopment of the existing systems.

Functional Size Measurement

An initial requirements specification for SSRM has been completed, and a functional size measure of the system has been carried out based on that specification. The function point sizing serves a number of purposes:

- Performing function point analysis helps to identify any missing, incorrect, or unnecessary requirements.
- The completed function point size and accompanying functional model will aid in scope management throughout the project by serving as a baseline against which any scope changes can be tracked and controlled.
- The function point size provides an objective measure of the system's size that can be obtained very early in the project life cycle and from which, with the addition of information from sources such as the ISBSG Repository, estimates of the project work effort and duration can be obtained.

The functional size of SSRM is determined to be *480 function points.* From past experience, Supersoft knows that requirements scope creep likely will increase the size of the system by around *12 percent* from the initial function point count to the final delivered size. An additional *60 function points* are therefore added to the functional size for use in estimating, to account for the likely scope creep.

Functional size from initial requirements specification:	*480 function points*
Likely functional size increase due to scope creep:	*12% × 480 = 57.6 ≈ 60 function points*
Functional size used in estimating:	*480 + 60 = 540 function points*

Project Work Effort and Duration Estimates

Supersoft has appointed Jenny to be the project manager for the development of SSRM. Jenny is an experienced software project manager and has managed the development of several similar systems in the past. Most members of Jenny's development team are also experienced in this type of software development.

One of Jenny's first tasks is to generate project work effort and duration estimates for the SSRM project. These will be used in the development of the project's schedule and budget.

Along with other members of her development team, Jenny plans to develop a complete work breakdown for the SSRM project and then to use a task-based micro-estimating technique to generate the estimates. From experience, however, Jenny knows that developing an accurate and complete work breakdown for a project such as this will take considerable time. Because she needs initial and indicative estimates more quickly than she can obtain them from the task-based micro-estimating technique, Jenny decides to use macro-estimating techniques, which do not require a complete work breakdown, to develop the initial estimates.

An additional benefit of using macro-estimating techniques is that when she comes to generate the full, task-based micro-estimates from the work breakdown, Jenny will be able to use the existing macro-estimates for validation. Any significant differences between the task-based micro-estimates and the macro-estimates can be investigated to ensure that no tasks have been inadvertently missed out, included without reason, or incorrectly assessed.

Ideally, Jenny would utilize historical data from completed Supersoft projects to generate the macro-estimates. Although Supersoft is an experienced software development company, it has only recently begun developing systems similar to SSRM and has therefore not yet developed a substantial repository of development information on such projects. Because Supersoft does not have its own repository, Jenny decides to utilize the ISBSG Repository as the source of historical data on completed projects from which to develop her project work effort and duration macro-estimates.

The remainder of this chapter describes how Jenny goes about developing the macro-estimates for the SSRM project using the ISBSG Repository.

By following the instructions within the text and utilizing project data from the ISBSG Repository, you can duplicate the steps Jenny carries out to generate the estimates. This will provide you with a practical introduction to using the macro-estimating techniques described in this book.

Example 1: Estimating Using Regression Equations

One of the quickest and simplest mechanisms for generating estimates of project work effort and duration is to utilize equations developed from regression analysis of completed software projects.

Linear regression equations have been developed from the data in the ISBSG Repository[2] for the following project classes:

- Projects classified by development platform: mainframe, midrange, PC, and multiplatform
- Projects classified by development language type: 3GL and 4GL
- Projects classified by project type: new development and enhancement
- Projects classified by a combination of development platform, development language type, and project type

In conjunction with a project's functional size, or a combination of functional size and maximum team size, the regression equations can be used to generate estimates for:

- Project delivery rate (PDR_{RE}), expressed in hours per function point
- Project work effort (PWE_{RE}), expressed in hours
- Speed of delivery (SD_{RE}), expressed in function points per month
- Project duration (PD_{RE}), expressed in months

Using Regression Equations to Generate Estimates for SSRM

Jenny uses the ISBSG regression equations to generate her first set of project work effort and duration estimates for the SSRM project.

Regression Equations: Functional Size

Because the ISBSG regression equations consider the project's development platform, Jenny must first decide which regression equations she should use to generate her estimates.

[2] The complete ISBSG project data is available on the "ISBSG Estimating, Benchmarking & Research Suite." The suite also includes the ISBSG Early Estimate Checker tool, which can be used to develop regression equation–based estimates. The suite can be licensed from www.isbsg.org or from ISBSG member organizations.

The project to develop SSRM will be a new development project. SSRM will be developed for a combination midrange and PC platform. Because all of the system's processing will occur on the midrange platform, with the PC platform limited to providing the standard web browser interface, Jenny initially decides to use the ISBSG regression equations for the class of new development projects developed for the midrange platform.

On viewing the ISBSG regression equations for this class of project, however, Jenny discovers that whilst a variation in functional size explains a reasonable variation in the project work effort, the same is not true for project delivery rate, speed of delivery, or project duration, where the equations' R2(Adj)[3] values are less than *0.25.* Jenny therefore decides to use the ISBSG regression equations for the class of new development projects developed for a multiplatform to estimate speed of delivery and project duration. These equations provide a reasonable match to her project and have substantially higher R2(Adj) values.

Jenny notes that none of the development platforms recorded in the ISBSG Repository can be used to generate effective project delivery rate estimates based upon functional size alone. In all cases they lead to R2(Adj) values of less than *0.25.* This is not too much of a concern for Jenny, however, because her goal is to determine estimates for project work effort and project duration, both of which she can do.

Using the selected regression equations for a project with a functional size of *540 function points,* Jenny obtains the following estimates:

Project Delivery Rate (Appendix C, Table C-2.0)	PDR_{RE}	There are no suitable ISBSG regression equations for estimating project delivery rate from functional size alone.
Project Work Effort (Appendix C, Table C-2.1)	PWE_{RE} *(New development/ Midrange)*	$= 19.08 \times Size^{0.883}$ $= 19.08 \times 540^{0.883}$ = 4,934 hours
Project Duration (Appendix C, Table C-2.2)	PD_{RE} *(New development/ Multi)*	$= 0.423 \times Size^{0.440}$ $= 0.423 \times 540^{0.440}$ = 6.7 months
Speed of Delivery (Appendix C, Table C-2.3)	SD_{RE} *(New development/ Multi)*	$= 2.367 \times Size^{0.560}$ $= 2.367 \times 540^{0.560}$ = 80 function points per month

[3] Adjusted Squared Multiple R = R2(Adj) is a measure of how much of the variability between different projects is actually explained by the equation. The maximum value is 1.00, which would occur when every project agreed exactly with the equation. The closer the value is to 1.00, the better. Even low values here can be meaningful; something is being explained, but randomness or variation in other predictive factors may have diluted the predictive effect. Low values do not tell you much (equations with an R2(Adj) less than 0.25 are not even reported in these tables). High values, such as 0.80, are extremely encouraging (but are not necessarily conclusive).

The regression equations based upon functional size for the midrange and multiplatform development platforms indicate that the SSRM project will require about *4,934 hours of work* and take 6.7 *months* to complete.

Regression Equations: Functional Size and Maximum Team Size

By combining these first estimates with her knowledge of the project's size and different project maximum team sizes, Jenny is able to both tune her estimates and investigate the relationship between project effort and duration.

First, Jenny uses her existing estimates of project effort and duration and her experience, which tells her that one full-time equivalent (FTE) resource equates to approximately *130 effort hours per month.*[4] She calculates a likely figure for the SSRM project's average monthly effort and hence an average team size of approximately *5.5 full-time equivalent resources*. Jenny performs the following calculations:

Resource to Effort Ratio (RER)	*1 FTE Resource = 130 hours per month*
Average Monthly Effort (AME)	$PWE_{RE} / PD_{RE} =$ *4,934 / 6.7 = 736 hours per month*
Average Team Size (ATS)	*AME / RER =* *736 / 130 ≈ 5.5 FTE resources*

Because Jenny knows that project resource levels are typically not constant for the entire project duration, but rather start at a low level, build up to a peak, and then decline, she also knows that the SSRM project's maximum team size will be greater than the average team size of *5.5* that she has already calculated. Based upon this and her experience, Jenny therefore chooses an initial maximum team size of *9 FTEs* for the SSRM project. Using this information, Jenny obtains the following additional estimates:

Project Delivery Rate (Appendix C, Table C-1.0)	PDR_{REMTS} *(New development/ midrange)*	$= 35.09 \times Size^{-0.597} \times$ *Maximum Team Size*$^{1.080}$ $= 35.09 \times 540^{-0.597} \times 9^{1.080}$ *= 8.8 hours per function point*
Project Work Effort (Appendix C, Table C-1.1)	PWE_{REMTS} *(New development/ midrange)*	$= 35.09 \times Size^{0.403} \times$ *Maximum Team Size*$^{1.080}$ $= 35.09 \times 540^{0.403} \times 9^{1.080}$ *= 4,752 hours*

[4] The ratio of one full-time equivalent resource equating to approximately 130 effort hours per month is based upon typical industry figures.

Speed of Delivery (Appendix C, Table C-1.3)	SD_{REMTS} *(New development/ midrange)*	There are no suitable ISBSG regression equations for estimating speed of delivery from functional size and likely maximum team size for midrange platform projects.
Project Duration (Appendix C, Table C-1.2)	PD_{REMTS} *(New development/ midrange)*	There are no suitable ISBSG regression equations for estimating project duration from functional size and likely maximum team size for midrange platform projects.

The regression equation for project work effort based upon SSRM's functional size and likely maximum team size indicates that the SSRM project will require around *4,752 hours of work*. There are no suitable regression equations for estimating project duration or speed of delivery. Because Jenny's new project effort estimate aligns closely to her initial estimate, however, she can reasonably assume that a new project duration estimate should align closely to her original project duration estimate of *6.7 months*.

To investigate the relationship between project effort and duration further, Jenny now recalculates the project effort estimate using a smaller maximum team size of *6 FTEs* as follows:

Project Work Effort (Appendix C, Table C-1.1)	PWE_{REMTS} *(New development/ midrange)*	$= 35.09 \times Size^{0.403} \times Maximum\ Team\ Size^{1.080}$ $= 35.09 \times 540^{0.403} \times 6^{1.080}$ $= 3{,}067$ *hours*

Based upon this smaller maximum team size, the regression equation indicates that the SSRM project would require around *3,067 hours of work*, a savings of *35 percent* over the previous estimate. Of course, this project effort savings must come at a cost. In this case, the cost is an increase in project duration. To obtain this reduction in project effort would require an increase in the project duration from a value of around *6.7 months* estimated using the maximum team size of *9 FTEs*. The ISBSG Repository contains insufficient data to determine the actual magnitude of the increase in project duration. Whether such an increase is acceptable is often driven by external factors such as time-to-market windows of opportunity or the availability of necessarily skilled development staff. If, for example, most members of the SSRM development team have no critical activities scheduled over the next *9 months*, then significant effort, and hence cost, savings might be made through utilizing a smaller project team coupled with a longer project duration.

The regression equations based upon the combination of functional size and maximum team size allow the project estimates to be tuned in a manner that investigates the relationship between project effort and project duration. These equations are best used in conjunction with the regression equations based upon functional size alone. This is because, if used with unrealistic or unachievable maximum team size values, or without some knowledge of the likely relationship between project effort and project duration, the regression equations based upon the combination of values may generate unachievable and unacceptable project delivery rate and work effort estimates.

Discussion

By utilizing the regression equations, Jenny has been able to quickly obtain indicative project effort and duration estimates for the SSRM project. She might use such initial estimates to establish project feasibility. She could decide that she is satisfied with these estimates and finish the analysis at this point. Alternatively, she could decide to fine-tune the estimates to address additional specific project attributes that so far have not been explicitly considered.

Because Jenny feels that the SSRM project has some other specific attributes that are likely to impact the total project work and duration, but that have not been explicitly addressed by the regression equations, she decides to fine-tune her estimates based upon the ISBSG Repository data. The following sections outline how she does this.

Example 2: Estimating Using Comparison

The most obvious limitation of using regression equations to estimate project work effort and duration is that the equations fail to address many specific project attributes that are known to impact work effort and duration. Although the provision of separate sets of regression equations for different development platforms improves this situation, the project delivery rate for an application developed using Lotus Notes is still likely to differ significantly from one developed using Java, even when they are both developed for the same midrange platform.

A further limitation of the regression equations as they were presented in the previous section is that they only provide a single value for each of the project estimates when, in many cases, a range of values would be more useful. Having a range of estimate values allows the project manager to consider both optimistic and conservative as well as likely estimates when devising or validating the project schedule and budget.

The estimating by comparison technique presented here addresses both these limitations of regression equation–based estimating by considering various specific project attributes and by generating a range of values for each of the project estimates.

The estimating by comparison technique begins by calculating *optimistic, likely,* and *conservative* project delivery rate and speed of delivery values for selections of projects from the ISBSG Repository that match the target project on a single attribute. The averages of the project delivery rates and speeds of delivery for all the selections are then calculated, and these values are combined with the target project's functional size to generate optimistic, likely, and conservative estimates for the target project's work effort and duration.

The estimating by comparison technique is described in detail in the following section.

The Estimating by Comparison Technique

Estimating by comparison utilizes the following approach to estimate project work effort and duration using data from the ISBSG Repository:

1. For the target project, determine its functional size and identify its project type and development platform.
2. Use the target project's functional size and development type and platform to select a subset of similar projects from the ISBSG Repository.[5] Estimates generated by the estimating by comparison technique will only consider the selected subset of projects.
    - The functional size used to select projects from the ISBSG Repository is expressed as a range of sizes rather than as a single value.
    - The estimator may choose not to restrict the set of projects for consideration based upon one or a selection of functional size and development type and platform. The reason for restricting the projects for selection in this way, however, is that analysis of the ISBSG Repository has shown that each of functional size, development type, and development platform has significant impact upon project work effort and duration. Restricting the estimating by comparison technique to consider only those projects of a similar functional size, and having the same development type and platform as the target project, should therefore provide more accurate estimates than simply considering all the projects in the repository.
3. For each of the target project's attributes recorded in the ISBSG Repository, calculate the optimistic, likely, and conservative

[5] The complete ISBSG project data is available on the "ISBSG Estimating, Benchmarking & Research Suite." ISBSG also provides the ISBSG Comparative Estimating tool. Both these products can be licensed from www.isbsg.org or from ISBSG member organizations.

project delivery rate and speed of delivery, based upon all the projects in the selected repository subset that exhibit that attribute.

- The median is used to calculate the likely value for project delivery rate and speed of delivery. The median is used instead of the mean to reduce the impact of outliers on the results.
- The 25th and 75th percentiles are used to calculate the optimistic and conservative values for project delivery rate and speed of delivery. Because a *lower* value indicates a *better* project delivery rate, the 25th percentile indicates the optimistic value for project delivery rate. However, because a *lower* value indicates a *poorer* speed of delivery, the 25th percentile indicates the conservative value for speed of delivery.

4. Estimate the project delivery rate and speed of delivery by calculating the averages of the project delivery rates and speeds of delivery for the sets of optimistic, likely, and conservative values.
   - The mean is used to determine the average values for the sets of project delivery rates and speeds of delivery.
5. Estimate the project work effort and duration by combining the project delivery rate and speed of delivery estimates with the project's functional size.

NOTE *Because estimating by comparison is an informal technique, it can be easily understood and applied by anyone with access to a database of historical project information, such as the ISBSG Repository. On the other hand, because estimating by comparison does not use formal statistical analysis, it is important that the estimator carefully assesses the type and number of individual projects that are contributing to an estimate to ensure that the basis for the estimate is valid.*

Using Estimating by Comparison to Generate Estimates for SSRM

Jenny begins the estimating by comparison task by restricting the projects from the ISBSG Repository that will be utilized to calculate the estimates to those that match SSRM's functional size, development platform, and project type, thereby selecting a suitable data set. She employs the following restrictions:

Attribute	Target Project Value	Matching ISBSG Projects
Functional Size	*540*	*250–750 function points*
Development Platform	*Midrange*	*Midrange*
Development Type	*New development*	*New development*

Next, Jenny identifies the SSRM project's values for a range of the project attributes included in the ISBSG Repository.

She then calculates the optimistic, likely, and conservative project delivery rate and speed of delivery values for the projects in the selected data set with matching project attribute values. If Jenny feels that for a particular project attribute, none of the values in the repository match, she simply ignores that attribute. Jenny also calculates the number of matches for each project attribute. These values will help her validate the viability of the final estimates. The following table displays the SSRM project attribute values and sets out the results of the calculations:

			Project Delivery Rate *(hours per function point)*			**Speed of Delivery** *(function points per month)*		
Attribute	**Target Project Value**	**Number of Matches**	**Optim (25th%)**	**Likely (median)**	**Conserv (75th%)**	**Conserv (25th%)**	**Likely (median)**	**Optim (75th%)**
Primary Programming Language	Java	*7*	*5.0*	*9.3*	*9.3*	*100.4*	*111.5*	*197.9*
Organization Type	Education	*0*						
Application Type	Management Information System	*2*	*7.9*	*8.4*	*8.9*	*38.1*	*38.1*	*38.1*
Maximum Team Size	5–8	*1*	*7.6*	*7.6*	*7.6*	*54.0*	*54.0*	*54.0*
Used Prototyping	Yes	*3*	*8.2*	*9.2*	*33.4*	*37.7*	*37.8*	*38.0*
Used JAD	Yes	*0*						
Web Development	Yes	*12*	*8.0*	*9.3*	*14.8*	*56.7*	*103.8*	*158.2*

The number of matches for the SSRM project's attributes ranges from *0* for *Organization Type – Education* and *Used JAD – Yes,* up to *12* for *Web Development – Yes.* Although Jenny would have preferred to have a larger number of matches for several of the project attributes, she decides that the total number of matching projects is adequate to provide indicative estimates. She also decides not to eliminate any further attributes from her analysis.

Jenny generates the SSRM project delivery rate (PDR_{CE}) and speed of delivery (SD_{CE}) estimates by calculating the averages (that is, the *means*) of the sets of project delivery rates and speeds of delivery for the conservative, likely, and optimistic values.

Finally, she combines the project delivery rate and speed of delivery estimates with SSRM's functional size of *540 function points* to calculate the estimates for project work effort (PWE_{CE}) and duration (PD_{CE}). She obtains the following results:

Project Delivery Rate	PDR_{CE}	= mean of optimistic/likely/ conservative project delivery rates
	$PDR_{CE\ optimistic}$	= 7.3 hours per function point
	$PDR_{CE\ likely}$	= 8.7 hours per function point
	$PDR_{CE\ conservative}$	= 14.8 hours per function point
Project Work Effort	PWE_{CE}	= $PDR_{CE\ I}$ × Size
	$PWE_{CE\ optimistic}$	= 3,954 hours
	$PWE_{CE\ likely}$	= 4,721 hours
	$PWE_{CE\ conservative}$	= 7,989 hours
Speed of Delivery	SD_{CE}	= mean of optimistic/likely/ conservative speeds of delivery
	$SD_{CE\ optimistic}$	= 97.2 function points per month
	$SD_{CE\ likely}$	= 69.1 function points per month
	$SD_{CE\ conservative}$	= 57.4 function points per month
Project Duration	PD_{CE}	= Size / $SD_{CE\ i}$
	$PD_{CE\ optimistic}$	= 5.6 months
	$PD_{CE\ likely}$	= 7.8 months
	$PD_{CE\ conservative}$	= 9.4 months

Estimating by comparison indicates that the SSRM project will require:

- Between *3,954* and *7,989 hours of work,* with a likely value of *4,721 hours*

  and

- Between *5.6* and *9.4 months,* with a likely value of *7.8 months* to complete

Discussion

Jenny has now completed the target project's estimation using the comparison technique. She has optimistic, likely, and conservative estimates for SSRM's project work effort and duration.

Of immediate interest is a comparison between the earlier regression equation estimates and the comparative estimates.

- The comparative estimate's likely project work effort estimate of *4,721 hours* aligns very closely with the regression equation estimate of *4,752 hours* (regression equation estimate considering both functional size and maximum team size).

- The comparative estimate's likely project duration estimate of *7.8 months* aligns reasonably closely (that is, is *16 percent* higher) to the original regression equation estimate of *6.7 months* (regression equation estimate considering functional size alone).

In other words, when several more of the SSRM's attributes were explicitly considered, they were found to support the regression equation estimate for project work effort and to suggest a slight increase for project duration.

Based upon her knowledge of the many other project attributes that were not addressed by the estimating by comparison technique, but which can also impact project work effort and duration, Jenny could now attempt to determine what actual value from within the estimate ranges she should select as the SSRM project estimates. Doing that, however, would limit the amount of information the estimating by comparison process has made available to her.

Jenny therefore chooses to focus on the full estimate range:

- If the project goes extremely well with no major problems, with less than the normal amount of holdups, scope creep, and rework, and no personnel changes, it should be possible to achieve the optimistic estimates.
- If the project follows the normal path, the likely estimates should be achievable.
- If, on the other hand, significant but surmountable problems and holdups occur during the project, it may be possible to achieve only the conservative estimates.

Utilizing the full range of estimate values, Jenny and the other Supersoft personnel in charge of the SSRM project can now consider the impact on their budget, resources, and the company's future of either a *highly successful, normal,* or *highly unsuccessful* SSRM project.

The full range of estimate values will also be more useful than a single estimate value to Jenny when she later uses the comparative estimates to help validate the task-based micro-estimates. If SSRM's task-based estimates fall within the comparative estimate ranges, Jenny can feel more confident that the task-based estimates are consistent with the values typically achieved by the industry for this type of project. If not, this will highlight the need to investigate whether there are valid reasons for SSRM being expected to have significantly better or worse project work effort or duration than is typically achieved.

Example 3: Estimating Using Analogy

The estimating by comparison technique just described allowed the estimator to "tune" the estimates calculated from the ISBSG Repository data to reflect the explicit attributes of a particular project. In doing so, however, estimating by comparison still relies upon calculating averages from a number of projects in the repository that are *somewhat* similar to the target project. Estimating by comparison does not attempt to find or to give additional weight to the one or small number of projects in the repository that are *most* similar to the target project. Its inability to focus on these *most* similar projects means that estimating by comparison may fail to properly consider the projects in the repository that can provide some of the most useful information.

The estimating using analogy technique presented here is a technique that focuses upon finding the project, or projects, in the repository *most* similar to the target project and then utilizing their actual values of project work effort and duration as estimates for the target project. These matching projects are known as *analogs.*

The estimating using analogy process is demonstrated in detail in the following section.

The Estimating by Analogy Technique

Estimating using analogy utilizes the following approach to estimate project work effort and duration using data from the ISBSG Repository:

1. Determine the target project's value for each of the project attributes recorded in the ISBSG Repository.[6]
2. Attempt to select a project analog from the ISBSG Repository that has the same attribute values as the target project. Ideally, this step will identify a single project analog. In reality, however, this is often not the case.

   If there is no single project analog in the repository, then it will be necessary to eliminate one or more of the recorded project attributes from the matching set until an analog can be found. Careful judgment needs to be exercised to determine which attributes should be eliminated from the matching set to ensure that those that have the most impact on the project work effort or duration are not eliminated. Another problem associated with selectively eliminating project attributes is that different subsets of matching attributes may identify different project analogs. Once again, careful judgment must be exercised to determine which subset of attributes is the most significant and hence, which analog should be selected.

   If matching all the project attributes identifies more than one project analog, then the estimator has the choice of either

[6] The complete ISBSG project data is available on the "ISBSG Estimating, Benchmarking & Research Suite" that can be licensed from www.isbsg.org or from ISBSG member organizations.

considering additional project attributes, in order to allow some of the first set of analogs to be eliminated, or of working with multiple project analogs. If the latter choice is made, the estimator might decide to use the averages of the analogs' project work effort and duration as the estimate values. Care must be taken with such an approach, however. If a small number of analogs display a wide variation in project work effort or duration values, then the estimating by comparison technique that also works with averages but considers a larger number of projects when determining those averages, may be a preferable approach.

3. Estimate the project work effort and duration for the target project from the analog project's actual values. It is often necessary to adjust the analog's values to account for any remaining differences between the target and the analog such as a variation in functional size.

Because estimating using analogy bases its estimates upon one or a small number of project analogs, it is more susceptible to errors resulting from selecting invalid project data points than the other techniques we have discussed. With these other techniques, the impact of a single invalid project data point will usually be quite small, because that data point is not considered individually, but always as one of a number of project data points that contribute to an average value.

For this reason, estimating using analogy should probably be used only when the estimator is confident of the accuracy and completeness of all the potential project analogs. Ideally, having selected an initial analog, the estimator would then be able to find out more about that project either through speaking to the project team members or by accessing the project documentation. This would allow the estimator to validate that the analog really did match the target project and that there were no extraneous issues to account for the achieved project work effort and duration.

Because this level of validation is not possible for projects in the ISBSG Repository, estimators need to be very careful in using the repository as a source of analogs. One way of minimizing this risk is to always use the estimating using analogy technique as a mechanism for validating existing estimates, rather than as the means for generating the estimates in the first place.

Using Estimating by Analogy to Generate Estimates for SSRM

Having generated estimate ranges for project work effort and duration using estimating by comparison, Jenny decides that she will now use estimating by analogy to validate her existing estimates.

Jenny's first task is to filter the ISBSG Repository to attempt to select a project analog that matches the target project on all of the recorded project attributes. The SSRM project attributes have the following values:

Attribute	Target Project Value
Functional size	*540 function points*
Development platform	*Midrange*
Project type	*New development*
Organization type	*Education*
Application type	*Management information system*
Maximum team size	*5 to 8*
Primary programming language	*Java*
Used prototyping	*Yes*
Used JAD	*Yes*
Web development	*Yes*

From her experience using the estimation by comparison technique, Jenny already knows that her copy of the ISBSG Repository contains no new development projects of between *250* and *750 function points,* developed for a midrange platform, that match *Organization Type – Education* or *Used JAD – Yes,* so she decides to eliminate those project attributes from the matching set.

When Jenny attempts to select an analog based upon the remaining SSRM project attributes, however, she discovers that there is still no analog to her target project in the ISBSG Repository. She therefore decides to eliminate and generalize more of the project attributes from the matching set in order to try to find an analog. This leads to the following reduced set of project attribute values:

Attribute	Target Project Value
Functional size	*250–750 function points*
Development platform	*Midrange*
Project type	*New development*
Primary programming language	*Java*

Using this reduced set of matching project attributes, Jenny identifies four matching projects and potential analogs in the ISBSG Repository. She considers each of these potential analogs individually, looking at their full set of attribute values, in order to determine which she should ultimately choose as the actual analog.

From this process Jenny eliminates the two potential analogs with *Organization Type – Manufacturing.* Jenny thinks that manufacturing and education organizations have very different focuses and that this may impact the way in which they develop and deliver software. The two remaining potential analogs both have *Organization Type – Professional Services,* which Jenny feels is a better fit to the SSRM project. These two remaining potential analogs have as their project activity scopes *Planning, Specification, Build and Test* and *Planning, Specification, Build, Test and Implement,* respectively. Because the SSRM project estimates must address all of the planning, specification, build, test, and implement phases, Jenny has no hesitation in choosing the latter project as her actual analog.

Jenny is now able to read values for the target project's delivery rate and speed of delivery estimates directly from the analog's own attributes.

Function Points	**Project Work Effort** *(hours)*	**Project Delivery Rate** *(hours per function point)*	**Speed of Delivery** *(function points per month)*	**Project Duration** *(months)*
435	4,045	9.3	111.5	3.9

Combining the analog's project delivery rate and speed of delivery with SSRM's functional size, Jenny calculates the following estimates:

Project Delivery Rate	PDR_{AE}	= *project analog value* = 9.3 *hours per function point*
Project Work Effort	PWE_{AE}	$= PDR_{AE} \times Size$ $= 9.3 \times 540$ = 5,022 *hours*
Speed of Delivery	SD_{AE}	= *project analog value* = 111.5 *function points per month*
Project Duration	PD_{AE}	$= Size / SD_{AE}$ $= 540 / 111.5$ = 4.8 *months*

Estimating using analogy indicates that development of SSRM will require around *5,022 hours of work* and will take *4.8 months* to complete.

Discussion

Jenny has now completed the estimation by analogy process. The estimated value for project work effort is around *6 percent higher* than the likely value calculated using estimating by comparison, so is well within the comparative estimate's likely to pessimistic range. On the other hand, the estimated value for project duration is around *38 percent lower* than the likely value calculated using comparative estimating and is even around *14 percent lower* than the comparative estimate's optimistic value.

For project work effort, the estimation by analogy value does appear to support the values calculated using estimation by comparison. The same is not true, however, for the project duration estimates. Because of her lack of knowledge as to whether the selected project analog is truly analogous to SSRM and because she is unable at this stage to discover any further information that would clarify this issue, Jenny decides not to utilize the analogy-based estimates to validate the planned task-based micro-estimates. In the future, when Supersoft has built up its own repository of completed project data, Jenny will be able to use that data to perform estimating using analogy more effectively.

Summary

Jenny has now completed her macro-level estimating for the SSRM project. She will use the comparative estimates as initial and indicative estimates of SSRM's required project work effort and duration to aid in constructing the project plan, schedule, and budget. She will also use the estimates to help validate the task-based micro-estimates that will be generated from the full work breakdown once it is completed.

When the development of SSRM is completed, Jenny submits a description of the project along with details of the actual project work effort and duration to ISBSG to be added to the ISBSG Repository. Each project added to the ISBSG Repository enhances its usefulness as an estimating tool and, hence, aids software practitioners in accurately determining project resource requirements and schedules and ensuring that they deliver their software on time and within budget.

CHAPTER 14

Estimating for Agile Software Development

Agile is an approach to software development and delivery that:

- Encourages a high level of customer involvement throughout the software process and tolerates—and even promotes—changes to the software's requirements during that process
- Delivers software via a series of short iterations—a couple of weeks to a couple of months—with outcomes that focus on the delivery of working software as opposed to descriptive specifications
- Is performed by largely self-organizing development teams where individual software developers take personal responsibility for the delivery of their components of the software product

The Agile approach is widely used throughout the world in a number of well-known and effective Agile software development and delivery methods and methodologies.

The way an Agile project is performed can differ markedly from a traditional software development or delivery project. In many cases, therefore, traditional software project estimation techniques are not the most appropriate or effective way of forecasting and managing an Agile project's schedule and budget.

This chapter introduces an estimation approach for Agile software projects.[1] It is important to note that while they align with the typical Agile approach to software development, a number of the estimation concepts presented here may also be applicable in other software projects that use more traditional development approaches.

Estimating an Agile Project

Before describing the Agile software project estimation approach, it is necessary to briefly outline how an Agile project is performed and to define a number of the key terms used.

Agile views a software *application* as comprising a number of features, and a software *project* as delivering a number of new or enhanced features into production. Estimation of an Agile project involves decomposing the project into the set of features to be delivered, as opposed to decomposing it into the set of work breakdown structure (WBS) tasks to be performed, as is often done in the traditional bottom-up approach to project estimation.

Different Agile methodologies and methods refer to project features by different names. Extreme Programming (XP) refers to features as *user stories* or just *stories.* This is the term used in this chapter.

An Agile project is performed by a development team as a series of short, fixed-length *iterations.* Iteration duration is typically between 2 weeks and 2 months. Each iteration delivers a number of stories (*features*).

A key aspect of Agile project estimation is determining which and how many stories can be delivered by each project iteration. Estimation requires methods for determining:

- The relative size of each of the project's stories (that is, how much software functionality each story delivers)
- The development team's velocity (that is, how quickly the team delivers the project's stories)

Various methods have been devised for measuring and expressing software size and velocity in general, and the size of stories and their delivery within Agile projects in particular. This chapter focuses on one of these techniques, the use of *story points.*

[1] This chapter provides a brief summary of estimation approaches for Agile software projects. The concepts and techniques included have been drawn from a number of sources. For more detailed and complete descriptions of estimation of Agile software projects, see the following:

Crystal Clear, by Alistair Cockburn (Addison-Wesley, 2005).
Agile Estimation and Planning, by Mike Cohn (Prentice Hall, 2004).
Planning Extreme Programming, by Kent Beck and Martin Fowler (Addison-Wesley, 2001).

This chapter also outlines how stories can be sized using Function Point Analysis (FPA) and how the data in the ISBSG Repository can be utilized to determine a project team's likely velocity. The decomposition of an Agile project into features using stories and then sizing those stories using story points can be viewed as similar to the way Function Point Analysis decomposes a software project into data and transactional functions and then sizes those functions using function points.[2] Likewise, the Agile estimation concept of *development team velocity*, expressed in terms of *story points (delivered) per iteration*, is similar to the Function Point Analysis–based estimation concept of *speed of delivery*, often expressed in terms of *function points (delivered) per month*.

Because an Agile project consists of a number of fixed-length iterations, it makes sense that Agile estimation focuses first on determining the number of iterations required. Once that number is known, it is usually a straightforward procedure to calculate estimates for both project schedule and cost by combining the required number of iterations with the iteration duration and the number and cost of development personnel involved.

Story Points

In an Agile project the relative size of each story to be delivered is measured using story points.

The Story Point Scale

Estimators allocate story points to stories from a fixed set of possible values. A commonly used set of values is a scale that begins with six numbers from the Fibonacci sequence and continues with one or two substantially larger numbers.

Example

Story point scale: *1, 2, 3, 5, 8, 13, 20, 50*

This approach allows estimators to allocate story points quickly, because they are working from only a small set of possible numbers, and confidently, because the magnitude of each number is significantly different from the numbers on either side of it. It is unnecessary and unhelpful to have a story point scale that continues with larger numbers than that proposed here. Any story allocated *50* or even *20* story points is too large for effective management and control within a single iteration. If any such stories are identified, they should be decomposed into a number of smaller and more manageable stories that are then reassessed to determine their story point size.

---

[2] *Function Point Counting Practices Manual: Release 4.3*, International Function Point Users Group (IFPUG), 2009.

Calibrating the Story Point Scale Using Past Projects

Story points are a relative size measure. This means that the same story delivered by different development teams could quite rightly be allocated different numbers of story points. To address the relative size issue, the story point scale to be used in Agile estimation must be calibrated to accurately reflect the size of stories typically delivered by the one or more development teams within an organization that plan to utilize that story point scale. In addition, it is necessary to ensure that all developers who will be involved in devising estimates have an effective understanding of the relative sizes within the story point scale.

Estimators must calibrate and understand the story point scale before using it to estimate a new project. Calibration begins by selecting one or more past projects. Selected past projects need both to be similar to the target projects to be estimated and to have had delivery that progressed at a typical rate. For the calibration projects, story points are retrospectively allocated to their stories based upon their *actual* delivery duration. All future estimators need to study the individual stories and their allocated story point values so as to gain a proper understanding of the relative sizes of stories associated with each of the values in the story point scale.

Example

Table 14-1 lists actual durations for the stories delivered for a project that has been completed in the past. Table 14-1 also shows the allocation of story points to each story based upon those actual durations. Future estimators would need to study these allocations along with the details of each story to gain an appropriate understanding of the relative sizes of stories associated with each of the values in the story point scale.

Prior to using the story point scale for estimation of new Agile projects, future estimators should gain expertise in the technique by practicing allocating story points to stories from other past projects where the actual story duration and, hence, likely allocated story point size, can be checked.

As an alternative to story points, stories can also be sized in function points using Function Point Analysis. This is done by applying the standard Function Point Analysis approach to each story.

An organization might choose to size its stories using function points for a number of reasons:

- The organization has substantial Function Point Analysis expertise.
- The organization wishes to utilize external sources (such as the ISBSG Repository) to determine likely speed of delivery (development team velocity).

Story	Actual Duration (*days*)	Allocated Story Points
1	1	1
2	1	1
3	1	1
4	2	1
5	3	2
6	3	2
7	4	2
8	4	2
9	4	2
10	4	2
11	4	2

Story	Actual Duration (*days*)	Allocated Story Points
12	6	3
13	7	3
14	7	3
15	8	3
16	8	3
17	10	5
18	11	5
19	11	5
20	12	8
21	15	8
22	15	8
23	17	13
24	19	13
25	19	13

TABLE 14-1 Investment Management System Upgrade Project: Story Durations and Story Points

- The organization wishes to use the size results for comparative benchmarking against either its own history of non-Agile projects or against projects from other organizations. Because story points are a relative size measure, they cannot be easily compared across organizations or even across different development teams within the same organization.

Development Team Velocity

To create Agile project estimates, it is necessary to know in advance how quickly the development team can deliver project stories. This speed is referred to as the development team velocity, or simply the velocity, and is expressed as *story points (delivered) per iteration.*

Velocity is used in conjunction with the story point sizes of a project's stories to both estimate overall project schedule and cost, and to allocate stories to individual project iterations.

Determining Development Team Velocity Using Past Projects

Velocity is ideally based upon past project performance from within the same organization and for the same development team. To determine the velocity achieved on a past project, determine its story point sizes, and calculate the average number of story points delivered by a project iteration.

To ensure that the determined velocity is appropriate, it may be necessary to consider several past projects. Once again, the past projects need to be both similar to the target projects to be estimated and to have had delivery that progressed at a typical rate. Remember, different types of projects are likely to have different velocities.

Example

Table 14-2 shows the stories and story points previously delivered by the completed Investment Management System Upgrade project across the project's five iterations. Based upon this data it appears that this development team has a typical velocity of around *22 story points per iteration.* Although this velocity could now be used for estimating future Agile projects, it would probably be wiser to investigate several more past projects before finalizing the velocity estimation figure.

For Agile projects sized using Function Point Analysis, it is possible to determine likely speeds of delivery (velocity) from external sources. This book includes descriptions of several different techniques to aid in selecting an appropriate speed of delivery from the ISBSG Repository.

Allocating Story Points to Stories

The Agile approach to software development requires that individual developers take personal responsibility for the delivery of their components of the software product. In keeping with this principle, all developers involved in a software project—or individual project iteration—are encouraged to actively participate in the estimation of that project or iteration. This, of course, requires that all developers have a clear understanding of what each of the story point sizes means in the context of their software projects.

Iteration	Number Stories per Iteration	Number Story Points	
		per Story	per Iteration
1	2	*13, 13*	26
2	3	*13, 8, 2*	23
3	6	*5, 5, 5, 3, 2, 2*	22
4	6	*8, 3, 2, 2, 2, 2*	19
5	8	*8, 3, 3, 3, 1, 1, 1, 1*	21
Total:	***25***		***111***
Average:	***5***		***22.2***

Table 14-2 Investment Management System Upgrade Project: Development Team Velocity

Agile project estimation utilizes a modified Wide-Band Delphi approach for allocating story point sizes to each of the project or iteration's stories. A typical Agile estimation session would progress as follows:

1. All the developers involved in the estimation session come together. An effective number of developers is between six and ten. One of the developers acts as a facilitator for the session. Business representatives may also attend the session. Their role is to provide explanation and clarification of the details of particular stories, not to participate in allocating story points or determining estimates.
2. The facilitator selects the next story to be estimated, and its requirements are discussed by the group. The discussion should be limited to a few minutes. If after this discussion, and input from the business representatives, the story's requirements remain unclear, the story is put aside—to be clarified later—and the next story is selected.
3. All developers now produce their estimates for the current story using the agreed story point scale. A useful tool is for each developer to have a set of cards, each card showing one of the numbers from the story point scale. When asked to produce his or her estimate, each developer simply places the card showing the chosen story point number face up on the desk in front of him or her.
4. The developers' story point estimates for the current story are now compared and assessed.

   If all the developers' estimates align, then the estimation process is completed for the current story. The number of story points allocated is recorded, and the next story is selected.

   If the developers' estimates do not align, then various techniques can be used to move the group toward an agreement:

   - If the estimates differ from each other by only one value on the story point scale, then one of the larger, smaller, or more frequently occurring values may be selected as the estimate. The rationale for selecting the larger value is that this is a safer, more conservative approach. The rationale for selecting the smaller value is that it encourages the estimators to think carefully before selecting smaller values, because they know that in doing so they may be committing themselves to the delivery of more functionality, and hence, more work, within an iteration. The rationale for choosing the more frequently occurring value is simply that it reflects the group's majority view.

- If the estimates differ from each other by more than one value on the story point scale, then the estimators with the largest and smallest estimates may be called upon to explain the rationales for their estimates. After this, the estimators will typically produce new estimates, and the process will be repeated.
- If after three iterations of the estimation process a unanimous agreement cannot be reached, then a decision should be made. This may involve eliminating any outliers or having the facilitator make the decision based upon his or her understanding of the story involved.

An important goal of the estimation process is that it should be done as quickly as is practicable.

Example

Table 14-3 shows the result of the first estimate round for a group of six developers allocating story points to story 12 from the planned Back Office Billing and Inventory project. In this case, story points are allocated using the scale beginning with six numbers from the Fibonacci sequence and then continuing with two larger numbers, that is, *1, 2, 3, 5, 8, 13, 20, 50.*

At this time, the developers' estimates do not align. Allocated story points range from *3* to *8*, a difference of two values on the story point scale. The developers who proposed the lowest and highest values are now called upon to explain the rationales for their choices. Following this discussion all the developers undertake a second estimate round.

The following table shows the result of the second estimate round for story 12.

Story	Estimate Round	Developer X Allocated Story Points					
		1	2	3	4	5	6
12	2	5	8	8	5	5	5

After this second estimate round, the developers' estimates differ by only one value on the story point scale. A third estimate round could now be undertaken to try and obtain universal agreement. Instead, however, the group chooses to select the smaller estimate of

Story	Estimate Round	Developer X Allocated Story Points					
		1	2	3	4	5	6
12	1	5	3	8	3	5	8

Table 14-3 Back Office Billing and Inventory Project: Allocated Story Points

5 story points. This choice is based upon the previously agreed upon procedure to select the smaller of the two estimates if those estimates only differ by one value on the story point scale. Doing this helps to ensure that the estimation process continues to progress quickly and effectively.

Having successfully allocated story points for story 12, the developers now move onto the project's next story.

Estimating Total Project Schedule and Cost at Project Initiation

Story points can be used to estimate the likely total project schedule and cost prior to the start of the project development iterations. Doing this requires that all of the project's stories have been identified and sized in story points and that the likely development team velocity is known.

Ideally, all the project developers will have participated in allocating the story points to the project's stories. However, it is not uncommon for the initial order of magnitude estimates devised at project initiation to be determined by a smaller group of key developers and project personnel.

The project schedule estimate is determined by combining the project iteration duration with its story point total divided by its likely velocity. The project cost can then be estimated based upon the required number of project iterations combined with the developer costs associated with a single iteration.

It is important to remember that estimates determined at project initiation should be viewed as order of magnitude estimates only. The full details and complexity of all the project stories may not yet be known. Their story point sizes may change once that information is available. Additionally, in an Agile project new stories may be identified as the project progresses.

Example

Table 14-4 shows initial project schedule and cost estimates for the Back Office Billing and Inventory project based upon the project size of *147 story points* and likely velocity of *22 story points per iteration.* These initial estimates suggest a project duration and cost of around *28 weeks* and *$262,500*, respectively.

For Agile projects sized using Function Point Analysis, the initial project schedule and cost estimates can be determined by combining the project's function point size with its likely speed of delivery and project delivery rate, respectively.

The project's cost can be estimated directly from its project delivery rate when the project delivery rate is expressed in terms of cost per function point (for example, *$1,500 per function point*). Often, however, the project delivery rate is expressed in terms of effort per function

Total Project Stories	*34*
Total Project Story Points (SP)	*147*
Development Team Velocity (V)	*22 story points per iteration*
Iteration Duration (D)	*4 weeks*
Developer Number (per Iteration) (DN)	*5*
Developer Cost (per Developer per Iteration) (DC)	*$7,500*
Estimated Iterations (I)	$= SP / V$ $= 147 / 22$ $= 6.7 \approx 7$
Estimated Schedule	$= I \times D$ $= 7 \times 4$ = *28 weeks*
Estimated Cost	$= I \times DN \times DC$ $= 7 \times 5 \times 7{,}500$ = *$262,500*

TABLE 14-4 Back Office Billing and Inventory Project: Initial Estimates

point (for example, *9.5 hours per function point*). In such cases, the project delivery rate must be combined with an additional project cost rate (for example, *$125 per hour*) in order to estimate the project's cost.

Allocating Stories to Individual Project Iterations

Prior to the start of each project iteration, story points can be utilized to help ensure that the appropriate number and size of stories are allocated to the iteration. Once again, this requires that all the project's stories have been identified and sized in story points and that the likely development team velocity is known.

To allocate stories to the next project iteration, select a group of stories with a total story point size approximately equal to the development team velocity. Of course, other constraints and dependencies beyond the story point size may impact which stories can or must be selected for inclusion within a particular iteration.

When allocating stories to a project iteration, either the developers can make use of the story point sizes determined at the project's initiation, or they can choose to reassess each potential story to determine anew its story point size. By reassessing the stories, the developers are able to consider any new or changed information they have acquired since the project began that may impact that size.

Example

Table 14-5 shows the allocation of a group of five stories to iteration *4* for the Back Office Billing and Inventory project.

Iteration Number	4							
Velocity	*22 story points per iteration*							
Allocated Stories	Story Number	*11*	*12*	*19*	*23*	*26*	**Total**	*5*
	Story Points	*5*	*8*	*3*	*5*	*3*	**Total**	*24*

TABLE 14-5 Back Office Billing and Inventory Project: Allocated Stories

Note that the total story point size for the five allocated stories is *24 story points,* which is two more than the likely velocity of *22 story points per iteration.* This highlights two factors. First, the likely velocity should be viewed as an average value only, and second, the number of story points allocated to any story is not so precise that it should necessarily restrict the inclusion of a story into an iteration if good reasons exist for that inclusion.

For Agile projects sized using Function Point Analysis, the likely speed of delivery can be used to allocate stories to an iteration.

First, however, the speed of delivery may need to be adjusted to address the iteration duration. If each iteration has a duration of 2 weeks, but the speed of delivery is expressed in function points per month (for example, *60 functions points month*), then the number of function points to be delivered needs to be halved to properly address the iteration duration (for example, *30 function points per 2-week iteration*).

Individual stories can then be allocated to each iteration in turn, up to the function point size limit for the iteration.

Reviewing the Process at Project Completion

The effectiveness of using story points for Agile project estimation can be continuously improved by ensuring that an estimation review always takes place after the project is completed.

The review should investigate the actual duration and cost required to deliver each story and should compare those actual values against the estimated values. Doing this will help the developers' understanding of how to effectively allocate story points to stories and will also help to fine-tune the likely development team velocity.

Benefits of Agile Software Estimation Using Story Points

For developers working with an Agile software development approach, using story points for project estimation offers a number of benefits over more traditional approaches. These include

- Story point–based estimation has been devised in conjunction with, and specifically for, the Agile development approach. The concepts and terminology used in story point–based estimation align with those used in Agile development. This alignment includes references to project iterations and stories.

- Story point–based estimation can be completed quickly and easily and does not require the developers responsible for the estimates to perform significant additional analysis or to have additional specialist skills. Estimation can be incorporated into the standard planning sessions prior to the start of each project iteration.
- Story point–based estimation supports the Agile principle of developers taking ownership and responsibility for the software they will deliver. Estimates are created by the developers themselves. Developers therefore understand that poorly considered estimates can have a direct impact on their own work situation.
- Story point–based estimation supports appropriate input into the estimation process by the different project roles. Once again, the developers who are required to deliver the software provide the development estimates. Occasional lapses of judgment or lack of understanding by an individual developer are mitigated through the use of a Wide-Band Delphi approach. Business representatives provide additional descriptions and clarifications of software requirements when and if needed.

Comparing Story Points and Function Points

Story point–based estimation is sometimes compared to and contrasted with Function Point Analysis–based estimation.

Both techniques focus on identifying, sizing, and devising size-to-effort, size-to-cost, or size-to-schedule ratios for the features that a software project will deliver into production. For story point–based estimation these features are the collection of project stories, whereas for Function Point Analysis–based estimation they are the collection of data and transactional functions.

Where story points differ most from function points, however, is that while function points endeavor to be an *absolute* measure of feature size, story points are explicitly a *relative* measure. This means that whereas applying Function Point Analysis to a particular collection of software requirements should *always* lead to identification of the *same* number of function points, determining the number of story points related to a particular collection of software requirements can lead to completely *different* numbers and depends entirely upon the story point scale used in each situation.

For story points, one claimed major advantage of being a relative sizing technique is that it can be quickly learned and applied as needed in a particular context. Unlike with Function Point Analysis, the use of story points does not require that estimators learn and understand a full set of sometimes complex and prescriptive rules and guidelines.

On the other hand, potential disadvantages of a relative sizing technique such as story points over an absolute technique such as Function Point Analysis are as follows:

- The use of story points requires recalibration within each organization and potential development team in which they are used.
- It is difficult to use external repositories as sources of information on likely development team story point velocity.
- Story points cannot be easily used for comparative benchmarking across organizations.
- There is no authoritative source against which to assess the correctness and consistency of project sizing.

Summary

The Agile approach to software development differs markedly from traditional development approaches such as Waterfall. As such, Agile requires its own method of estimation. In this chapter we have provided a brief introduction to Agile software development estimation and described the sizing process using either story points or function points.

CHAPTER 15

A Guide to Estimating Project Cost Using ISBSG Data

Although the ISBSG collects the costs incurred by projects as a project attribute in its repository, it is very difficult to standardize these costs as a ratio of "dollar cost per function point delivered" that can be used to predict the likely cost of a newly planned project. Difficulties in using other projects' total costs arise due to the following factors:

- The costs submitted to the ISBSG are provided in a wide range of currencies.
- Projects are submitted to the ISBSG over many years, and the currency conversion rates to a "standard" currency such as the euro or U.S. dollar vary significantly as economies strengthen and weaken relative to each other.
- Since the dates that the project costs were collected are not known, it is not possible to allow for any subsequent inflation that may have occurred.

It is therefore recommended that in order to estimate your project's costs, you should use the predicted project effort, and convert the effort to cost using current relevant personnel resource costs. That is, use the effort predicted by the PDR combined with the hourly charge-out rates for the particular project team in the currency in which they will be paid, allowing for the inflation over the proposed project duration.

This chapter explains how this can be done and the types of considerations that need to be allowed for prior to committing a monetary value to a project.

Hourly Charge-Out Rate

The way charge-out rates are calculated varies for different countries and organizations. It also depends on whether the development organization is selling its development services or building the software as an internal asset for its own organization.

The next two sections describe how to calculate internal project and external project charge-out rates.

Internal Project: Building Software for Your Own Organization

Your internal accounts department should be able to provide the internal charge-out rate for each project team member. The charge-out rate is the direct labor cost, that is, the *cost of the employee to the organization*. This is usually calculated using the employee's hourly pay rate plus on-costs. *On-costs* are all non-salary employee costs. Typically, these include such overheads as payments for sick leave, recreational leave, public holiday, superannuation, insurance, fringe benefits, payroll tax, and so forth. On-costs vary from country to country and in different employment situations. They may add as much as 15–40 percent to the hourly rate paid to the employee. On-costs plus the annual hourly rate paid for hours worked make up the employee's *salary package.*

For example: If the hourly pay rate is $40 an hour, then on-costs could vary between $6 and $15. Therefore, the internal charge-out rate for that employee could be from $46 to $56 an hour depending on the employee's employment/contract benefits.

External Project: Building Software for an External Organization

Where an organization sells software development services, the *rates that it charges the customer* (charge-out rates) need to cover the cost of the employee, plus a profit margin. Charge-out rates are calculated taking into account:

- The utilization rate of the staff, that is, the number of revenue earning days compared to the total number of days they are paid.
- The company overheads (equipment, telephones, utilities, rent, office and administration costs, insurance, and so on). This also applies in many organizations that are not commercial software development companies, but where IT services are treated as a cost center and where *internal* projects include company overheads in the project costs.
- Total employee salary package costs.
- Profit margin required.

As a rule of thumb the external charge-out rate is 2.5 to 3 times the employee's hourly pay rate, but may be up to 6 times for larger corporations.

For example: if the hourly pay rate paid to the supplier organization's employee is $40 an hour, then the rate charged by the supplier to the client, for that employee's time spent on the project, could be between $120 to $240 per hour.

Refining Hourly Charge-Out Rate for Project Team Structure

The size and structure of the project team, and the individual roles required for the project, will depend on many factors, including the size of the project, type of project, project risk factors, type of organization, and the maturity and rigor of the development process. There may be up to a fourfold difference in the rates charged for personnel performing the different roles, and the number of people performing each role will vary from project to project.

To estimate total cost for a project, you first need to determine the likely project team structure (number of people performing each role) and their respective charge-out rates. For internal projects this is straightforward. To determine the charge-out rate for external projects, you may need to reference industry sources such as job advertising sites on the Internet, IT industry surveys, and government web sites, or you can simply ask your suppliers.

Total effort hours for the project are calculated from the project delivery rate (PDR), therefore it is important to try to assign the projected effort hours across the different project roles in order to more accurately predict costs. Figure 15-1 shows the percentage breakdown of effort of the various project roles for an in-house, new development project. The ISBSG provides similar charts for enhancements and outsourced new developments in the subscriber section of its web site.

Use an appropriate role ratio breakdown for your particular software development, and then apply your charge-out rates to the different roles.

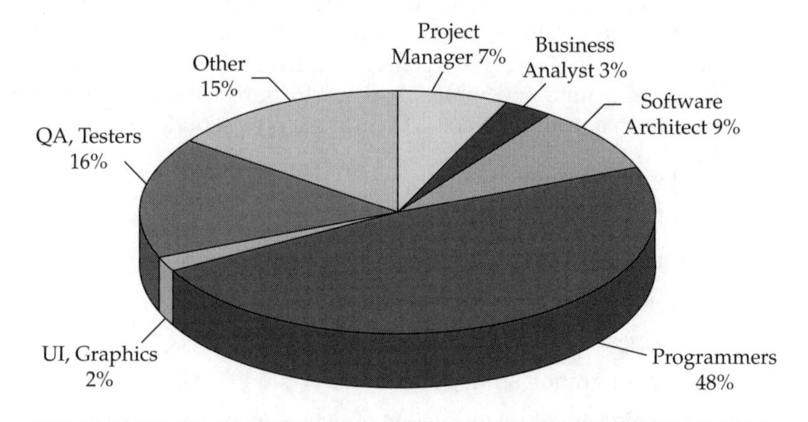

FIGURE 15-1 New development role ratios for in-house development

Indexing the Charge-Out Rate for Inflation and Currency Movements

Global software development projects, the impact of financial crises on different economies, and development teams spread across continents, all make predicting costs for projects with long durations a more complex task.

If the project duration is estimated to be more than one year, then it is recommended that you factor the predicted inflation rate—for the country where the employees are paid—into the charge-out rates. Compound for each of the successive project years.

If the currency that is funding the project is different from the currency being used to pay the project team, then currency projections may also need to be taken into consideration when calculating the charge-out rates.

Additional Cost Considerations

So far we have concentrated on the costs that are associated directly with the project team that is developing the software. There are other costs that lie outside the development team; these are discussed in the following sections.

Costing Activities Outside Project Development Tasks

When converting functional size to effort using the appropriate ISBSG PDR in hours per function point, it is important to understand exactly which project activities the effort hours correspond to in order to understand what proportion of the total project costs the PDR-based cost estimate is predicting and what has been omitted.

The hours collected by the ISBSG and used to calculate industry PDR values are specifically for the following activities in the software development life cycle, as shown in Table 15-1.

Any effort estimates—and their corresponding cost estimates derived from the PDR—can cover only the software development activities shown in Table 15-1, and consequently these *exclude* other fixed price, and time and materials costs, to purchase other project-related items that need to be considered in the project budgets, such as:

- Hardware/networks
- Software-licensing fees/software product costs
- Software utilities/development tools
- Strategic planning
- Business process reengineering
- Data migration strategy/data conversion
- Planning and implementation of change management strategies

Project Activity	Possible Activity Components
Plan	Preliminary Investigations Overall Project Planning Feasibility Study Cost Benefit Study Project Initiation Report Terms of Reference
Specify	Systems Analysis Requirements Specification Review & Rework Requirements Spec Architecture Design/Specification Review & Rework Architecture Spec
Design	Functional/External Design Create Physical/Internal Design(s) Review and Rework Design(s)
Build	Package Selection Construct Code & Program Software Review or Inspect & Rework Code Package Customization/Interfaces Unit Test Integrate Software
Test	Plan System or Performance Testing System Testing Performance Testing Create & Run Automated Tests Acceptance Testing
Implement	Prepare Releases for Delivery Install Software Releases for Users Prepare User Documentation Prepare & Deliver User Training Provide User Support

TABLE 15-1 ISBSG Activities Where Effort Is Recorded for PDR

- Training requirements
- System deployment to multiple sites
- Internal client effort—for example, the execution of UAT (user acceptance testing)
- Enhancement of external systems to provide interfaces that are not included in this project's functional size scope
- Decommissioning of existing or interim systems

If your project will need to fund any of the preceding activities, then these will need to be costed separately and then added to the PDR-based cost estimates.

Costing Effort Contributed by Personnel Not Included in the PDR

The PDRs published by the ISBSG typically only include the Level 1 Effort[1] of the project development team, that is, the effort hours recorded by those people responsible for the delivery of the application under development. The project development team includes those individuals who specify, design, build, test, and implement the software.

Consequently, the effort established using the PDRs typically does *not* include the effort hours expended by the:

- IT administrative and support people who enable the project development team to do their job; that is, it excludes the operations people on hardware support, database administration staff, and so on.
- Business users or software users, that is, those individuals responsible for defining the requirements of the applications and sponsoring/championing the development of the application, acceptance testing the software, and actually using the software.

If the project budget is required to pay for the effort expended by these non–development team members, then this will need to be estimated and costed separately from the effort costs derived from the PDR.

Summary

The following steps detail the procedure to calculate project cost using the published PDRs:

1. Determine the functional size relevant to project scope (function points measured for each project component that is implemented using different cost drivers, for example, different platforms, languages, and so on).
2. Determine the most likely software delivered size for each component by predicting the percentage of likely scope creep caused by requirements changing and/or incomplete specifications. For early estimates this may be as much as 30 percent growth on measured size (Function Points Measured × % growth = Project Predicted Delivered Size).

[1] Refer to "work effort breakdown" in the Glossary.

3. Determine the appropriate project delivery rate for the software component (effort hours per function point).
4. Calculate the effort (PDR × Predicted Delivered Size = Total Software Effort Hours).
5. Steps 1 through 4 need to be completed for each software component to determine the Total Effort Hours.
6. Determine the project team role profile, and allocate the percentage contributions for each role.
7. Allocate effort hours to each role using the percentage contribution (Total Project Effort Hours × % Role Contribution = Hours for Role).
8. Determine the charge-out rate for each role.
9. Calculate the cost of the effort for each role (Role Charge-Out Rate × Effort Hours for Role) allowing for currency movements and inflation if applicable.
10. Sum the Project Cost for each role to calculate the Total Project Cost based on PDR.

Additional Steps to Calculate Non-PDR-Related Project Costs

11. Calculate the costs for activities not included in the ISBSG Project Activities in Table 15-1.
12. Calculate the costs for people to be paid for by the project budget but whose effort was not included in the PDR-derived effort, typically Level 2 and above.
13. Total the costs for steps 10 through 12 to determine total costs for input into the project budget.

NOTE *The figure calculated in Step 13 is the most likely project cost.*

Project cost estimates should not be presented as a single number but always as a range—for example, best case, likely case, worst case—in order to appropriately manage expectations and to obtain approval for realistic budget allocations.

CHAPTER 16

Creating a Software Project Estimation Framework Using the ISBSG Repository

A key solution to the problem of poor software project estimation is to create a software project estimation framework for your development team. A software project estimation framework comprises a set of templates or tables, combined with a supporting procedure, that allow you to estimate the effort and duration of a software project.

Once you have established an estimation framework, you can enter measures of the scope for a new project into the framework to obtain a project effort and duration estimate.

If you have an environment where your development team has developed multiple projects over a few years, then the ultimate estimation framework is one based on data from the team's past projects, in other words, your organization's own software measurement data.

However, few organizations have long-term development teams—or more commonly—the necessary skills to collect and maintain their own project history over several years. So in the absence of an organization's own experience data, you can use past projects from a public project database such as the ISBSG Repository.

NOTE *A software project estimation framework comprises a set of templates or tables, combined with a supporting procedure, that allow you to estimate the effort and duration of a software project.*

You can use a number of sources of ISBSG data for your framework:

- The appendixes of this book. You will find a set of project delivery rate tables showing PDR by category. These tables have been derived from the ISBSG Repository.
- The ISBSG Development and Enhancement Repository. Release 11 of the ISBSG Repository contains data from over 5,000 software projects.
- The ISBSG Special Report series of publications and the Web Subscription service. These provide discussions on the factors that have a major impact on project delivery rate, duration, defect densities, and other topics.[1]

Using the ISBSG PDR Tables to Create Tables for Your Estimating Framework

You can use the following procedure to establish an estimation framework using the ISBSG tables in Appendix B:

1. Identify which development platforms your software development group is likely to use on future projects.
2. From Appendix B extract PDR distributions for your team's development languages for the relevant development platforms (Tables B-17, B-18, B-19, and B-20).
3. Next consider the impact of the likely project maximum team sizes on the PDR distributions.
4. Examining the PDR distributions extracted will reveal that they are too broad for practical use. Consequently, the next step is to refine them by benchmarking a small number (one to five) of your group's typical projects against the extracted PDR distributions.
5. Finally, use the PDR values at the top and bottom of your group's benchmark quartile from each extracted PDR distribution to create the PDR tables for your estimation framework.

To estimate a specific project using the framework, you apply the following equation:

$$\text{Effort (in hours)} = \text{FPs} \times \text{PDR}$$

You measure FPs from whatever form of specification about project scope that you have available. The level of detail in this specification

[1] The ISBSG Special Reports are available to ISBSG web subscribers. Reports are produced regularly based on analysis of the ISBSG data.

influences how precise your FP measurement is and the actual steps necessary to obtain that measurement. You select the PDR from the table(s) you create by following the preceding steps.

Working through an example development team, we can construct appropriate estimating framework tables. Our example development team develops small-scale applications using Microsoft Visual Basic (.NET) technology. It links some of these applications to database and mail servers running on the Windows Server platform. It also develops applications using Java and JavaScript tools to run across the Internet in HTML browsers using a multitier architecture of Windows Server computers.

Step 1. Identify the Development Platforms

The ISBSG divides its project delivery rate (PDR) data into four platforms: mainframe, midrange, PC, and multiplatform. ISBSG analysis of its project data shows development language as one of the three factors that make the most impact on project delivery rate. (The other two factors are team size and, once you allow for team size impact, project size.)

Identifying the operating system platform for which your team is developing software helps improve the precision of the estimating framework. Consequently, before you extract PDR values for the development languages that your team uses, you need to identify the development platforms for the software.

For our example team a complete estimation framework will examine two PDR tables in Appendix B, Table B-20 for multiplatform development projects using Java and .NET tools, and Table B-19 for PC development projects using Microsoft Visual Basic.

Step 2. Extract PDR Distributions Based on Development Languages

Locate Tables B-17, B-18, B-19, and B-20 in Appendix B that present "Project Delivery Rate by Language" for the development platforms that your group uses, and extract the PDR distributions for the programming languages that your group is likely to use on future projects.

For our example team, developing PC-based systems using Visual Basic, we extract the highlighted PDR distribution. This gives one row in the team's PDR table shown in Table 16-1.

If your team's specific programming languages do not appear, then use the "3rd generation language" and "4th generation language" PDR distributions in Tables B-12, B-13, B-14, and B-15. Alternatively, use the values for those languages that are similar to the ones that your team uses. For example, Borland Delphi is a similar development tool to Microsoft Visual Basic, so its PDR distribution is likely to be similar to that shown for Visual Basic.

	N	Min	P10	P25	Median	P75	P90	Max	Mean	Std Dev
ASP	11	2.2	2.6	2.7	5.9	7.8	9.5	14.3	6.0	3.8
C++	15	4.0	8.6	9.3	11.4	18.5	27.8	60.1	16.5	13.9
COBOL	18	2.8	4.2	5.2	10.4	19.7	24.0	35.1	12.7	9.4
Java	26	1.9	3.0	5.7	7.7	10.9	19.0	25.3	9.3	6.1
Oracle	16	1.2	2.3	3.7	9.0	13.5	19.8	33.8	10.6	8.8
Visual Basic	48	1.0	1.9	3.2	7.2	9.5	13.8	24.4	7.4	5.0
Other	59	1.0	2.2	3.6	7.3	14.6	25.6	49.8	11.2	11.5

Table 16-1 Project Delivery Rates by Language—PC Platforms

Step 3. Adjust the Extracted PDR Distributions According to Team Size

The total team size has the most significant impact on the productivity of a development project. The detrimental impact of larger teams on productivity is so significant that it is the main reason why projects delivering several thousand FPs have such poor productivity compared with smaller scope projects. Team-size impact overrides any productivity benefits from a specific development language. Consequently, any estimating framework must take into account the maximum team size the development team needs to deliver the project.

Use the appropriate median values from Table B-45, "Effect of Maximum Team Size and Project Size," to refine the PDRs extracted from the tables showing PDR by language. This has to be done with some judgment when considering highly productive development languages such as Microsoft ASP or Visual Basic (.NET). Note too that you need to consider the *maximum* team size, which may include several technical specialists or QA people who have only a part-time role on the project. A lot of development teams bring in several people for small roles on a project without considering whether their impact on overall productivity may negate any quality benefit.

In addition, you need to consider the typical size of the projects developed by your team. Smaller projects tend to have lower productivity. If your team develops projects of significantly different sizes, then you may need to add this as another factor to be taken into consideration. However, it is probably more effective to combine the project size and team size factors together, as most development teams link the two when planning projects. Our example team does a lot of projects around 400 FPs with small teams plus the occasional project of greater than 1,000 FPs. They never use a team of more than eight people.

The data in Table B-45 states that using a team size of one to four has a median impact of reducing the development language's PDR by 5.1. In other words, the one- to four-person team will expend 5.1

hours less effort per function point produced than is typical for all projects. However, if the example project team used only one- to four-person teams on its Visual Basic–PC projects, adjusting the median PDR down by 5.1 hours per function point would result in a PDR of 2.1 hours per function point. This is close to the productivity of the best VB projects in the ISBSG database, which is likely to be unachievable. In this situation, our example development team would be better off making a more conservative adjustment to the PDRs for smaller team sizes, such as the P75 value of –2.1.

Examining Table B-45 shows that a team of five to eight on a project of more than 1,000 FPs is unusual. Only 4 of the 1,681 projects had such a small team on a project of that scope. This is too small a sample to provide usable statistics. The PDR improvement values (that is, the negative values) in this table also show that this team size on large projects generally achieves high productivity. However, once again you need to take care in selecting the PDR adjustment value. For our example team, a value of –3.3 from the Max column seems appropriately conservative. Using these figures will result in the following PDR table for the team.

Step 4. Benchmarking Your Projects' PDR

Without benchmarking your projects, you will find it difficult to use these PDR ranges extracted from the ISBSG tables. The range of the PDRs present in Appendix B will likely be too wide for commercial acceptability. You will need to benchmark whatever projects exist in your team's history, or to narrow the range arbitrarily.

To benchmark a few of your team's projects, perform the following steps:

1. Calculate each project's PDR, in hours per function point. When doing this, consider the scope of activities included in the PDR. The effort figure used for the calculation should cover the full development life cycle.
2. Decide the development language and platform for each project. This will determine the set of PDR distributions you will extract from Appendix B to use for benchmarking (Tables B-17, B-18, B-19, and B-20). Also identify the maximum team size for each project.
3. Based on a project's language and team size, select the appropriate PDR distribution you have extracted from the ISBSG. Our example team would compare the PDR for a four-person project that used Java with the PDR distribution on the first row of Table 16-2. This will place the team's project within one of the quartiles of the PDR distributions. Our example team's project had a PDR of 4.1 hours per FP, which places it in the P25-to-median quartile.

	Min	P10	P25	Median	P75	P90	Max
Java – Multiplatform	3.1	3.3	4.0	4.3	6.0	9.7	17.1
Visual Basic – Multiplatform	0.9	2.5	4.2	6.5	16.5	34.7	60.9
Visual Basic – PC	1.0	1.9	3.2	5.1	7.4	11.7	24.4

TABLE 16-2 Project Delivery Rates by Language for 1–4 Team Size

4. Perform this comparison for each project PDR that you have available from the projects that your team has completed. This is likely to reveal that most projects sit within the same quartile of the relevant row in the draft PDR table. This is your team's benchmark quartile, and consequently provides a narrower range of PDR values for use in the estimating equation.

Benchmarking your team's projects against the ISBSG data will show that this data can provide only approximate PDR tables. A team's own project history would produce much more accurate PDR tables.

Step 5. Construct the Estimation Framework

After benchmarking one or more of your projects against the PDR distributions extracted from the ISBSG tables, you can construct the estimation framework. Typically, you can create one PDR table that has Team Size across the columns and Languages down the rows. In each table cell are the appropriate top and bottom PDR values from your group's benchmark quartile.

For our example development team, the estimating framework PDR table would be as shown in Table 16-3.

When using these tables, remember that projects delivering under 400 function points typically have distinctly worse PDRs, and projects delivering more than 1,000 FPs typically have distinctly better PDRs. The cause of this impact is unclear, but it probably relates to "economies of scale." Doing a larger amount of work as a coherent whole can typically proceed more efficiently than a smaller amount of work. Remember that this impact of project size occurs *after taking into account the impact of team size.* Because team size has such a large negative impact on productivity, it counters the beneficial impact of

Language	Team Size 1–4 (<400FP Project)	5–8 (>800 FP Project)
Java – Multiplatform	3.6–4.3	3.1–4.8
Visual Basic – Multiplatform	4.2–6.5	4.2–5.3
Visual Basic – PC	3.2–5.1	

TABLE 16-3 PDRs Chosen from the ISBSG Tables for Example Development Team

project size. Consequently, you do need to take into account the impact of project size on your team's PDR if you are estimating a project with a size that is unusually larger, or more importantly, unusually smaller, than you would normally assign to a team of a given size.

The example development team can now use this PDR table in its estimation framework. However, while building up its project history, the example development team can refine this table using the history from each project that it completes.

To calculate an estimate, use the attributes of the planned project to select a pair of PDR values, and then multiply these by the measured FP scope for the project. This provides a "best case" and "worst case" estimate. Which estimate you actually use on a project depends upon risk and commercial factors. For example, for a project that you think faces several risks of high probability and impact, you may choose to use the worst case figure.

Estimates Are Targets, Not Predictions

Remember that project estimates represent a target for the team that is performing the project. They are not predictions that will come true as a matter of course. The key issue for estimating software projects is setting realistic targets that your development team can reasonably expect to achieve. Estimates based purely on professional judgment are notoriously optimistic. Estimates also set the customer's expectations; the first published estimates are usually the ones that are remembered.

Using the information in Appendix B, you can construct a useful estimation framework for a development team. This framework will produce estimates that have a higher likelihood of being achieved than any form of estimating based purely on professional judgment.

Calculating a Benchmark Estimate for a Planned Project

It is advisable to calculate a second estimate for a planned project. Ideally, the second estimate should have a high degree of independence from the first. The following is a simple, fast, estimating procedure that you can use to calculate a "benchmark" estimate for a project. This procedure produces a benchmark PDR and so needs a measure of the software size in function points.

The procedure results from an ISBSG analysis of greater than 500 projects in the ISBSG Repository.[2] These software development

[2] A four-step analysis was performed that (1) estimated PDR as the average of the selected data set; (2) adjusted the PDR according to the effect of the expected team size, by adding the tabulated value to the current estimate; (3) further adjusted the PDR, according to the effect due to the estimated project size (expressed in UFP), by adding the tabulated value to the current estimate; and (4) further adjusted the PDR according to the effect of the programming language, by adding the tabulated value to the current estimate.

Team Size	Median	Mean
1 to 4	–3.09	–4.54
5 to 8	–0.06	–1.45
9 or more	6.12	4.37

TABLE 16-4 Maximum Team Size

Project Size	Median	Mean
1 to 200	2.96	3.88
201 to 400	–0.05	0.01
401 to 600	–1.95	–4.68
601 to 800	–4.3	–6.91
801 to 1,000	–5.56	–8.73
>1,000	–6.76	–9.52

TABLE 16-5 PDR Adjustment Factor

projects have high quality data covering all the important factors impacting productivity. You start the benchmark estimate calculation with these two PDR values that cover all 500 projects:

10.43 hours per FP (median) and 14.92 hours per FP (mean)

Step 1. Adjust PDR for Team Size

Decide the appropriate maximum team size for the planned project, and select from Table 16-4 the applicable adjustment factor for the PDR.[3]

If our example project team needs to put a maximum of four people on a project, this adjusts the median PDR downwards to 7.32 hours per FP. Be careful to note that this is the maximum team size, not the core team size—part-time people add to the team size.

Step 2. Adjust PDR for Project Size

Next, you extract the adjustment factor that applies to the size of the project as measured in function points (see Table 16-5).

If our example project team has an 800 FP project, this adjusts the median PDR downwards further to 3.02 hours per FP. There is a relationship between project size and maximum team size, but other factors also influence the maximum team size on a project, such as development process and role division across the team.

[3] Tables 16-4, 16-5, and 16-6 were derived from the ISBSG analysis referred to earlier.

Language	Median	Mean
ABAP	0.93	–1.29
Access	–3.23	–7.92
ADS	–4.36	–8.80
ASP	–1.81	–5.71
C	0.96	0.66
COBOL	3.67	6.17
C++	–1.26	3.63
C#	2.38	3.45
Datastage	0.51	2.10
Java	–0.53	–1.33
Lotus Notes	–4.00	–7.00
Natural	–2.82	–4.46
Oracle	–2.85	–4.92
Other 3GL	–0.60	–0.26
Other 4GL	2.31	0.70
PL/I	3.03	–0.06
Powerbuilder	–3.13	–4.10
Scripting	3.28	5.76
SQL	0.23	–1.42
Visual Basic	–3.77	–4.89

Table 16-6 Programming Language Adjustment Factor

Step 3. Adjust PDR for Development Language

For the final adjustment, you extract the factor that applies to the planned development language. Table 16-6 represents the most commonly used languages for the projects in the ISBSG Repository.

Our example project team plans to use Java for this project, which adjusts the median PDR downwards further to 2.49 hours per FP. This PDR is significantly lower than the range of 4.0 to 4.7 from the team's estimating framework, and so indicates that the estimating framework calculates more conservative, but commercially safer, estimates.

Step 4. Calculate Effort Estimate and Consider the Range of Probable Values

Applying the estimating equation gives a median effort estimate for our example of 1,992 hours. A median estimate represents a 50 percent probability of the project delivering its planned scope by providing that much effort. There is a 71 percent confidence level to achieve the project within a range of 50 percent to 200 percent of this value.

In other words, the range of likely PDRs for a project of these characteristics and scope is 1.29 to 4.98 hours per FP. The estimating framework falls within this range, even though it is large, and this increases the confidence in the estimate values. In other words, the team's estimating framework does set reasonable targets.

Summary

Creating a software project estimation framework for your development team will provide a tool that will allow you to more accurately estimate effort and duration for software projects. The framework that you create will be tailored to suit your environment and team and will therefore provide more accurate estimates that if you simply used available industry data.

CHAPTER 17
Functional Size Measurement Methods in Use Today

The past three decades of use of functional size measurement (FSM) have shown that it is currently the only proven method of sizing software that gives consistent and reliable results for project estimation and productivity comparisons. The FSM method for sizing is supported and continually enhanced by the international community and is the method of choice for major software estimation tools and benchmarking organizations.

How Many FSM Methods Are There?

Currently, five FSM methods are recognized by the International Organization for Standardization (ISO):

- **COSMIC-FFP** ISO/IEC 19761:2003 Software engineering. A functional size measurement method.[1]
- **FiSMA FSM** 1.1 [3]. ISO/IEC 29881:2008 Information technology—Software and systems engineering—FiSMA 1.1 functional size measurement method.
- **IFPUG CPM** 4.3 [11]. ISO/IEC 20926:2009 Software and systems engineering—Software measurement—IFPUG functional size measurement method 2009.

[1] A revised COSMIC standard is due for release in 2010: ISO/IEC 19761:2010 COSMIC functional size measurement method v 3.0 [10]. Information technology—Software and systems engineering—COSMIC-FFP—A functional size measurement method.

- **Mk II Function Point Analysis** 1.3.1 Unadjusted [12]. ISO/IEC 20968:2002 Software engineering—Mk II Function Point Analysis—Counting Practices Manual.
- **NESMA FPA Method** 2.1 Unadjusted [13]. ISO/IEC 24570:2005 Software engineering—NESMA functional size measurement method version 2.1—Definitions and counting guidelines for the application of Function Point Analysis.

The major steps in the methods as per their official specifications are described next. Because Mk II is no longer regularly used, no description has been provided. For analysis purposes the ISBSG combines IFPUG and NESMA sized projects, because these two methods are similar.

IFPUG From the IFPUG 4.3 Counting Practices Manual, the major process steps are the following:

1. Gather available documentation.
2. Determine the counting scope and (application) boundary and identify functional user requirements.
3. Measure (identify and size) the data functions. Data functions are either internal logical files (ILFs) or external interface files (EIFs).
4. Measure (identify and size) the transactional functions. Transactional functions are either external inputs, external outputs, or external inquiries.
5. Calculate the functional size.

The IFPUG 4.3 method can be used to determine the functional size of both software applications and software projects.

NESMA From the NESMA 2.1 Guidelines, the major process steps are as follows:

1. Identify the transactional and data functions within the scope of the enhancement project and determine their functional size.
2. Determine which transactional and data functions are to be added.
3. Determine which transactional and data functions are to be deleted.
4. Determine which data functions are to be changed and determine the impact factor.
5. Determine which transactional functions are to be changed and determine the impact factor.
6. Calculate the number of enhancement function points.

The NESMA 2.1 method is specifically for sizing enhancement projects.

COSMIC From the COSMIC 3.0.1 Measurement Manual, the major steps are the following:

1. Measurement Strategy Phase:
   a. Define the purpose of the measurement.
   b. Define the scope of the measurement.
   c. Identify the functional users.
   d. Identify the level of granularity.
2. Mapping Phase:
   a. Identify functional processes.
   b. Identify objects of interest and data groups.
   c. Identify data attributes.
3. Measurement Phase:
   a. Identify data movements.
   b. Apply measurement function.
   c. Aggregate measurement results.

The COSMIC FSM method can be used to determine the functional size of both software applications and software projects.

FiSMA From the FiSMA 1.1 Functional Size Measurement Method document the major steps are summarized as follows:

1. Gather documentation and software development artifacts to describe the functional user requirements for the software (to be or already) developed.
2. Determine the scope of the functional size measurement.
3. Determine which are the functional user requirements to be measured.
4. Identify the base functional components within the functional user requirements in two main parts: (a) measuring the end-user interface services, and (b) measuring indirect services.
5. Classify the base functional components into the appropriate base functional component type services.
6. Assign the appropriate numeric value to each base functional component.
7. Calculate the functional size.
8. Document the instance of the FiSMA 1.1 count details.

The FiSMA FSM method can be used to determine the functional size of both software applications and software projects.

Which FSM Method Should I Choose?

ISO has published a guide[2] to choosing the method most appropriate for your needs. Key points to be considered:

- **Availability of Equivalent Industry Data** If you need to use industry data for comparison of productivity, or as input into estimates, then this may be a deciding factor. The ISBSG Repository Release 11 contains the following breakdown of FSMs:

IFPUG 4+	3,379 projects
FiSMA	478 projects
COSMIC	335 projects
NESMA	130 projects

  Other approaches represented in the repository include Mark II and Feature Points, but there are few such projects.

- **Availability of FSM Tools and Training** Most of the industry-leading tools have been written to measure using the IFPUG method, but several have a roadmap that will incorporate other methods.
- **Availability of Trained Experienced Certified Metrics Experts** Currently, the highest number of people are trained and certified in the IFPUG/NESMA method, which is offered in most countries. COSMIC training and certification is now being offered in India, Japan, Europe, North America, and Australia.

How Hard Is It to Measure Functional Size?

Functional size measurement requires specialized training of two to three days. After training, it typically takes several months using the technique, measuring in a variety of situations, to become proficient. International accreditation usually requires the measurer to have at least two years experience with the technique. Organizations either train a select group of software developers for the measurement role or use the services of a specialist software metrics consulting company.

[2] ISO/IEC 14143-6:2006. Information technology—Software measurement—Functional size measurement—Part 6: Guide for use of ISO/IEC 14143 series and related International Standards.

Successful functional sizing is similar to other specialist activities such as database design in that it requires a person skilled in business analysis who has a high attention to detail.

What Sort of Accuracy Can I Expect from an FSM Measurement?

For current FSM methods two trained counters typically achieve size figures within +/– 10 percent of each other if the functional user requirements are known and well specified. This is based on tests performed during more than 150 software estimation training courses.[3] Other tests indicate that if ten project managers from different business areas try to estimate project effort without a systematic approach, such as an FSM method, the typical ratio between the smallest and largest estimate is 1 to 6, the worst as high as 1 to 12.

Accuracy and repeatability of measuring functional size has been shown to increase when the measurer has acquired:

- Formal training by an experienced certified trainer
- At least one year's experience measuring at least 15,000 function points
- Use of a purpose-built functional size measurement tool with inbuilt validation and measurement rules
- Several years IT experience in analysis and design of software

The Value of FSM as a Size Measurement

FSM is heavily used by mature software development organizations worldwide that are interested in producing accurate estimates, benchmarking, and process improvement. FSM has proven to be a reliable and effective method that allows organizations to estimate software and to compare productivity. The various bodies responsible for FSMs continue to work on improving and certifying FSM-related methods, tools, training, and standards.

Summary

Functional size measurement of software provides a reliable and consistent way to express how big a piece of software is, or will be. A functional size can then be used in estimating, benchmarking, project planning, and analysis.

[3] Pekka Forselius of FiSMA ran the course and the tests referred to.

CHAPTER 18

A Brief Tutorial on Functional Size Measurement (FSM)

This chapter provides a brief introduction to the fundamental principles behind the concept of *functional size* of software. It is intended for anyone using the ISBSG database who needs to understand what functional size measurement is, the various standardized measurement methods and their respective units of measure, and how functional size fits in with project estimating. This chapter is not intended as a primer of the specific rules involved in any of the five functional size measurement (FSM) methods standardized by the International Organization for Standardization (ISO). For your reference, however, we have provided website addresses for each of the methods. Note that ISBSG accepts projects sized using all five ISO/IEC FSM methods plus a variety of other software-sizing methods.

ISO/IEC Definitions

The terms *functional size* (FS), *functional size measurement* (FSM), and *functional user requirements* (FUR) are defined by the ISO/IEC 14143-1:2007 Functional Size Measurement: Part 1 Definition of Concepts: (ISO/IEC, 2007):

- **Functional Size** Size of the software derived by quantifying the functional user requirements
- **Functional Size Measurement (FSM)** Process of measuring functional size

- **Functional User Requirements** Subset of the user requirements describing what the software does, in terms of tasks and services

  Note that functional user requirements include but are not limited to:

  - Data transfer (for example, Input customer data, Send control signal)
  - Data transformation (for example, Calculate bank interest, Derive average temperature)
  - Data storage (for example, Store customer order, Record ambient temperature over time)
  - Data retrieval (for example, List current employees, Retrieve aircraft position)

  User requirements that are not functional user requirements include but are not limited to:

  - Quality constraints (for example, usability, reliability, efficiency, and portability)
  - Organizational constraints (for example, locations for operation, target hardware, and compliance to standards)
  - Environmental constraints (for example, interoperability, security, privacy, and safety)
  - Implementation constraints (for example, development language, delivery schedule)

It is important to remember that functional size alone does not adequately reflect the size of all aspects of software requirements. Functional size measurement is just one software sizing tool that forms part of the software project management toolkit. The benefit of FSM in estimation comes when functional size is used along with other project attributes to estimate work-effort and project duration. See Chapter 1 for an explanation of the three levels of requirements that form the inputs to the project work-effort estimation (including functional size).

This chapter provides project managers with sufficient base knowledge about functional size measurement to be able to understand the ISBSG database variables (columns) that contain functional size values and the value adjustment factor (VAF)[1] values. An illustration of how to measure functional size is provided in this chapter using the IFPUG Function Point method. Examples and case studies of how to measure functional size using each of the methods represented in the ISBSG Repository are provided in following chapters. ISO/IEC

[1] The value adjustment factor (VAF) can be used to reflect the user non-functional requirements or complexity of the developed software.

standardized functional size measurement methods each have their own rules and measurement units for assessing the functional user requirements for a piece of software to arrive at a functional size. The goal of all functional size measurement methods is similar: to evaluate the functional user requirements for a piece of software and to determine its functional size. Functional size is an important and objective measure that a project manager can use as part of estimating, planning, tracking, and controlling software projects.

What Is Functional Size?

Functional size represents the size of the subset of user requirements known as the functional user requirements (that is, the functions that the software must support) and excludes the other user requirements (often referred to as quality and technical requirements). Functional size measures the size of a software project's work output or work product. FSM methods establish the size of the functional user requirements that are supported or delivered by the software. They do this by sizing the *functional area* part of the project. In simplistic terms, functional size is the size of *what* the software must do from an external, user perspective, independent of how the software is constructed or how well it must perform. This is similar to sizing a building based on its floor plan, expressed in units of square meters (or square feet). Functional size reflects the size of the software's functional user requirements. Because most software (no matter how large or how small) is developed to address functional "user" requirements, all software has a functional size.

Analogies to Illustrate Functional Sizing

The relationship between functional size and software development can be described analogously with square meters and construction. Table 18-1 provides a few comparisons.

The Key to Functional Size Measurement Is to "Think Logical"

A fundamental principle to remember about functional sizing is that everything is counted from a logical user perspective, based on the functional user requirements.[2] This can be a paradigm shift for software developers who are well versed in programming and

[2] In the early stages of software development, it may be necessary to estimate the requirements or to make assumptions about the functional user requirements, and to subsequently use shortcut methods based on these assumptions to arrive at an approximate functional size. Refer to the March 1998 issue of *IT Metric Strategies* for the article "Requirements are (the Size of) the Problem," by Carol Dekkers, which further explores the topic, and *The IT Measurement Compendium,* by Manfred Bundschuh and Carol Dekkers (Springer, 2008) for further information.

Metric	Construction Units of Measure	When Is It Important to Measure?	Software Functional Size Units of Measure	When Is It Important to Measure?
Estimated (functional) size	Square meters (or feet)	When floor plan is available	Function points	When FUR (functional user requirements) are known or at contract stage
Unit delivery rate (or unit labor cost) & overall effort (or labor) cost	Hours per square meter (or $ per square meter) & total hours (or total $)	When builder is selected or construction contract is negotiated	Hours per FP (Labor $ per function point) & total hours (and total labor $)	At contract signing; at go or no go development decision
Estimated work effort (duration)	Person-months and move-in date	Throughout construction (adjusted whenever change orders accepted)	Person-months (or person-hours) and delivery date	Throughout development (adjusted whenever change requests are accepted)
Size of change orders	Square meters (or feet), hours or $ (impact)	Whenever change identified	FP, hours, or $ (impact)	Whenever change identified

TABLE 18-1 Analogies Between Building Construction and Software Development

physical configuration management, because functional size does not vary with the relative ease or difficulty involved in building the software. It is irrelevant to the functional size whether it takes a thousand lines of COBOL code and eight subroutine calls or a hundred lines of C++ code to implement a function; the functional size does not vary (it is the same no matter *how* the software is built) because the user functionality is the same.

Functional size, like the square meters or square feet of a building, is not equal to work effort. Here is the relationship:

- **Functional Size (for example, FP)** = An INDEPENDENT measure of the software's LOGICAL size (based only on the functional user requirements).
- **Work Effort (in Hours)** = A DEPENDENT measure of how long the software will take to develop. It depends on many factors (functional size as well as, for example, project type, programming language, hardware platform, team skills, methodology, team size, risks, and many more).
- **Productivity (for example, Hours per FP)** = A DEPENDENT result, dependent on all of the same factors as work effort.

NOTE *An INDEPENDENT variable (FP) divided by a DEPENDENT variable (Hours) yields a DEPENDENT result.*

These relationships tell us that just as factors such as the quality of the raw materials, the piping configuration, the configuration of the floors (how many stories in the building), and the overall layout all affect the work effort and duration of a building project, so too do the programming language and other physical attributes affect the software development effort and duration. However, regardless of how the building is constructed, the floor plan size of the building stays the same. With software, the software's functional size remains the same even when there is variation in the programming language, skills, physical configuration, and other factors used in its development.

Counting in FSM: An Example Using IFPUG Function Points

For illustration purposes, IFPUG (International Function Point Users Group) function points will be used to demonstrate one approach to functional size measurement. The ISBSG database has a number of variants of IFPUG FP units of measure, each relating to a particular release of the IFPUG Counting Practices Manual (CPM). Higher numbered releases supersede prior releases. All IFPUG FP data in the ISBSG database includes the specific IFPUG release number that was used to count a project's functional size. At this printing, the current IFPUG release is 4.3, which was released in September 2009.

The process to calculate IFPUG function points is maintained by the International Function Point Users Group and is documented in the Counting Practices Manual (CPM).[3]

IFPUG Function Point Components

To count IFPUG function points, we evaluate five *logical* components of the software based on the functional user requirements:[4]

- **Internal logical files (ILF)** Logical, persistent entities maintained by the software application. (Note that "code/description" tables are considered to be implementations of technical user requirements rather than functional and are therefore excluded as countable functionality. Thus, they are neither ILF nor EIF.)

[3] The International Function Point Users Group (IFPUG) Counting Practices Manual Release 4.3 contains the rules for counting function points. To obtain a copy of the Counting Practices Manual, contact IFPUG at www.ifpug.org.

[4] The components listed are taken from the International Function Point Users Group (IFPUG) Counting Practices Manual 4.3 (IFPUG, 2004). The explanatory text is the author's own wording to describe each component.

- **External interface files (EIF)** Logical, persistent entities that are referenced only by the software application, but are maintained by another software application.
- **External inputs (EI)** Logical, elementary business processes whereby data crosses into the application boundary to maintain data on an internal logical file or to ensure compliance with user business requirements (for example, control data).
- **External outputs (EO)** Logical, elementary business processes that result in data leaving the application boundary to meet a user requirement that involves at least one of (a) a calculation; (b) derivation of data; (c) update of one or more ILFs; (d) controlling the behavior of the software (for example, summarized reports, output data files with derived data, output tapes where an ILF was updated during the process, screen alerts involving calculation(s)).
- **External queries (EQ)** Logical, elementary business processes that result in data leaving the application boundary to meet a user requirement, which involves retrieving data from at least one ILF or EIF, but which cannot perform any of the processing listed clauses *a–d* of an external output (for example, output files where no data is derived or calculated, detail reports, pure data extracts from ILFs/EIFs, and data browse displays).

Note that these five types of *logical* components are not the same as physical components. When we talk about "internal logical files," for example, it does not necessarily mean physical files or data sets. "Internal logical files" refers to the logical, persistent entities maintained through a standardized function of the software. In other words, ILFs are the stand-alone, logical entities that would typically appear on a logical entity relationship diagram (ERD). For example, in a human resources application, an associate or employee entity is one of the typical entities that would be maintained. This entity would be counted as an ILF.

Another illustration of counting *logical* components is when we refer to the transactional functions of external inputs, external outputs, or external queries. External inputs are the logical, elementary business processes that maintain the data on an internal logical file or that control processing. The logical business process of adding an associate (an employee) would be one elementary user function, and therefore in function point counting we would count one external input. The size in function points for this one external input would be the same regardless of how we physically implemented it, because in every implementation it performs one logical user function. For example, the count for "Add employee" is the same regardless of the number of physical screens, keystrokes, batch programs, or pop-up data windows we need to complete the process.

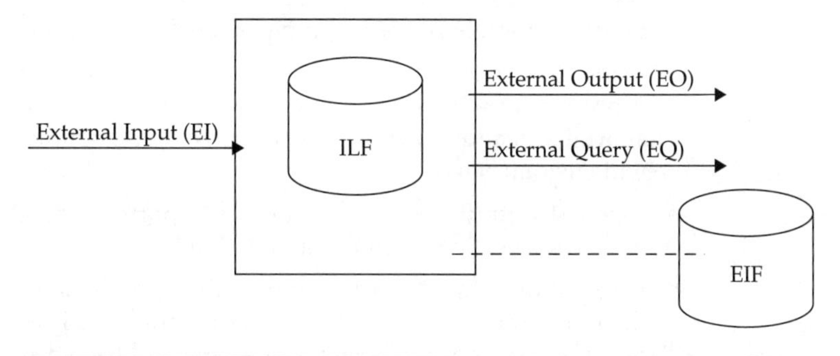

Figure 18-1 Context diagram for IFPUG FP

What Is Involved in IFPUG Function Point Counting?

The basic steps[5] involved in the IFPUG methodology for function point counting include

1. Determine type of count (can be a new development project, an application or base count, or an enhancement project count).
2. Determine the project scope and the purpose for measuring the functional size. This step identifies exactly what is to be counted. For example, if a piece of software is to be delivered incrementally over five releases, and we need to estimate the effort to deliver phase 1, then we would want to know the functional size of the functional user requirements that would be delivered by phase 1. The remaining functional user requirements would be out of scope of the phase 1 functional size.
3. Identify the application boundary (that is, the functions the software must perform. This creates a context diagram for the application or project as illustrated in Figure 18-1).
4. Identify the function types and establish complexity:
   a. Count the data function types (self-contained, persistent logical entities):
      - Internal logical files (ILF), which are logical data groups maintained within the application boundary
      - External interface files (EIF), which are used only for reference by the application and are maintained within another software's application boundary

[5] These steps are a condensed version of the full FP counting method included in the IFPUG Counting Practices Manual. Additionally, there are full case studies of FP counts done at differing phases of application development that can also be ordered through the IFPUG office.

b. Count the transactional function types:
    - External inputs (EI), which include the elementary processes for which data entry is their primary intent, as well as stand-alone controlled inputs (for example, add customer)
    - External outputs (EO), for example, reports or data displays where calculations are involved
    - External queries (EQ), for example, direct retrieval of data from one or more of the entities identified as ILFs or EIFs, and no additional processing as described earlier

c. Evaluate the "complexity" of each of the five function types identified earlier. IFPUG provides several simple matrixes to determine whether a function is Low, Average, or High complexity, based on data element types (user-recognizable, nonrecursive data fields), record element types (subsets of user-recognizable data), and file types referenced (number of logical data groupings required to complete a process). Table 18-2 summarizes the number of function points assigned to each function type.

d. Following the IFPUG guidelines, count and rate all of the identified functions, and add the function points together. The resultant number is called the *unadjusted FP count* and is the functional size of the project.

5. The next step is an *optional* step in the IFPUG function point method because it goes beyond the determination of functional size. It attempts to quantify a portion of the non-functional user requirements by evaluating 14 factors of the software. This step determines a factor called the value adjustment factor (VAF), which reflects the user non-functional requirements or complexity for the developed software. The VAF is calculated via an equation (VAF = 0.65 + (Sum of General System Characteristics × 0.01)) and involves a simple evaluation of 14 general

Function Type	Low	Average	High
EI	×3	×4	×6
EO	×4	×5	×7
EQ	×3	×4	×6
ILF	×7	×10	×15
EIF	×5	×7	×10

Table 18-2 Unadjusted FP Assigned to IFPUG Function Types

systems characteristics (GSCs). Specific evaluation guidelines for the following GSCs are provided in the IFPUG Counting Practices Manual (IFPUG, 2009):

- Data communication
- Distributed data processing
- Performance
- Heavily used configuration
- Transaction rate
- Online data entry
- End user efficiency
- Online update
- Complex processing
- Reusability
- Installation ease
- Operational ease
- Multiple sites
- Facilitate change

6. The final step is also optional in the IFPUG CPM because it too goes beyond what is considered functional size. It "adjusts" the functional size (Step 4) and the non-functional VAF (Step 5) together using: Adjusted FP = unadjusted FP * VAF.

NOTE *The ISBSG records the* functional size *in units of unadjusted FP and records the VAF as a separate and distinct project value.*

While some organizations find value in using the adjusted FP count in their project work, the majority of the established estimating toolsets, including the ISBSG, report the functional size (unadjusted FP) separately from the non-functional measure (VAF).[6]

The Logical Boundary

One of the first steps to measuring functional size using any of the functional size measurement methods is to identify the logical "boundary" around the software application. This boundary separates the software from the user domain (remember that users can be people, things, other software applications, departments, other organizations, and so on). As such, the software may span several

[6] At this writing, IFPUG has a working group working on a Software Non-functional Assessment Framework Project (SNAP) to provide a sizing method for non-functional requirements.

physical platforms and include both batch and online processes. The software boundary is *not* drawn in terms of how the physical system is implemented, but rather in terms of how an experienced user would view the software. This means that a single application boundary can encompass several hardware platforms (for example, mainframe and PC hardware used to provide an accounts receivable application would both be included within the single application boundary).

ISO and IFPUG have identical definitions for (application) boundary (IFPUG, 2009; ISO, 2007):

> Boundary, a conceptual interface between the software under study and its users
> (IFPUG added the following note: "Prior versions of this International Standard used the term application boundary.")

Where Does Functional Size Fit in with the ISBSG and Software Project Estimating?

After we have determined that the software project involves the new delivery or enhancement of functional user requirements (that is, functionality), we can measure the software's functional size. If a project does *not* involve the delivery or enhancement of software functionality—for example, it simply involves maintenance/fixes of already delivered functionality, or upgrades the technical or non-functional requirements, or is a pure documentation project, and so on—then it cannot be sized using functional size measurement and must be estimated using some other estimation equations based on other input measures.

Once we have the functional size for a project or application (in functional size units), we have established the "functional" size of the project work product. If we choose to evaluate the VAF, we then also have a numerical value for the influence of non-functional quality types of requirements for the application.

Just as the square meters (or feet) size of a house does *not* equal the speed at which a house can be built or its construction duration, the functional size does *not* equal delivery rate or work effort. Functional size measures the size of *what* the software does, rather than *how* it is developed or implemented (technical requirements) or *how* it must operate (quality requirements). This means that given a common set of functional user requirements, the functional size of the software will be the same whether it is developed using COBOL or Java, or using rapid application development (RAD) or waterfall or agile development methods.

Functional size (and even IFPUG's optional VAF) provides us with objective software size measures for use in work-effort estimating equations (together with other factors) or to normalize productivity or quality ratios. The value in using functional size lies in the ratios and normalized comparisons between ratios. Process improvements can be found when normalized ratios are compared and their underlying project attributes assessed for their impact on the project.

NOTE *In 2008 IFPUG launched a project to address the measurement of non-functional requirements within IS projects and applications. The SNAP (Software Non-Functional Assessment Process) project will release an Assessment Practices Manual (APM) in 2010 to be reviewed and tested by the IFPUG membership. The APM will enable the usage of the SNAP sizing method. This will include the assessment itself, instructions on the completion of the assessment, and guidance on how to utilize and apply the results of the assessment. In addition, common terms and definitions will be provided within the APM.*

Summary

Functional size measurement and functional size provide an objective, repeatable process for assessing the logical size of software based on its functional user requirements. Functional size provides us with a standard, normalized measurement value of the work product. Together with other measures, such as the value adjustment factor and project attributes, functional size–based software metrics can highlight process improvement opportunities and are a proven approach to increasing the accuracy of software work-effort estimating precision and accuracy.

CHAPTER 19

An IFPUG Function Point Case Study

This chapter outlines and demonstrates how functional size measurement can be applied to determine:

- The functional size of a sample set of new development user requirements
- The functional size of a sample set of enhancement user requirements

Once the functional user requirements for each sample set are identified, functional size measurement is done using one of the ISO-recognized functional size measurement methods. This case study uses the IFPUG method.[1]

You should read the preceding chapter, "A Brief Tutorial on Functional Size Measurement (FSM)," before reading this chapter.

New Development Case Study

For the first example we will establish the functional size for the new development of a piece of software. We have chosen the planned development of an Employee Records Management system for our case study. This relatively straightforward system provides a good framework on which to display how to go about functional sizing.

[1] See ISO/IEC 20926: 2009 Software engineering—IFPUG 4.3 Functional Size Measurement Method—Counting practices manual.

Sample Set of User Requirements

The following list represents a sample set of user requirements for a new development software project:

1. The software application must store and maintain employee information consisting of the following data fields: name, employee number, rank, street address, city, state, ZIP code, date of birth, phone number, office assigned, and the date the employee data was last maintained.
2. The software application must provide a means to add new employees, update employee information, terminate employees, and merge duplicate employee records (in cases where all fields other than employee number are identical).
3. The software application must provide a scheduled weekly report. Its header includes the Report Period and provides a retrieved list of all employees (Name and Employee Number) where information has changed within the previous 7 calendar days (report period).
4. The application must provide a means for the end user to view an employee's data.
5. User security data (user ID, password) is referenced from the security application for user logon security validation.
6. Complex algorithms are used to encrypt the employee date of birth so that it cannot be directly read from the information stored for an employee.
7. The software application must provide subsecond response time for data maintenance processes during the peak business hours between 8 A.M. and 5 P.M. Eastern USA Standard Time (GMT – 5).
8. The software application must use programming language(s) that are compatible with open systems design and Oracle databases.

Functional User Requirements

Functional size represents the size of the subset of user requirements known as the functional user requirements (that is, what functions the software must support), which excludes quality and technical requirements.

Of the preceding list of user requirements, 1 through 5 represent the functional user requirements, while 6 through 8 are nonfunctional (quality and technical) requirements. Only requirements 1 through 5 will be used to determine the functional size of the software.

Functional Size Measurement Using ISO/IEC 20926: 2009 – IFPUG 4.3

Functional Size Measurement Method: IFPUG 4.3 identifies the following five base functional components for determining functional size:

NOTE *The terms* application *and* software application *are used interchangeably in the following narrative.*

- **Internal logical file (ILF)** This persistent logical entity is maintained by a standard elementary process (function) of the software application.
- **External interface file (EIF)** This persistent logical entity is maintained by another software application, and referenced only by this software application.
- **External input (EI)** This elementary process of the application has the primary purpose of processing data entering the application boundary and either maintains the data contained in an ILF or controls the behavior of the application.
- **External output (EO)** This elementary process of the application has the primary purpose to present data to a user (that is, data exits the application boundary to a "user"). At least one (or more) of the following logic steps must be part of the elementary process:
  - Calculation
  - Derivation of data
  - Update of at least 1 ILF
  - Control of the behavior of the application
- **External query (EQ)** This elementary process of the application retrieves data from at least 1 ILF or EIF for presentation to a user. The elementary process cannot include any calculations, derived data, updating of an ILF, or control of the application's behavior.

Determining the Functional Size

Without getting into the specifics of how the IFPUG 4.3 method rates a specific base functional component as Low, Average, or High, the following example illustrates the basic steps to arrive at the functional size (in units of function points) for the sample set of functional user requirements previously discussed.

The function point components to be counted based on the preceding include

- **Internal logical file (ILF)** *Count 1 ILF* for the Employee data group because it is a persistent logical entity maintained by the application. Based on the function point counting rules, the complexity of this function would be Low (refer to ISO 20926: 2009 for detailed counting rules):

  1 Low ILF = ***7 FP***

- **External interface file (EIF)** *Count 1 EIF* for the externally maintained Security logical entity. It is a Low complexity EIF:

  1 Low EIF = ***5 FP***

- **External input process(es) (EI)** *Count 4 EIs:* one EI each for the elementary processes of Add Employee, Update Employee, Terminate Employee, and Merge Duplicate Employee Records. Each EI accesses only one FTR (file type referenced) and meets the IFPUG requirements for a Low complexity EI function:

  4 Low EI (of 3 FP each) = **12 FP**

- **External output process(es) (EO)** *Count 1 EO* for the user to browse an employee's data (which includes the step of using an algorithm to decrypt the date of birth for display). The report accesses 1 FTR and has less than 19 DETs and is therefore a Low complexity EO:

  1 Low EO = ***4 FP***

- **External query process(es) (EQ)** *Count 2 EQs: 1 for the Weekly Report (listing) and 1 for the User Security Logon function.* Each of these elementary processes meets the requirements for an EQ. Based on the IFPUG 4.3 rules, they are classified as a Low EQ:

  2 Low EQ (of 3 FP each) = ***6 FP***

The total functional size expressed in function points is the sum of the individual components:

Functional size = ILF + EIF + EI + EO + EQ
= 7 + 5 + 12 + 4 + 6
= 34 FP (IFPUG 4.3)

Figure 19-1 shows the context diagram for the functional user requirements included in this functional size.

The full details and FP counting procedure are contained in the *IFPUG Function Point Counting Practices Manual 4.3,* available through ISO (www.jtc1-sc7.org/) or from the International Function Point Users Group (IFPUG) at www.ifpug.org.

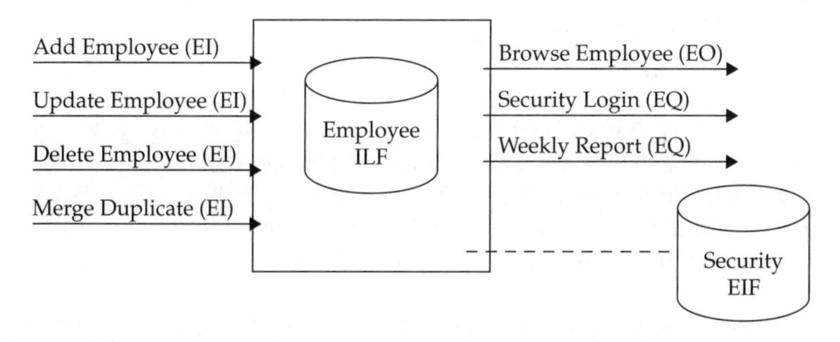

FIGURE 19-1 Sample new development functional user requirements using IFPUG 4.3 functional size measurement method

Enhancement Case Study

For this example we will establish the functional size for the enhancement of a piece of software. For this case study we have chosen the enhancement of the Employee Records Management system used in the first example.

Sample Set of User Requirements

The following list represents a sample set of user requirements for the enhancement of the newly developed software described previously:

1. The *add new employee* function will now include additional logic steps to validate fields that were not validated in the first release of the software.
2. The scheduled weekly report will now include a calculated value that sums the total number of employees listed.
3. The software application will now include a navigational menu for users to select the data maintenance function they wish to perform on the employee data.

No other changes will be made.

Functional User Requirements

Functional size represents the size of the subset of user requirements known as the functional user requirements (that is, what functions the software must support), which excludes quality and technical requirements.

Of the listing of user requirements, 1 and 2 represent the functional user requirements, while 3 is a nonfunctional requirement to provide end-user friendliness (navigational aids). Therefore, only the first two requirements will be included in the determination of functional size.

Determining the Functional Size

The IFPUG 4.3 method counts an enhancement project's functional size by identifying any function that is New (added), Modified (changed), or Removed (deleted) and including it as part of the functional size. Once again IFPUG 4.3 rates each specific base functional component impacted by the project as Low, Average, or High, and the following example illustrates the basic steps to arrive at the enhancement project's functional size (in units of function points).

The function point components to be counted based on the functional user requirements include

- **Internal logical file (ILF)** No ILFs are New, Modified, or Removed as part of the functional user requirements.
- **External interface file (EIF)** No EIFs are New, Modified, or Removed as part of the functional user requirements.
- **External input process(es) (EI)** *Count 1 EI* for the modified Add Employee EI where the processing logic has been enhanced. This was (and remains) a Low complexity EI function and results in:

  1 Low EI = ***3 FP (modified)***
- **External output process(es) (EO)** *Count 1 EO* for the modified Weekly Report function that now includes a calculation step and a new data field. The report is a Low complexity function and would result in:

  1 Low EO = ***4 FP (modified)***

  Note that this function existed as an EQ in the first software release and has been modified (additional logic whereby a calculation is now performed); therefore it is now classified as an EO as a result of the enhancement project. It is *not* counted as a removed EQ function and a new EO function—rather it is a single modified function and counted as an EO in the enhancement project.
- **External query process(es) (EQ)** No EQs are New, Modified, or Removed as part of the functional user requirements (see EO earlier for the treatment of the Weekly Report).

The total functional size expressed in function points is the sum of the individual components:

Functional size = New + Modified + Removed Functions
= (3 + 4) modified
= 7 FP (IFPUG 4.3)

Figure 19-2 shows the context diagram for the functional user requirements included in this functional size.

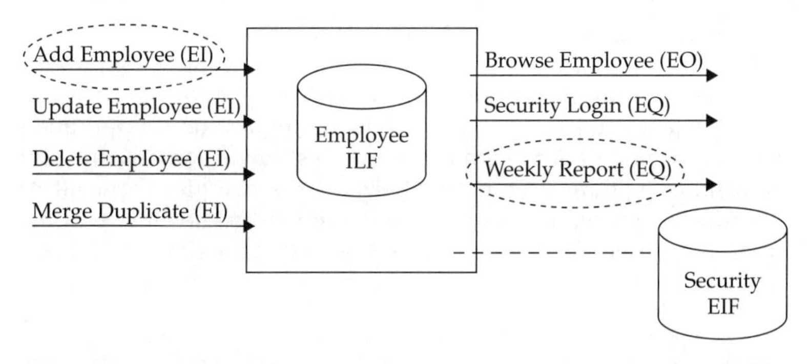

FIGURE 19-2 Sample enhancement functional user requirements using IFPUG 4.3 functional size measurement method

Types of Functional Size

It is worth noting that functional size is typically used in two major areas. (Note that in the ISBSG software project database, only the functional size for new development, redevelopment, or enhancement software projects is included.)

- **Application or base software functional size** This measure represents the functional size of an installed base software application. (Think of it in terms of square meters of a constructed building.) The base functional size is a point-in-time snapshot of the current size of an application. This number is useful whenever comparisons are required between different installed applications (for example, defects/base FP).
- **New development or enhancement project functional size** This measure reflects the size of the functional area impacted by a new development or enhancement project. An enhancement project size is the result of summing the New functions added in the project, plus the functions Removed from the application by a project, plus the functions Changed (modified) by the project. (Think of this count in terms of a renovation project where the square meter size of the project equals the sum of the area of a New living room, a Removed bathroom, and a Remodeled kitchen.) This measure is useful in project-based metrics (for example, relative cost in $/development FP).

  For a new development project, all of the functional user requirements are New—therefore, there are no removed or changed functions to be sized, only new (added) functionality.

At the end of a new development or enhancement project, the Application or Base FP count must be initialized for new development or updated (if it is an enhancement project) to reflect the actual functional size *of the application* at this time.

Note that in addition to adding, removing, and modifying application functionality, new development and enhancement projects may also include the development or delivery of conversion functionality required to convert data from one application or application version to another. Although the size of this conversion functionality *is* included within the functional size of the new development or enhancement project, it *is not* included in the functional size of the impacted application for the simple reason that the conversion functionality in question is not part of the application's functionality.

Summary

This chapter has provided a practical introduction to software sizing using functional size measurement. It has demonstrated how functional size measurement can be applied to both new development and enhancement projects. Readers should refer to the counting practices manuals, or equivalent, for the particular functional sizing methodology that they plan to use.

CHAPTER 20

The COSMIC Functional Size Measurement Method

The idea of measuring a size of the functional user requirements (FUR) of a piece of software in terms of its *functionality* as opposed to its physical components was first put forward by Allan Albrecht of IBM in 1979. He proposed the method called *Function Point Analysis,* which has since evolved into the *IFPUG* method—see Chapter 19 of this book.

Albrecht's clever piece of lateral thinking laid the foundations for the subject of functional size measurement (or FSM), and it is a great tribute to his original idea that his method is still widely used today. (And if the IFPUG method gives satisfactory results for performance measurement and estimating, then there is little incentive to change.)

However, the COSMIC functional sizing method was developed by the Common Software Measurement International Consortium to offer an alternative to IFPUG. The logic behind, and the reasons for, the development of the COSMIC method are explained on the web site: www.cosmicon.com.

The COSMIC method has been accepted as an international standard (ISO/IEC 19761: 2003) and at this writing is proceeding through the ISO process to be aligned with version 3.0 of the COSMIC method.

The method is now used in major corporations and public sector organizations around the world for software project performance measurement and for estimating in all the domains for which it was designed.

Overview of the COSMIC Functional Size Measurement Method

The COSMIC method defines the principles, rules, and a process for measuring a standard functional size of a piece of software. *Functional size* is a measure of the amount of functionality provided by the software, completely independent of any technical or quality considerations.

Applicability of the Method

The common characteristic of the types of software for which the COSMIC method was designed (business applications, real-time software, infrastructure software, and hybrids of these) is that they are dominated by functions that input data, store and retrieve data, and output data. In common with the other FSM methods covered in this book, the COSMIC method is not designed to size software that is dominated by functions that manipulate data, as in typical scientific and engineering software.

Subject to the preceding, the method may be applied to measure the FUR of software:

- At any level of decomposition, for example, a "whole" piece of software or any of its components, subcomponents, and so on
- In any layer of a multilayer architecture
- At any point in the life cycle of the piece of software

The Principles for Measuring the COSMIC Functional Size of a Piece of Software

The COSMIC method measures a size as seen by the "functional users" of the piece of software to be measured, that is, the senders and/or intended recipients of the data that must enter or exit from the software, respectively. Functional users may be humans or other pieces of software, or may be hardware devices that interact directly with the software being measured, as defined in the FUR. Different sizes may result depending on the defined functional users, since the different types can "see" different functionality.

The method uses a model of software known as the COSMIC Generic Software Model (see Figure 20-1).

This model is based on fundamental software engineering principles, namely:

- The FUR of a piece of software can be analyzed into unique functional processes, which consist of subprocesses. A subprocess may be either a data movement or a data manipulation.

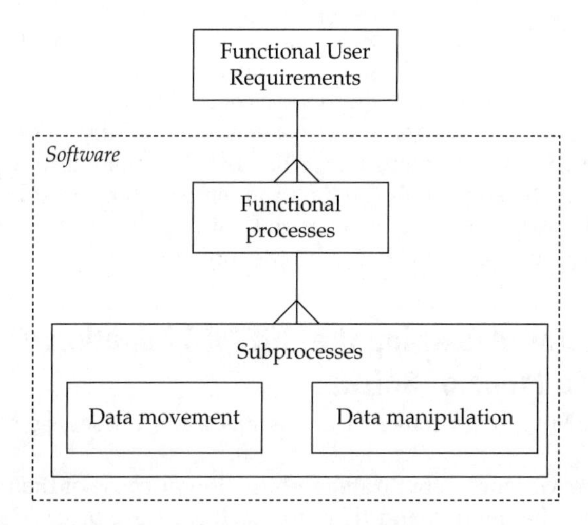

FIGURE 20-1 The COSMIC Generic Software Model

- Each functional process is triggered by an Entry data movement from a functional user that informs the functional process that the functional user has identified an event to which the software must respond.
- A functional process is complete when it has done all that is required to respond to the event.
- A data movement moves a single data group of attributes describing a single "object of interest," where the latter is a "thing" of interest to a functional user.
- There are four types of data movement subprocesses. An Entry moves a data group into the software from a functional user, and an Exit moves a data group out. Writes and Reads move a data group to and from persistent storage, respectively.

As an approximation for measurement purposes (and given the applicability of the method, described earlier), data manipulation subprocesses are not separately measured. The method assumes that data manipulation is accounted for by the data movement that it is associated with.

The size of a piece of software is then defined as the total number of data movements (entries, exits, reads, and writes) summed over all functional processes of the piece of software. Each data movement is counted as one COSMIC function point (CFP). The size of a functional process, and hence the size of a piece of software, can be a minimum of 2 CFP, with no upper limit. This is a very important factor. Most functional processes typically have a few data movements, say in the range of 2–10 CFP. But sometimes software has some much larger (more "complex"?) functional processes; examples have been measured of up to 70 CFP in a banking business application and over 100 CFP for a single functional process in the avionics of a military aircraft.

The size of changes or enhancements required for existing software can also be measured. The size of a change to a piece of software is the sum of all the data movements that must be added, changed, or deleted, where "changed" also includes changes to the data manipulation associated with the movement.

The Process for Measuring the COSMIC Functional Size of a Piece of Software

The COSMIC measurement process has three phases, as shown in Figure 20-2.

In the Measurement Strategy phase, the purpose of the measurement must be defined and then, for each separate piece of software that must be measured, the following information is needed:

- The layer of the architecture where it resides
- Its scope (what functionality is included)
- Its functional users
- Its level of decomposition (care must be taken in summing sizes of pieces of software at different levels of composition)

In the Mapping Phase, the artifacts of the FUR of the software to be developed/enhanced and measured are analyzed to determine:

- The separate events that trigger functional processes
- The functional processes
- The objects of interest to the functional users, the data groups describing those objects of interest that will be moved, and the data movements

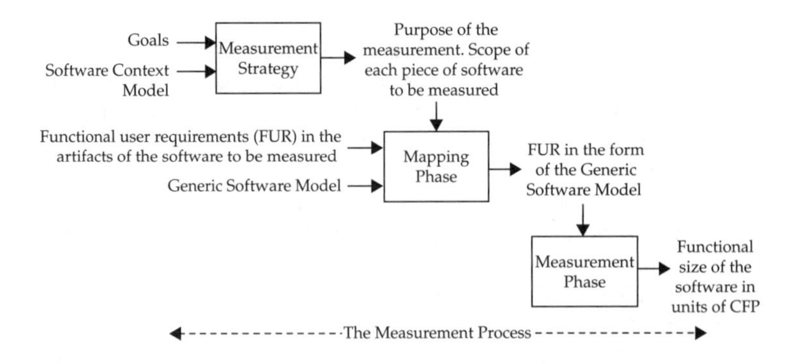

FIGURE 20-2 COSMIC measurement process phases

In the Measurement Phase, the functional processes are measured by counting the data movements and summing them appropriately to give the size of the pieces of software in units of CFP. The measurement must be well documented for future use and interpretation.

COSMIC Method Documentation

For the detailed measurement rules, see "The COSMIC Functional Size Measurement Method v3.0.1: Measurement Manual, the COSMIC Implementation Guide for ISO/IEC 19761:2003." Three other important documents are in the v3.0 series:

- "Method Overview - v3.0" (a more detailed overview of the method than is given here)
- "Documentation Overview and Glossary of Terms - v3.0.1"
- "Advanced and Related Topics - v3.0"

Full documentation is available for free download from www.cosmicon.com including translations in Arabic, Chinese, Dutch, French, Turkish, and Japanese.

A wide range of supporting services and tools is available for the COSMIC method, for example:

- The International Standard ISO/IEC 19761:2003, obtainable from www.iso.org (updated in 2009 to align with v3.0.1 of the COSMIC method).
- A "Method Overview" document aimed at those who need an introduction to the method.
- Specialist Guidelines, that supplement the Measurement Manual with guidance and many examples for various special types of software. Guidelines exist for sizing business applications and data warehouses. Other guidelines are in preparation, for example, for sizing components in an SOA architecture.
- Guidance and formulae for converting sizes from first-generation methods.
- Certification examinations.
- Suppliers of consulting and training services, worldwide.
- Case studies.
- Estimating tools.
- Benchmark data (in the ISBSG database and reports, from www.isbsg.org).

Summary

This chapter has provided an introduction to, and an explanation of, the COSMIC functional sizing method. For additional information readers should refer to "The COSMIC Functional Size Measurement Method v3.0.1: Measurement Manual, the COSMIC Implementation Guide for ISO/IEC 19761:2003" and associated documentation.

CHAPTER 21

A COSMIC Function Point Case Study

In this chapter the same case study used in Chapter 19 (an IFPUG function point case study), is used here, this time measured using the COSMIC FSM method. The version of the method used is as defined either in the ISO/IEC standard 19761:2010 or as in the COSMIC Measurement Manual version 3.

Those unfamiliar with the COSMIC Functional Size Measurement (FSM) method, should read Chapter 20 for an overview. More details of the COSMIC FSM method may be obtained from the ISO standard (ISO/IEC 19761:2010) via www.iso.org or full details can be obtained by free download of the COSMIC Measurement Manual, v3.0.1, and all other documentation from www.cosmicon.com.

For the functional user requirements of the case study to be measured, please see Chapter 19.

Analysis of the Size of the New Software to Be Developed

The purpose of the measurement is to determine the functional size of the stated functional user requirements 1–8 of the new development project.

The scope of the size measurement of the new software to be developed includes all the functional user requirements of this case study, that is, all the specified requirements of the project, but recognizing that the non-functional requirements (7 and 8) do not contribute to the functional size.

For requirement 5 (which states: "User security data (user ID, password) is referenced from the security application for user logon security validation") it is assumed that a new functional process must be provided to enable a user to log on by entering his ID and password in order to obtain authorization from the security application to proceed.

Requirements 1 and 6 include the "data manipulation" subprocesses of validation and encryption. These operations are part of the logical processing of their associated data movements. They are not measured as a separate subprocess.

The last two requirements, 7 and 8, are non-functional and not measured as part of the functional sizing.

All the software to be measured lies within one application layer. The functional users of the software to be developed are

- A human user of the software
- The security access control application that maintains the file of authorized users

The Maintain Employee Data application has one object of interest, namely Employee. The security application has one object of interest, namely Authorized User, but since the case study is only concerned with measuring the maintain employee application, and the Authorized User data is only accessible by calling on the second functional user (the security application) to retrieve the relevant data on behalf of the maintain employee application; no direct Read or Write data movements are associated with the Authorized User object of interest.

The Employee object of interest is associated with a single Data Group, Employee.

The functional processes for the new development are shown in Table 21-1. Where an error message is identified and counted, this is an assumption, since the treatment of input errors is not stated in the requirements.

Reqt. No.	Name of Functional Process	Data Movement Type (and Data Group)	Total CFP
5	User security logon	Entry (User ID, password) Exit (request to security application to authorize user) Entry (receipt of authorization, or not) Exit (authorize user, or not, and inform user)	4
1, 2	Add New Employee	Entry (Employee data) Read (Employee data)—next number Write (Employee data) Exit (Employee number) Exit (confirmation or error message)	5
1, 2	Update Employee data*	Entry (Employee data) Write (Employee data) Exit (confirmation or error message)	3

TABLE 21-1 Functional Processes—New Development

Reqt. No.	Name of Functional Process	Data Movement Type (and Data Group)	Total CFP
1, 2	Terminate Employee*	Entry (Employee number) Write (Employee data) Exit (confirmation or error message)	3
1, 2	Merge duplicate Employee records	Entry (Select to Merge) Read (Employee data)—find duplicates Write (Employee data)—remove duplicate record(s) Exit (error/confirmation message)	4
3	Scheduled weekly report (on Employees whose data has changed in the past week)	Entry (end-of-week timing signal) Read (Employee data) Exit (Report Period) Exit (Employee ID, name) Exit (error/confirmation message to application management)	5
4	View Employee	Entry (Employee Name/Number) Read (Employee data) Exit (Employee data) Exit (error message)	4
Total size of the new software to be developed in COSMIC function points =			28 CFP

*Normally these functional processes would be preceded by a "retrieve Employee data" functional process, to ensure that the correct employee had been selected for update or deletion. We assume that the View Employee functional process is used for this purpose.

Table 21-1 Functional Processes—New Development (*Continued*)

Analysis of the Size of the Enhancement to the Software

The purpose of the measurement is to determine the functional size of the stated functional user requirements 1–3 of the enhancement project.

The scope of the size measurement of the software enhancement includes all the functional user requirements included in the enhancement requirements (that is, 1 and 2) of this case study. Requirement 3 concerns implementation of navigational features that are considered non-functional with respect to the functional users of this software.

- All the software to be measured lies in the one application layer.

Reqt. No.	Name of Functional Process That Is to Be Changed	Data Movement Type (and Data Group) That Is to Be Changed	Total CFP
1	Add new Employee	*Entry (Employee data)	1
2	Scheduled weekly report	Exit (Report Period and Report total number of Employees)	1
The total size of the required enhancement in COSMIC function points =			2 CFP

*It is assumed that the data validation is changed for the Entry, but although the error message may have new values, its data manipulation logic, formatting, and presentation are not changed.

TABLE 21-2 Functional Processes—Enhancement

- The functional user of the software to be enhanced is a human user of the software.
- The Maintain Employee Data application has one object of interest, namely, Employee.

The functional processes of the enhancement are shown in Table 21-2. Where an error message is identified and counted, this is an assumption, since the treatment of input errors is not stated in the requirements.

Note that the COSMIC FSM method measures the size of the required changes to the functional user requirements (not the size of the functional processes that are changed).

It is likely that the new validation rules would also be applied to the Modify Employee details requirement. This needs to be verified with the users and added to the impacted data movements if it also is impacted by changes in the validation rules.

Overall Size of the Software After the Enhancement

The size of the Maintain Employee Data application software after the enhancement project has finished has not changed from 28 CFP, since only existing data movements were changed and no new data movements were added or existing ones removed.

Summary

This chapter provides a simple example of how to size both the new development of a piece of software and the enhancement of a piece of software using the COSMIC FSM method. By reading Chapter 20 and this chapter the reader will gain a sound understanding of the COSMIC sizing method. As this chapter uses the same example set of user requirements as those used for the IFPUG and FiSMA methods, the reader can also make comparisons to understand the differences in the three sizing approaches.

CHAPTER 22

A FiSMA Function Point Case Study

In this chapter the same case study is used as in Chapter 19 (an IFPUG function point case study), this time measured using the FiSMA FSM method. The version of the method used is as defined either in the ISO/IEC standard 29881:2010 or as in the "FiSMA 1.1 Functional Size Measurement Method" document that is publicly available on the www.fisma.fi/in-english.

For those unfamiliar with the FiSMA 1.1 Functional Size Measurement (FSM) method, we introduce the main characteristics here:

- FiSMA 1.1 is based purely on functional user requirements.
- FiSMA 1.1 is applicable to measure all software in any functional domain.
- FiSMA 1.1 identifies 28 distinct Base Functional Component (BFC) types.
- FiSMA 1.1 identifies seven BFC classes.
- Each BFC class has a specific counting rule for determining the functional size of any functional component within the class.
- Parameters in FiSMA 1.1 counting rules are "number of data elements," "number of reading references," "number of writing references," and "number of operations." One or more parameter types may occur in any of the BFC classes.

The seven FiSMA 1.1 BFC classes with their *relevant counting parameters* (1.) and *examples of BFC types* (2.) are

- Interactive navigation and query services for end users
    1. Number of data elements and number of reading references

2. Seven BFC types, for example, inquiry screens, menus, browsing screens

- Interactive input services for end users
  1. Number of data elements and numbers of writing and reading references
  2. Three BFC types: 1-functional, 2-functional, and 3-functional input screens (functionality depending on the capability to create, update, and delete)
- Non-interactive output services for end users
  1. Number of data elements and number of reading references
  2. Four BFC types, for example, reports, static output forms, e-mails
- Interface services to other applications
  1. Number of data elements and number of reading references
  2. Three BFC types, for example, online messages and batch records
- Interface services from other applications
  1. Number of data elements and numbers of writing and reading references
  2. Three BFC types, for example, online messages and batch records
- Data storage services
  1. Number of data elements
  2. Two BFC types, entities, and other persistent data records
- Algorithmic and manipulation services
  1. Number of data elements (variables) and number of operations
  2. Six BFC types, for example, calculation routines, security routines, formatting rules

All FiSMA 1.1 counting rules follow the same type of formula, and its size measurement scale is continuous. This means that every additional data element, reference, or operation increases the functional size of the functional component. The common formula for the FiSMA 1.1 counting rules is

Size = A + Number of data elements / D + Number of references (or operation) / C where A, D, and C are class-specific constants. For example, for the navigation and query services, the calculation rule is

Size = 0.2 + N/7 + R/2

For example: size of an inquiry service with 21 data elements (N) on the screen, read from 4 entities (R), would be 0.2 + 21/7 + 4/2 = 5.2 FFP (FiSMA function points).

Size Measurement of the New Software to Be Developed

The purpose of the measurement is to determine the functional size of the stated user requirements of the new development project. In the next paragraphs we go through the set of requirements from 1 to 8, collecting all base functional components and counting their sizes based on the given information.

In all tables below the column identifiers are

- Base Functional Component type (one of 28 BFC types)
- N = number of data elements
- W = number of writing references
- R = number of reading references
- O = number of operations
- FFP = size in FiSMA Function Points

1. *The software application must store and maintain employee information consisting of the following data fields: name, employee number, rank, street address, city, state, ZIP code, date of birth, phone number, office assigned, and the date the employee data was last maintained.*
    - This requirement indicates that there will be a persistent data storage service with only one ENTITY with 11 data elements.

Base Functional Component type:	N	W	R	O	FFP
ENTITY	11	—	—	—	3.7

2. *The software application must provide a means to add new employees, update employee information, terminate employees, and merge duplicate employee records (in cases where all fields other than employee number are identical).*
    - This requirement indicates that there will be an INPUT screen for creating, updating, and deleting employees. There will be fields for ten employee data attributes and some other data elements on the screen (for example, screen title, different buttons, probable error message, and

so on). We think that the total number of data elements will be 18. The result will be written into the employee record, and the software will read system parameters when displaying this screen.

- The requirement also reveals that the user has specified an algorithmic RULE for comparing employee records and merging the duplicates. Not knowing the exact rule yet, we expect that ten different variables and three different operations will be needed.

Base Functional Component type:	N	W	R	O	FFP
3-FUNCTIONAL INPUT SCREEN	18	1	1	—	14.9
DATABASE CLEANING RULE	10	—	—	3	3.1

3. *The software application must provide a scheduled weekly report. Its header includes the Report Period and provides a retrieved list of all employees (Name and Employee Number) where information has changed within the previous 7 calendar days (report period).*
    - This requirement indicates that there will be a REPORT with approximately five data elements. To provide this report, the application must read employee data and system parameters.

Base Functional Component type:	N	W	R	O	FFP
REPORT	5	—	2	—	3.0

4. *The application must provide a means for the end user to view an employee's data.*
    - This requirement indicates that there will be a BROWSING SCREEN for finding and selecting the employee whose detailed information will then be displayed on an INQUIRY SCREEN. We expect that there will be eight data elements on the browsing screen and ten on the inquiry screen. Provision of both screens requires reading the employee data and system parameters.

Base Functional Component type:	N	W	R	O	FFP
BROWSING SCREEN	8	—	2	—	2.3
INQUIRY SCREEN	10	—	2	—	2.6

5. *User security data (user ID, password) is referenced from the security application for user logon security validation.*
    - This requirement indicates that there will be a LOG-ON screen with approximately five data elements that reads the system parameters.

- Because the security data is maintained and administered by another application, our application must send an ONLINE MESSAGE TO the security application and then receive the answer by an ONLINE MESSAGE FROM the same security application. With both these messages our application needs to refer system parameters, but no other entities.

Base Functional Component type:	N	W	R	O	FFP
LOG-ON	5	—	1	—	1.4
ONLINE MESSAGE TO	4	—	1	—	1.6
ONLINE MESSAGE FROM	4	1	0	—	1.7

6. *Complex algorithms are used to encrypt the employee date of birth so that it cannot be directly read from the information stored for an employee.*
   - This requirement indicates that there will be a SECURITY ROUTINE for encryption. Without knowing the exact rules, we assume five variables and five different operations needed.

Base Functional Component type:	N	W	R	O	FFP
SECURITY ROUTINE	5	—	—	5	2.8

7. *The software application must provide subsecond response time for data maintenance processes during the peak business hours between 8 A.M. and 5 P.M. Eastern USA Standard Time (GMT – 5).*
   - A non-functional user requirement that does not contribute to the functional size.
8. *The software application must use programming language(s) that are compatible with open systems design and Oracle databases.*
   - A technical requirement that does not contribute to the functional size.

The total functional size of this new development expressed in FiSMA function points is the sum of the individual components:

3.7 + 14.9 + 3.1 + 3.0 + 2.3 + 2.6 + 1.4 + 1.6 + 1.7 + 2.8 = 37.1 FFP

Size Measurement of the Enhancement to the Software

The purpose of the measurement is to determine the functional size of the stated requirements of the enhancement project. In the next paragraphs we go through the set of requirements from 1 to 3, collecting all base functional components and counting their sizes based on the given information. In the FiSMA 1.1 method the enhancement size is measured using a "touch" convention. The number of data elements is the number of added, deleted, modified, or moved data elements. The numbers of references and operations are the numbers of those impacted by the change, that is, all the counting parameters that are touched are counted.

1. *The* add new employee *function will now include additional logic steps to validate fields that were not validated in the first release of the software.*

    - The user will specify a new algorithmic RULE with probably five variables and five operations. This requirement does not change the input screen.

Base Functional Component type:	N	W	R	O	FFP
OTHER ALGORITHMIC RULE	5	—	—	5	2.8

2. *The scheduled weekly report will now include a calculated value that sums the total number of employees listed.*

    - This requirement indicates adding one new data element on the REPORT. It has no impact to the reading references on that report.
    - Calculating the sum of employees listed is a new CALCULATING ROUTINE with about three variables and two operations.

Base Functional Component type:	N	W	R	O	FFP
REPORT	1	—	0	—	1.2
CALCULATING ROUTINE	3	—	—	2	1.3

3. *The software application will now include a navigational menu for users to select the data maintenance function they wish to perform on the employee data.*

    - This requirement indicates that there will be a main MENU with three possible alternatives (Update employee, Merge duplicates, or Browse employees). The only entity referenced will be the system parameters.

Base Functional Component type:	N	W	R	O	FFP
MENU	3	—	1	—	1.1

The total functional size of this enhancement expressed in FiSMA function points is the sum of the individual components:

2.8 + 1.2 + 1.3 + 1.1 = 6.4 FFP

Overall Size of the Software After the Enhancement

The size of the Maintain Employee Data application software after the enhancement project is finished has changed from 37.1 FFP to 42.4 FFP. All three new functions (two algorithms and one menu) increase the size directly, but the changed functions must be re-measured based on the current values of counting parameters. In this example case the size of the report increases from 3.1 to 3.2 FFP.

Summary

This chapter has provided a practical example of the application of the FiSMA FSM method using the same case study that we have used to demonstrate the use of other FSM methods. Further information is available on the www.fisma.fi/in-english web site.

APPENDIX A

What Is in the ISBSG Repository?

Data Availability

ISBSG data can be licensed in two ways, via a data suite release or via a corporate subscription:

- **Data Suite Release** You can license an extract of all the projects held in the repository. This extract is called the "Estimating, Benchmarking & Research Suite" and is issued with a release number. New releases are made available when the number of projects in the repository has increased significantly. These releases can be licensed either through your local ISBSG member or via the ISBSG web site (www.isbsg.org). You can use the Estimating, Benchmarking & Research Suite to help you with your own software estimation, project planning and management, benchmarking your projects against similar ones in the repository, or conducting your own research.

  The suite contains a data subset of more than 100 fields for all the projects in the repository. Each release contains a detailed description of the data that is included in the suite.
- **Corporate Subscription** A corporate subscription is an extract of all the projects held in the repository at the time of the subscription. The subscription is annual, providing annual updates to the data and e-mail support and advice. The data set provided via the corporate subscription is a much larger field subset than that provided in the data suite releases and can be tailored to suit the licensee.

Data Quality

Each project submitted to the ISBSG Repository is validated against specified quality criteria and accorded a rating of "A," "B," "C," or "D":

- **Rating A** The data provided was assessed as being sound with nothing being identified that might affect its integrity.
- **Rating B** While assessed as being sound, there are some factors that could affect the credibility of the data provided.
- **Rating C** Due to significant data not being provided, it was not possible to assess the integrity of the data provided.
- **Rating D** Due to one factor or a combination of factors, little credibility should be given to the data provided.

Other than rating submitted projects, as just described, the ISBSG does not normally verify data that is submitted for inclusion in the repository in any other way. This means that there may be some data in the repository that appears to be questionable. It is important to make your own decision about the usefulness, or otherwise, of the data that you choose to use from the repository.

The repository data is provided in an MS Excel spreadsheet to allow you to select cases that you consider relevant to your situation and to do your own analysis.

What the ISBSG Data Can Be Used For

The ISBSG data can be used for more than software estimation: it can help you with project planning and management; you can benchmark your projects against similar ones in the repository; you can do your own research on topics of particular interest to you; or it can be used for academic research with the objective of improving IT practices and performance.

You can download a presentation on the ways that the ISBSG data can be used at www.isbsg.org/isbsg.nsf/weben/Repository%20info.

Considerations

If you intend using the ISBSG data for benchmarking or to help you with software estimation, then you need to be aware of the likely maturity level of the companies that submitted the project data that you are benchmarking against.

If you are a researcher who is going to use the ISBSG data for work that will report on the performance of the IT industry, you need to consider whether the ISBSG data (and particularly a selected subset of it) is representative of the industry.

ISBSG Project Data Positioning

The ISBSG project data is not necessarily representative of the software industry. The ISBSG believes that the projects in the repository are representative of the more productive projects in the industry, rather than of industry norms. There are a number of reasons for this.

Some organizations simply cannot contribute to the repository. The criteria for including a project in the repository generally exclude organizations that do not use functional size measurement (FSM).[1] They also exclude projects for which work effort (in person-hours) is not available.

Only organizations that collect the necessary metrics can contribute to the repository. Organizations with software metrics programs are likely to be among the more mature software development organizations.

Organizations also choose which of their projects they submit. They might choose typical projects, but they might choose only their best projects.

It is also worth noting that the majority of the projects in the repository are less than 2,000 function points in size. Very few are really big projects.

These considerations do not lessen the value of the data in the repository. The focus of the repository is as much on understanding best practice in the IT industry as on overall averages.

However, the key metrics have been studied and tested. The results of this work demonstrate that the sample represented by the repository is self-contained, internally consistent, and contains no apparent anomalies. The repository is therefore a very valuable collection of data for a number of avenues of analysis, benchmarking, and estimation.

Comparing Apples with Apples

When performing statistical analyses, it is very important to make sure that like is compared with like, that "apples are not compared with oranges." For this reason, it should be rare to find the entire repository analyzed as a single sample. Subsets of projects should be analyzed, so that it makes sense to compare projects within a subset.

Selecting a Suitable Data Subset

It is important to give careful thought to the project data that you will include in any data set that you plan to use. You need to think about the meaning of the data, not just to treat it as numbers to be used without selectivity. What project types can be legitimately compared or analyzed together?

---

[1] Although the repository does accept projects that have been sized using methods other than functional units (for example, LOC and use case points), the ISBSG does not perform validation on these size measures; it simply records them for general information.

Here are some examples:

- **Functional sizing methods** You shouldn't mix pre-IFPUG V4 projects with V4 and post-V4 (the sizing changed with that release). New development projects sized using the NESMA standard can be included with IFPUG V4+ projects. Use the *Count Approach* field in the data (and perhaps also the *FP Standards* and *Reference Table Approach* fields), to select projects that use the same sizing method that you use.
- **Normalized Effort**[2] For effort, give consideration to what risk and gain is involved in using normalized effort. The *Summary Work Effort* shown in the data is the total effort for the project. What is counted within that total varies, because different projects record effort at different levels of detail (see the *Resource Level* and *Recording Method* fields).

A resource level of "1" means that only the effort of the development team is recorded; "2" means that support team effort is also recorded; "3" adds computer operations; and "4" adds effort expended by the end user or client.

Two things you might do to make sure you compare effort appropriately:

- Select only those projects that record the same effort detail as you do.
- You don't have to ignore every other project—you can use rules of thumb to translate approximately between different levels of effort.

Previous analysis of projects in the ISBSG Repository shows that Level 2 effort is about 10–12 percent more than Level 1, Level 3 adds about another 1 or 2 percent, and Level 4 is about 20–25 percent more than Level 1.

NOTE *If you use approximations like this, you add uncertainty to your data and add risk to any conclusions that you draw. However, you may still be able to learn a lot from these projects; just be wary of placing too much reliance on your conclusions.*

- **Project Rating** The ISBSG considers that projects with a data quality rating of A or B are suitable for statistical analysis. Projects rated C or D may still provide valuable data, but uncertainty about some of their size or effort values means that it is best not to include them in statistical analyses.

---

[2] Refer to "Normalized work effort" in the Glossary.

- **Lines of Code** Although the ISBSG Repository does include projects that are sized using LOC, these are not validated and should not be used for benchmarking.

Unless your aim is to benchmark your project or organization against the entire repository, you are probably not interested in projects that are very different from your own.

You will want to select projects that are similar to yours in important project attributes.

The ISBSG suggests that the most important criteria for selecting projects are:

- **Size** If yours is a really large project, there is not much value to you in studying small ones and vice versa.
- **Development type** New development, enhancement, or redevelopment.
- **Primary programming language or language type** For example, 3GL, 4GL.
- **Development platform** Mainframe, midrange, or PC.

Other criteria that may be important are organization type, business area type, application type, user base, and development techniques.

Bear in mind that as you add more selection criteria, the number of projects selected inevitably gets smaller. You can end up with small groups of projects, or perhaps even no projects that satisfy all criteria. How important the group size is will depend on what you want to do with the data.

It is important that the data subset you use have integrity. The key points are that you choose only appropriately rated data; measurements are defined the same way (that is, IFPUG versions and effort measures with different time units); and measurements apply to the same thing (that is, effort normalization and effort levels).

Many practitioners will want to compare their IT development performance with "relevant" projects in the data set. For many, the analysis process will consist of selecting projects based upon multiple criteria, followed by some form of summary analysis. Some may wish to use regression analysis to derive the equation of the line of best fit through the data points and to use this equation as an estimating device.

When performing such analyses, it is worthwhile bearing in mind that use of many selection criteria could result in a very small or even zero sample size. A sample size of more than 20 should provide reasonable results; however, not much can be concluded from a sample size of 5 or fewer.

It is not uncommon for people to use a mean or median value, or to use a regression line for estimation purposes. Bear in mind that estimation parameters derived from a sample of the population may not have much relevance to a particular project. It may well be that population surveys show that x percent of males will suffer a heart attack by the time they are 60 years of age. This percentage does not indicate the probability that you will suffer a heart attack before you are 60. Consequently, a regression line, even if derived from a sample of projects with similar characteristics to your own, may not be a good estimation tool unless you have reason to believe that your attributes are broadly similar.

Means, medians, and regression lines should be used with great caution, especially where sample sizes are small and variances or standard deviations are high.

What You Can Find in the ISBSG Repository

At the time of writing, the ISBSG Repository contained data on more than 5,500 projects. In this section we provide details of the various project data types that are included in the ISBSG. The demographics published here reflect the contents of the repository contained in Release 11. You will note that the project totals shown at the bottom of the tables rarely equal the 5,052 projects in that release. This is because submitters do not necessarily provide project data for all the data fields that ISBSG offers. The "Data Field Descriptions" document available from www.isbsg.org explains the contents of the various data fields in the data releases that can be licensed.

By studying the demographics that follow, you will be able to establish the areas that are of specific interest to you. We recommend that you read the "Guidelines for use of the ISBSG data" document before you do any analysis, estimation, or benchmarking using the data.

The projects in the repository have come from 24 countries, with 70% of the projects being less than 9 years old. This is what makes the ISBSG Repository unique. A broad range of project types from many industries and many business areas is available for you to use for estimating, awareness of trends, comparison of platforms, and languages or benchmarking.

Demographic Summary

The projects in the repository cover a broad cross-section of the software industry. In general, they have a business focus.

Project Origin

- The projects have been submitted from 24 countries. Major contributors are the United States (31% of all projects), Japan (17%), Australia (16%), Finland (10%), the Netherlands (8%), India (6%), Canada (5%), Denmark (3%), Brazil (2%), the United Kingdom (2%), and China (1%).

- The projects were "built" in 29 different countries. Major contributors are Finland (18% of all projects where the country of effort is known), the Netherlands (14%), Australia (13%), India (11%), Japan (10%), the United States (10%), Canada (5%), Denmark (5%), the United Kingdom (4%), Brazil (3%), China (2%), and France (2%).

Project Context

- Organization type: Major types are communications (22% of all projects where the organization type is known), insurance (17%), banking (13%), government (12%), business services (10%), and manufacturing (8%).
- Business area: Major areas are telecommunications (25% of all projects where the business area is known), banking (12%), insurance (12%), finance (8%), manufacturing (8%), engineering (5%), accounting (4%), and sales and marketing (4%).

Type of Project

- Development type: 59% are enhancement projects, 39% are new developments, and 2% are redevelopments.
- Intended market: 85% of projects are developed for internal use (that is, for the organization that contributed the project to the repository), and 15% are developed for other organizations. 48% are developed in-house and 52% are outsourced. In total, 41% are developed in-house for internal use.
- Team size: 36% of projects have up to four people in the development team, 38% have five to nine people, and 28% have ten or more people.

Type of Product

- Product size: While IFPUG projects dominate the repository, COSMIC, NESMA, and FiSMA are all well represented. Among the IFPUG projects, 30% of projects have fewer than 100 FP, 22% have 100–200 FP, and 13% have 200–300 FP. The median size is slightly under 200 FP.
- Application type: 16% are information systems; 48% are transaction-processing systems.
- Architecture: 51% of projects for which this information is available have a client-server architecture, and 20% have a multitier architecture (there is some overlap between these groups of projects). 40% are stand-alone systems.
- Web development: 17% of the projects in the repository are web developments.

Development Environment

- Platform: 39% are mainframe projects, 10% midrange, and 18% PCs. 33% of projects involve multiple platforms.
- Language: Over 100 programming languages are represented. 3GLs represent 64% of projects, 4GLs 33%, and application generators 3%. Major languages are COBOL, C/C++/C#, Java/J2EE/JavaScript, Visual Basic, PL/I, PL/SQL, Oracle, .Net, SQL, NATURAL, Access, Powerbuilder, ASP, and Lotus Notes.

Development Method

46% of projects that say anything about techniques report using a waterfall model or "traditional" methods, but give no further details of techniques used.

Of the projects that report the use of particular techniques:

- Classical system modeling techniques are used in 46% of them. The most common single technique is data modeling, used in 36% of projects.
- RAD/JAD techniques are used in 18% of the projects.
- Object-oriented techniques are used in 18% of the projects.
- Prototyping is used in 18% of the projects.
- Standards are used in 24% of the projects, with CMMI the most common.
- Testing-oriented techniques, reviews, and inspections are used in 49% of the projects.

Project Origin

Projects have been contributed from 24 different countries.

Country of Origin

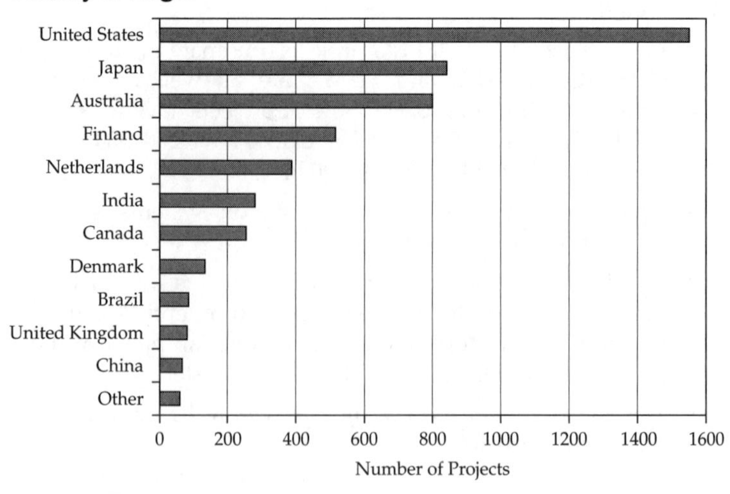

Country of Origin	Projects	Percent
United States	1548	30.7%
Japan	841	16.7%
Australia	801	15.9%
Finland	515	10.2%
Netherlands	389	7.7%
India	280	5.5%
Canada	252	5.0%
Denmark	131	2.6%
Brazil	87	1.7%
United Kingdom	82	1.6%
China	65	1.3%
Other	58	1.1%
Total	5049	

Country of Effort

Twenty-eight countries are represented in the repository.

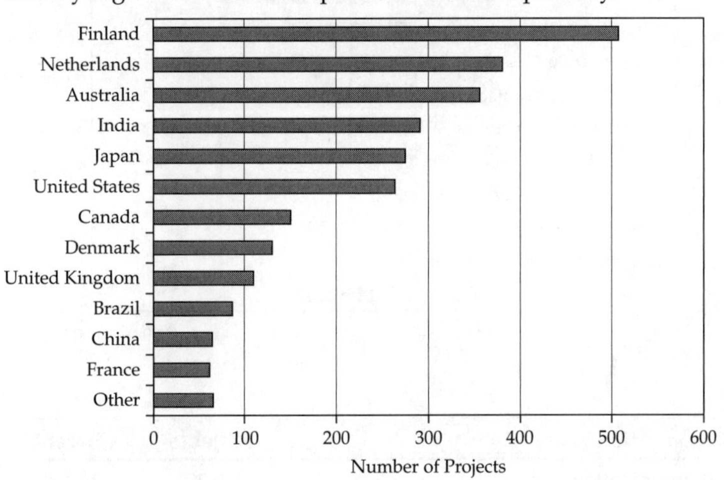

Country of Effort	Projects	Percent
Finland	508	18.5%
Netherlands	381	13.9%
Australia	356	13.0%
India	291	10.6%
Japan	275	10.0%
United States	264	9.6%

Country of Effort	Projects	Percent
Canada	151	5.5%
Denmark	131	4.8%
United Kingdom	110	4.0%
Brazil	87	3.2%
China	65	2.4%
France	62	2.3%
Other	66	2.4%
Total	2226	

Project Context

Organization Type

The organization type defines the industry, or type of organization, for which each project has been developed.

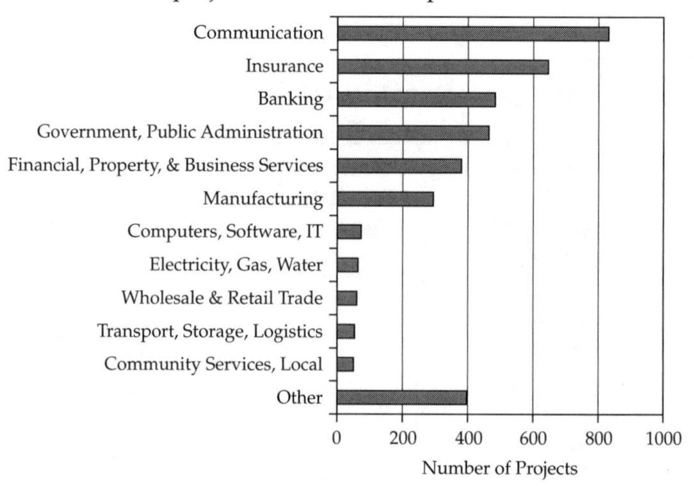

Organization Type	Projects	Percent
Communication	828	21.9%
Insurance	644	17.0%
Banking	482	12.8%
Government, Public Administration	462	12.2%
Financial, Property, & Business Services	380	10.0%
Manufacturing	293	7.8%
Computers, Software, IT	72	1.9%
Electricity, Gas, Water	62	1.6%

Organization Type	Projects	Percent
Wholesale & Retail Trade	59	1.6%
Transport, Storage, Logistics	53	1.4%
Community Services, Local	50	1.3%
Other	396	10.5%
Total	3781	

Business Area

This is the business area within the organization/industry that the project/application will be supporting.

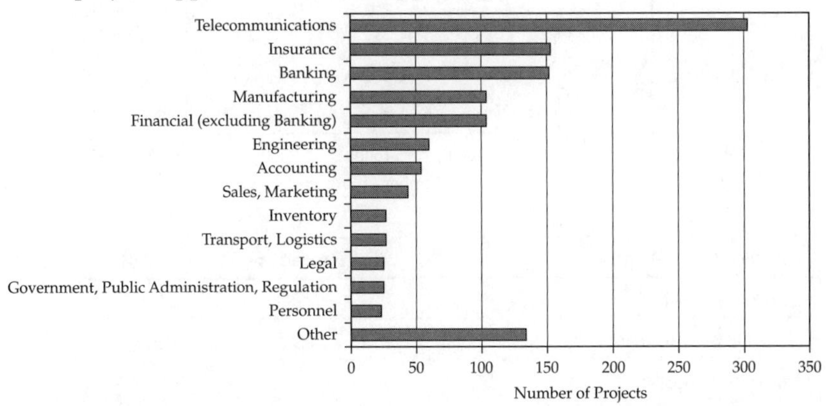

Business Area	Projects	Percent
Telecommunications	303	24.6%
Insurance	153	12.4%
Banking	152	12.3%
Manufacturing	104	8.4%
Financial (excluding Banking)	103	8.4%
Engineering	60	4.9%
Accounting	54	4.4%
Sales, Marketing	44	3.6%
Inventory	27	2.2%
Transport, Logistics	26	2.1%
Legal	25	2.0%
Government, Public Administration, Regulation	25	2.0%
Personnel	23	1.9%
Other	134	10.9%
Total	1233	

Type of Project

Development Type

A detailed explanation of the development types is given in the ISBSG Glossary of Terms.

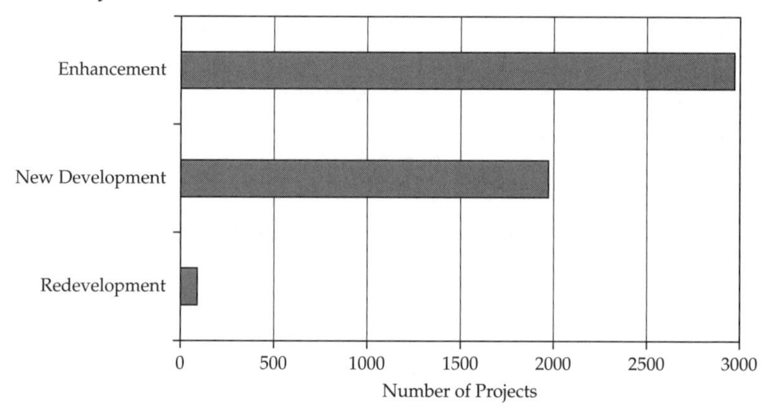

Development Type	Projects	Percent
Enhancement	2969	58.9%
New Development	1971	39.1%
Redevelopment	89	1.9%
Other	8	0.2%
Total	5037	

Intended Market

This defines the relationship between the customer, the project/application developer, and the application user. If the customer and the developer are in the same organization, it is assumed to be an in-house development; if the customer and user are in the same organization, it is assumed that the development is for internal use.

As can be seen from the figures that follow, most of the projects in the repository (for which this information is available) have been developed for an internal business unit. Outsourced developments slightly outnumber in-house developments.

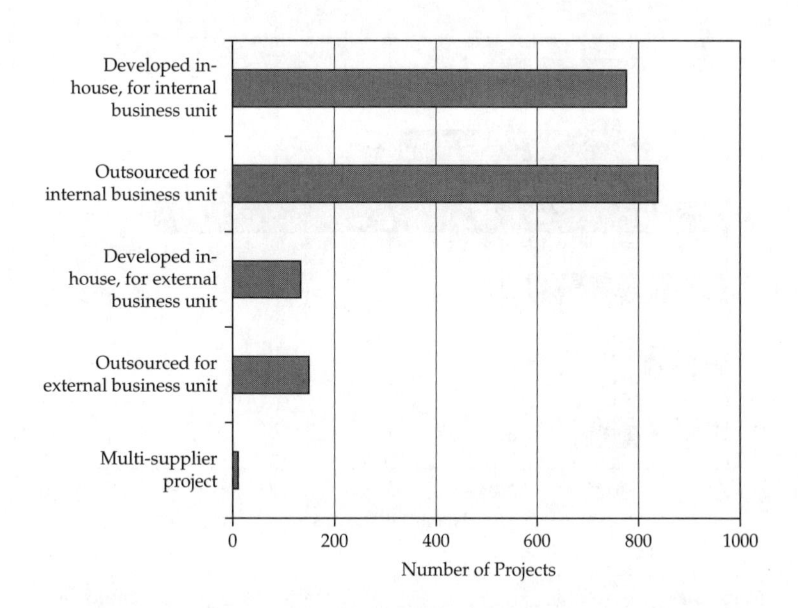

Intended Market	Projects	Percent
Developed in-house for internal business unit	776	40.6%
Outsourced for internal business unit	838	43.9%
Developed in-house for external business unit	135	7.1%
Outsourced for external business unit	150	7.8%
Multi-supplier project	12	0.6%
Total	1911	

Team Size

This is the maximum number of people in the development team at any given time in the project. Teams of two through five people are about equally common. Five is most common (by a small margin).

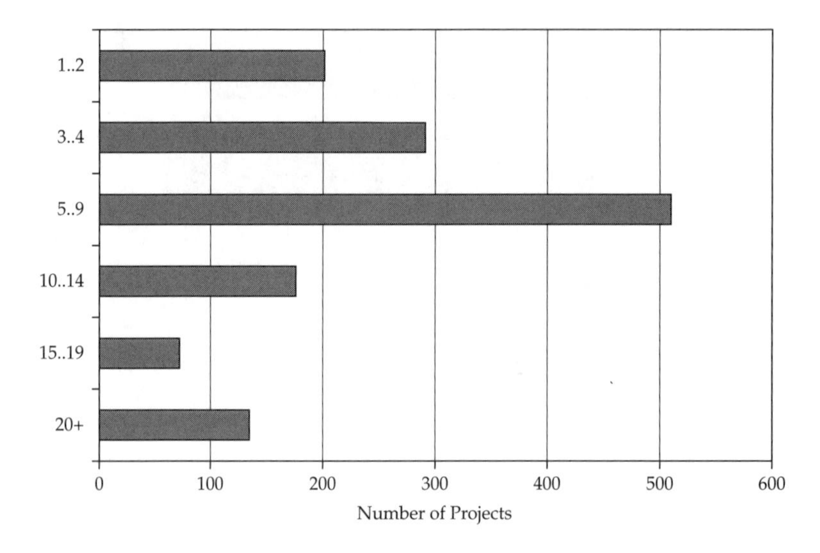

Team Size	Projects	Percent
1 or 2	216	14.0%
3 or 4	316	20.5%
5 to 9	583	37.8%
10 to 14	197	12.8%
15 to 19	86	5.6%
20 or more	143	9.3%
Total	1541	

Type of Product

Product Size

Size is measured in function points. The four main function point–counting approaches represented in the repository are IFPUG, COSMIC, FiSMA, and NESMA. Other approaches represented in the repository include Mark II and Feature Points, but there are few such projects, and very few have been contributed to the repository in recent years.

IFPUG projects dominate the repository. The numbers of COSMIC, FiSMA, and NESMA projects are steadily increasing.

The following tables and histograms show the range of project sizes for each of these four function point–counting approaches. (Projects sized with other approaches, or that have low data quality ratings, are not included.)

IFPUG

Projects sized with outdated versions of IFPUG function points (IFPUG 2, IFPUG 3) are excluded from the figures that follow. The table shows the sizes (in UFPs) of projects sized with IFPUG function points that are known or presumed to have been sized using CPM 4.0 or later.

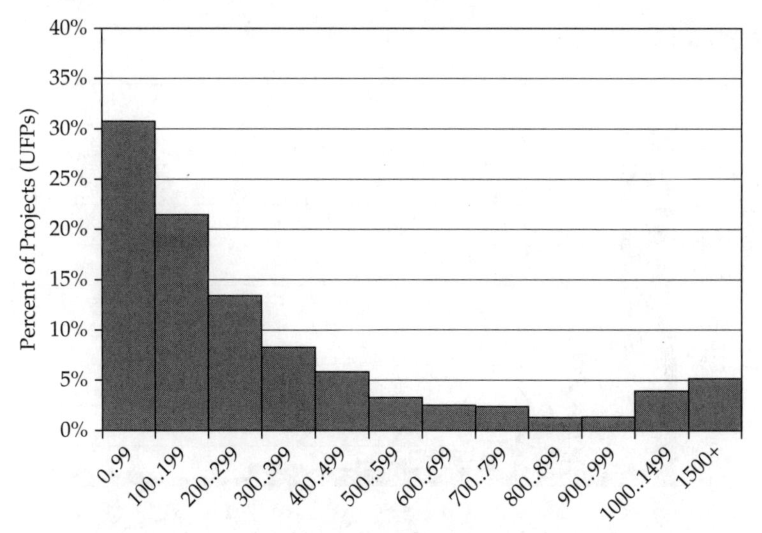

Size in IFPUG 4 Function Points	Projects (UFPs)	Percent (UFPs)	Projects (AFPs)	Percent (AFPs)
0 to 99	818	30.6%	1108	32.8%
100 to 199	576	21.6%	740	21.9%
200 to 299	360	13.5%	442	13.1%
300 to 399	220	8.2%	282	8.3%
400 to 499	155	5.8%	173	5.1%
500 to 599	89	3.3%	103	3.0%
600 to 699	70	2.6%	76	2.2%
700 to 799	65	2.4%	82	2.4%
800 to 899	35	1.3%	52	1.5%
900 to 999	37	1.4%	36	1.1%
1000 to 1499	106	4.0%	123	3.6%
1500 or more	138	5.2%	162	4.8%
Total	2669		3379	

Smaller projects are more common. Size ranges from 3 to 16,148 UFPs (3 to 20,000 AFPs). The median size is 186 UFPs (171 AFPs).

For enhancement projects, the range is 3 to 7,134 UFPs with a median of 125 UFPs (3 to 20,000 AFPs with a median of 119 AFPs). For new developments, the range is 6 to 16,148 UFPs with a median of 312 UFPs (6 to 16,148 AFPs with a median of 311 APFs).

COSMIC

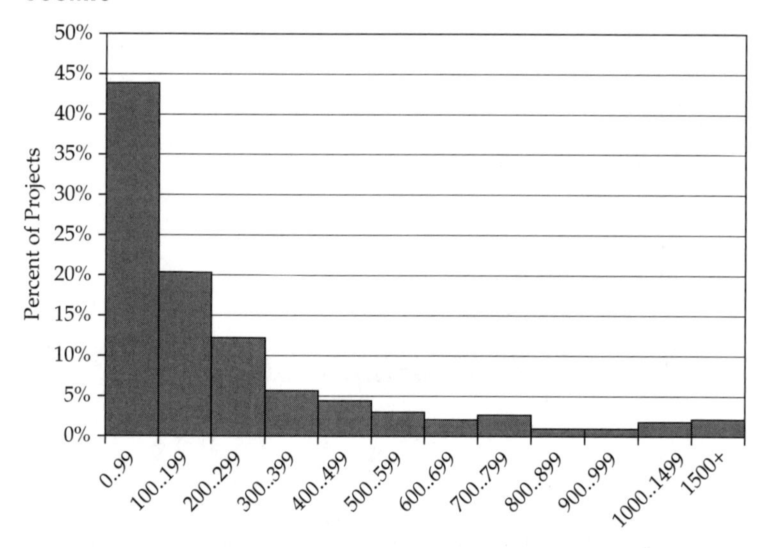

Size in COSMIC Functional Size Units	Projects	Percent
0 to 99	147	43.9%
100 to 199	68	20.3%
200 to 299	41	12.2%
300 to 399	19	5.7%
400 to 499	15	4.5%
500 to 599	10	3.0%
600 to 699	7	2.1%
700 to 799	9	2.7%
800 to 899	3	0.9%
900 to 999	3	0.9%
1000 to 1499	6	1.8%
1500 or more	7	2.1%
Total	335	

Again, smaller projects are much more common. Size ranges from 5 to 2,090 cfsu. The median size is 122 cfsu. For enhancement projects the range is 3 to 2,003 cfsu (median 95). For new developments the range is 8 to 1,670 cfsu (median 181). (The 2,090 cfsu project is one of a small number of redevelopments.)

NESMA

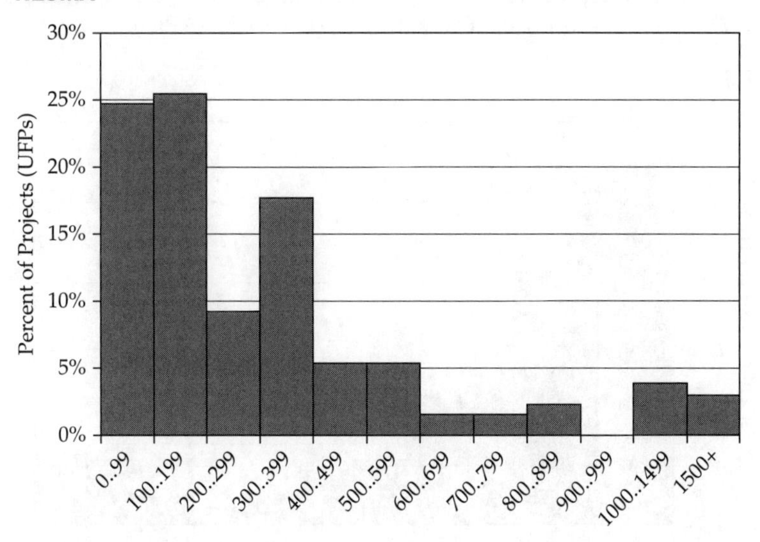

Size in NESMA Function Points	Projects (UFPs)	Percent (UFPs)	Projects (AFPs)	Percent (AFPs)
0 to 99	32	24.6%	32	24.6%
100 to 199	33	25.4%	33	25.4%
200 to 299	12	9.2%	12	9.2%
300 to 399	23	17.7%	23	17.7%
400 to 499	7	5.4%	7	5.4%
500 to 599	7	5.4%	7	5.4%
600 to 699	2	1.5%	1	0.8%
700 to 799	2	1.5%	3	2.3%
800 to 899	3	2.3%	3	2.3%
900 to 999	0	0.0%	0	0.0%
1000 to 1499	5	3.8%	5	3.8%
1500 or more	4	3.1%	4	3.1%
Total	130		130	

Smaller projects are more common, as usual, but there appears to be a broader spread than with the IFPUG or COSMIC approaches. Size ranges from 14 to 1,924 UFPs (14 to 1,828 AFPs). The median size is 206 UFPs (205 AFPs).

For enhancement projects, the range is 28 to 1,468 UFPs with a median of 198 UFPs (28 to 1,468 AFPs with a median of 196 AFPs). For new developments, the range is 14 to 1,924 UFPs with a median of 230 UFPs (14 to 1,828 AFPs with a median of 230 APFs).

FiSMA

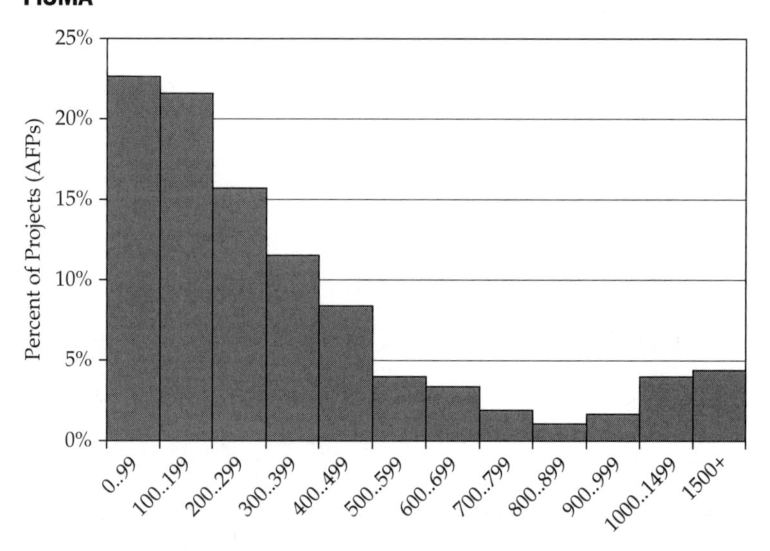

Size in FiSMA Function Points	Projects	Percent
0 to 99	108	22.6%
100 to 199	103	21.5%
200 to 299	75	15.7%
300 to 399	55	11.5%
400 to 499	40	8.4%
500 to 599	19	4.0%
600 to 699	16	3.3%
700 to 799	9	1.9%
800 to 899	5	1.0%
900 to 999	8	1.7%
1000 to 1499	19	4.0%
1500 or more	21	4.4%
Total	478	

The FiSMA projects all report size in adjusted function points only. As with the NESMA projects, smaller projects are more common, but there appears at the moment to be a broader spread than with the IFPUG or COSMIC approaches. Size ranges from 6 to 9,390 AFPs. The median size is 235 AFPs. For enhancement projects, the range is 6 to 1,843 AFPs with a median of 142 AFPs. For new developments, the range is 18 to 9,390 AFPs with a median of 320 AFPs.

Application Type

This defines the project/application type within the business area and organization/industry type. For example, a project/application could be a Decision Support system for Manufacturing within the Automotive industry. More detailed descriptions are provided in the ISBSG Glossary of Terms.

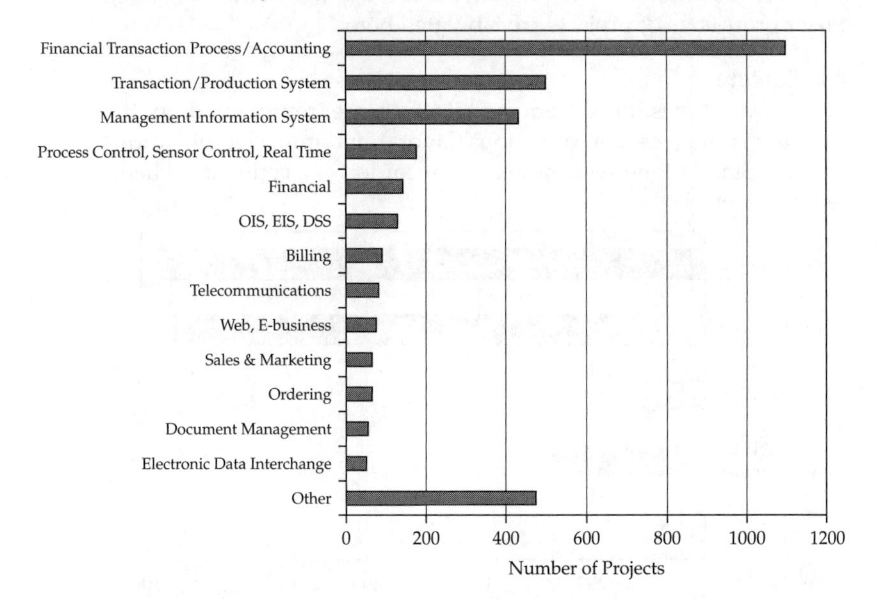

Application Type	Projects	Percent
Financial Transaction Process/Accounting	1095	32.0%
Transaction/Production System	499	14.6%
Management Information System	432	12.6%
Process Control, Sensor Control, Real Time	176	5.1%
Financial	142	4.1%
Office information system, executive information system, decision support system	128	3.7%
Billing	90	2.6%

Application Type	Projects	Percent
Telecommunications	81	2.4%
Web, E-business	75	2.2%
Sales & Marketing	65	1.9%
Ordering	64	1.9%
Document Management	54	1.6%
Electronic Data Interchange	50	1.5%
Other	475	13.9%
Total	3426	

Over 100 different application types are recorded in the repository. Major groupings of projects are tabulated here.

Architecture

Two broad types of system architecture are represented in the repository: client-server (of various flavors), and multitier (of various flavors). Stand-alone systems are also recorded as a contrast to client-server systems.

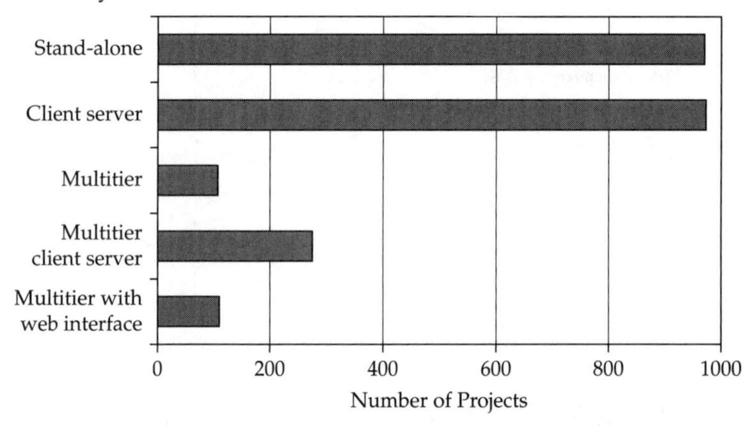

Architecture	Projects	Percent
Stand-alone	971	39.8%
Client server	972	39.9%
Multitier	108	4.4%
Multitier client server	276	11.3%
Multitier with web interface	111	4.6%
Total	2438	

Taken together, 20% of projects in the repository (for which this information is known) have a multitier architecture, and 51% of projects have a client-server architecture.

Development Environment

Development Platform

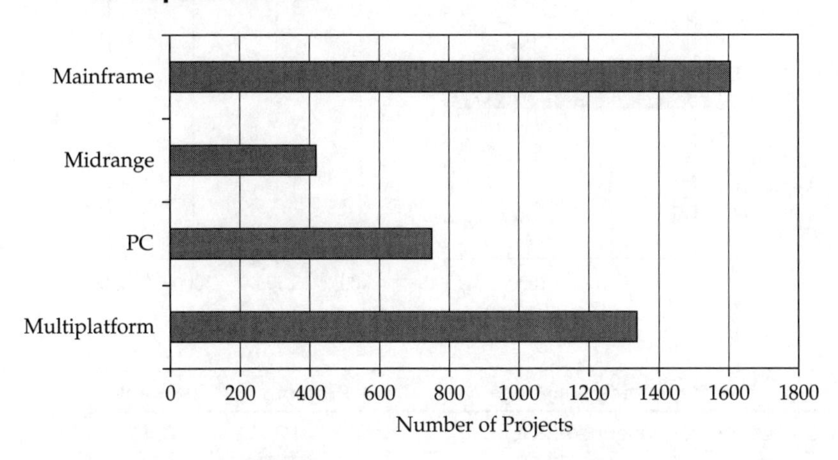

Development Platform	Projects	Percent
Mainframe	1604	39.1%
Midrange	418	10.2%
Personal computer	750	18.3%
Multiplatform	1336	32.5%
Total	4108	

Multiplatform developments are increasingly common and may soon overtake mainframe developments in the repository.

Type of Programming Language

A large number of languages are recorded in the repository. This can make it difficult to compare some projects. Consequently, languages are classified by type, as shown next.

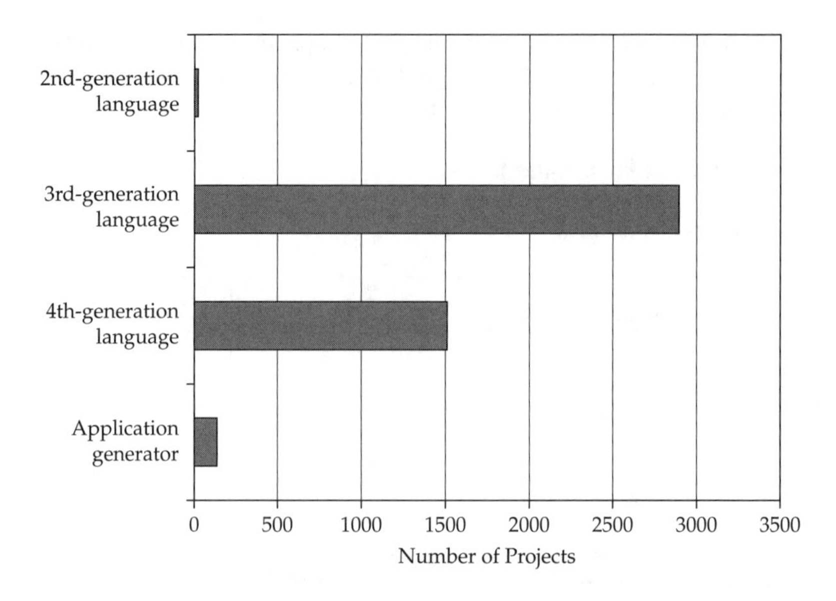

Type of Programming Language	Projects	Percent
2nd-generation language (2GL)	19	0.4%
3rd-generation language (3GL)	2893	63.5%
4th-generation language (4GL)	1507	33.1%
Application generator	136	3.0%
Total	4556	

Over 100 programming languages are represented in the repository. 3rd-generation languages dominate, but 4th-generation languages are also very well represented.

Some languages (for example, Visual Basic, Visual C++) were nominated sometimes as 3GLs and sometimes as 4GLs. The preceding table tallies the language types as originally nominated. In the following tables, each language is consolidated under a single type.

Primary Programming Languages: 3GLs

This is the programming language that has been nominated by the project submitter as the primary programming language.

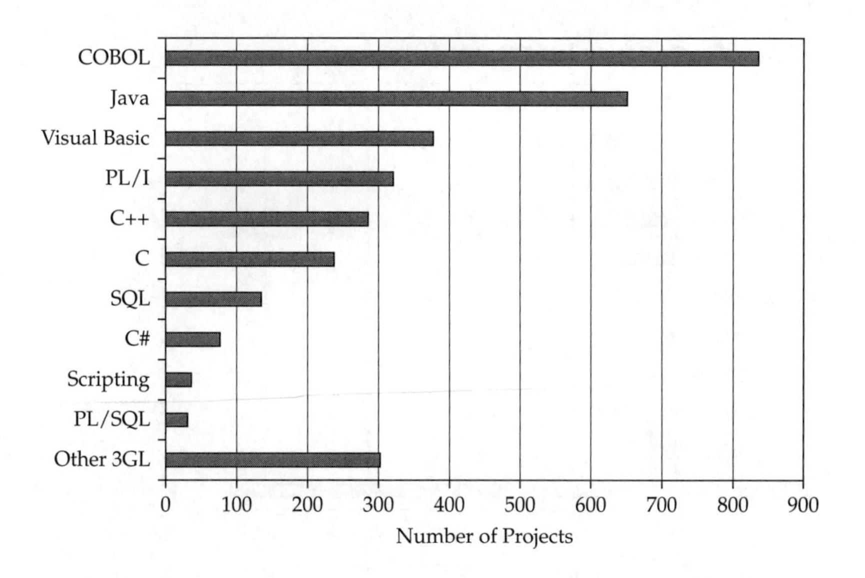

3rd Generation Languages	Projects	Percent
COBOL	837	28.2%
Java	652	19.8%
Visual Basic	377	11.5%
PL/I	321	9.8%
C++	285	8.7%
C	237	7.2%
SQL	134	4.1%
C#	76	2.3%
Scripting	35	1.1%
PL/SQL	30	0.9%
Other	301	9.2%

Other 3GLs in the repository include JavaScript, Smalltalk, HTML, Ada, Pascal, Periphonics, and FORTRAN.

Primary Programming Languages: 4GLs

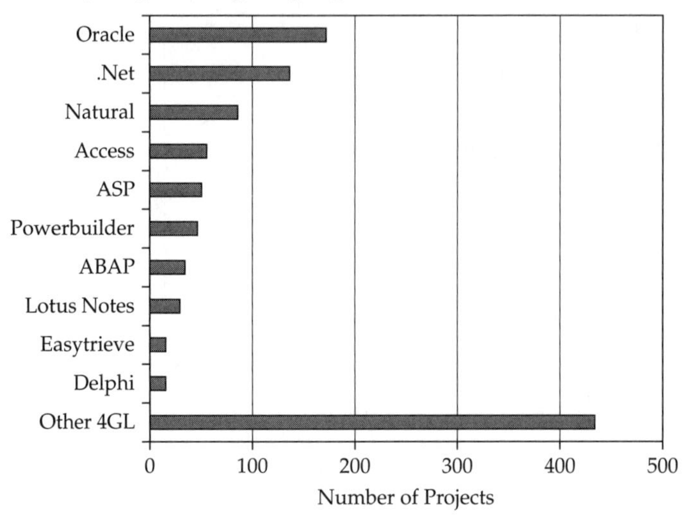

4th Generation Languages	Projects	Percent
ORACLE	172	16.0%
.Net	136	12.7%
NATURAL	86	8.0%
ACCESS	56	5.2%
ASP	51	4.7%
Powerbuilder	47	4.4%
ABAP	34	3.2%
Lotus Notes	29	2.7%
Easytrieve	15	1.4%
Delphi	15	1.4%
Other 4GL	434	40.4%

The "Other 4GL" count is high because many projects do not specify the language, other than that it was a 4GL, and numerous languages are represented by only a small number of projects. Other 4GLs represented in the repository include CLIPPER, ColdFusion, Ingres, FOCUS, IDEAL, and RALLY.

Application Generators

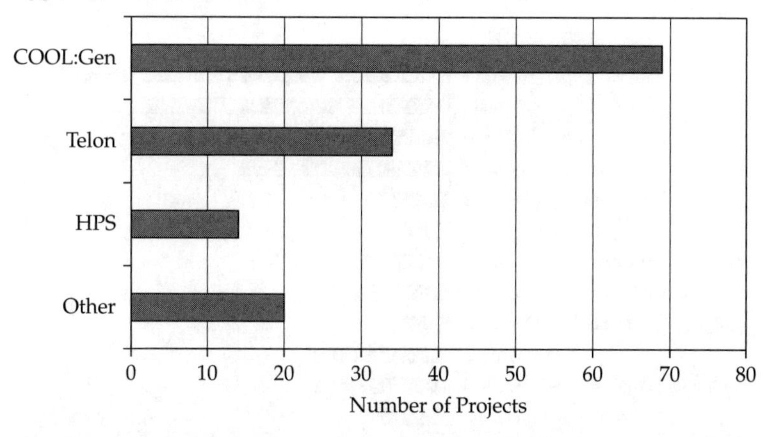

Application Generators	Projects	Percent
COOL:Gen	69	50.4%
TELON	34	24.8%
HPS	14	10.2%
Other	20	14.6%

Few projects that used application generators have been contributed to the repository in recent years.

Methods and Tools

Three fields are used to describe the various techniques that may have been used during the execution of a project: Specification Techniques, Design Techniques, and Development Techniques.

The following graph and table combine information from all three fields.

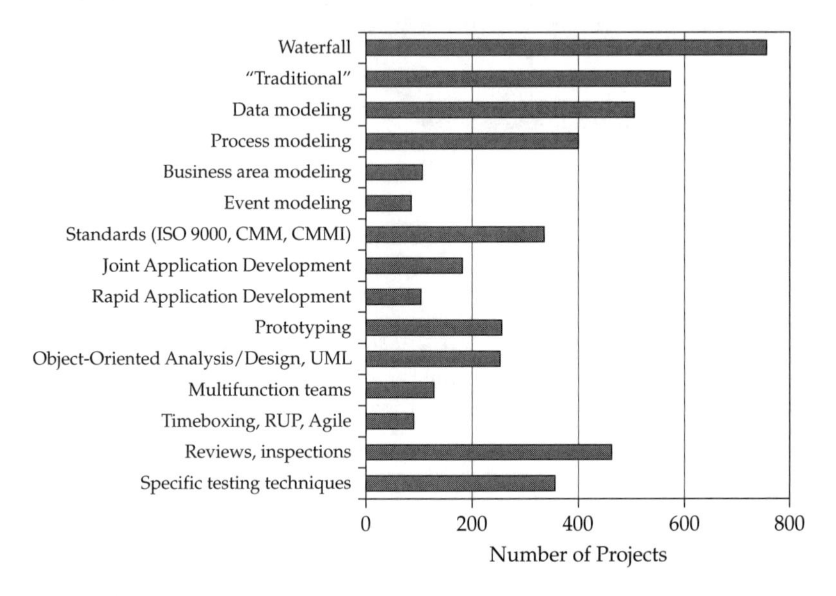

Development Techniques	Projects	Percent
Waterfall	745	
"Traditional"	713	
Data modeling	505	36.5%
Process modeling	399	28.8%
Business area modeling	106	7.7%
Event modeling	85	6.1%
Standards (ISO 9000, CMM, CMMI)	335	24.2%
Joint Application Development	181	13.1%
Rapid Application Development	103	7.4%
Prototyping	255	18.4%
Object-Oriented Analysis/Design, UML	252	18.2%
Multifunction teams	127	9.2%
Timeboxing, RUP, Agile	89	6.4%
Reviews, inspections, walkthroughs	462	33.4%
Specific testing techniques	356	25.7%

745 projects report using a waterfall process, of which 593 give no further information about specific techniques used. 573 further

projects report using a "traditional" process, but give no further details of specific techniques used.

There are 1,384 projects that list specific techniques. Between them the classical techniques of data modeling, process modeling, business area modeling, and event modeling are listed in 643 projects (46%).

The most common single technique is data modeling, used in 36% of these projects. RAD and/or JAD techniques are used in 18% of these projects. Object-oriented techniques are used in 18% of these projects. Testing-oriented techniques, reviews, and inspections are listed in 49% of these projects.

Many of the projects that have been contributed recently to the repository make use of standards (ISO 9000 series, CMM, CMMI). Of the 335 projects in the repository that used standards, 248 (74%) used CMMI, 74 (22%) used CMM, and 74 (22%) used ISO 9000 series standards. 50 projects (15%) used ISO 9000 and one or both of CMM/CMMI.

Summary

The ISBSG project history data is a very valuable resource for analysis, benchmarking, and estimation, but it must be used carefully and with an understanding of what it does and does not represent.

Additional Documentation

The following documents are available for download from the Downloads section of www.isbsg.org.

- Glossary of Terms
- Data Field Descriptions
- The ISBSG Repository Demographics
- The ISBSG Repository Field Descriptions

APPENDIX B

Project Delivery Rates by Category

This appendix summarizes project delivery rates in a number of categories. You can use these tables as a base for your estimates and to help you build an estimation framework, as described in this book.

The tables are based on analysis of 1,681 projects, out of the 5,052 projects in the repository. These projects all have a high data quality rating (A or B), size measured with IFPUG or NESMA function points, and normalized work effort at resource level 1 (development team only). Extreme outliers are not included. Projects completed more than ten years ago are not included.

The ranges of project characteristics are as follows:

- All are sized with IFPUG function points, version 4 or later, or are new developments sized using the NESMA approach.
- All have high data quality rating (A or B).
- 25 <= Size (UFP) <= 4,200 FP.
- 80 <= Effort <= 61,500 hours.
- Maximum team size <= 52.
- 0.5 <= Duration < 34 months.
- 0.65 <= PDR <= 80 Hrs/FP.
- 4.5 <= Speed of delivery (for the entire project team) < 520 FP/month.
- 0.7 <= Speed of delivery (per project team member) < 45 FP/month/person.

- Project completion date is 1999 or later.
- (Normalized effort for development team / reported effort for development team) < 1.25.

Presentation of Statistics

This section briefly describes the tables in this appendix.

Throughout the appendix, each table indicates the number of projects represented (N). This number is important, because care must be taken not to draw unwarranted conclusions from small samples of projects.

In the tables that follow, no group of projects is tabulated in its own right unless N is at least 10 (that is, at least 10 projects are represented in every group).

The total number of projects in each table varies. This is because the values of a number of variables are not known for projects submitted to the repository (that is, submitters do not provide data for every field).

Small inconsistencies between numbers of projects tabulated are due to missing values of variables selected for tabulation; for example, in some cases in the repository the Development Platform is given as "Unknown."

NOTE *When you are using the tables, always check the number of projects represented. Don't jump to conclusions based on a small number of projects.*

Explanation of Tables

In this appendix, tables are frequently used to summarize some key statistics about the data for the topic being analyzed. The following header is common to all of the tables presented:

N	Min	P10	P25	**Median**	P75	P90	Max	Mean	Std Dev

- *N* is the number of projects or data instances in the sample.
- *Min* is the minimum value found in the sample.
- *P10* is the 10th percentile and is that value which is greater than the values of 10 percent of the members of the sample.
- *P25* (often also written as *Q1*) is the 25th percentile or first quartile. It is that value which is greater than the values of 25 percent of the members of the sample or subsample.

- *Median* (sometimes written as *P50*) is the middle value; half the values in the data sample or subsample are below this value, while the other half are above it.
- *P75* (often also written as *Q3*) is the 75th percentile or third quartile. It is that value which is greater than the values of 75 percent of the members of the sample or subsample.
- *P90* is the 90th percentile and is that value which is greater than the values of 90 percent of the members of the sample or subsample.
- *Max* is the maximum value found in the sample.
- *Mean* is the arithmetic mean or average.
- *Std Dev* is the standard deviation.

Use of the Statistics

In most cases we have focused upon the median rather than the mean. However, the mean is always noted in addition to the median. The median is the more useful measure when the data contains outliers or when it is strongly skewed.

NOTE Mean *is the* average *of all the values. The* median *is* middle *value of all the values.*

Using the *mean* or *average* can be misleading when the data is skewed. One huge number can distort the mean, so that it is no longer a fair representation of "average." This is common in software engineering data sets, so the median is usually preferred.

Standard deviation is a measure of how wide the spread of values is. A small standard deviation means that most numbers fall into a narrow band around the average, and a large standard deviation means there is a wide range of values. A small standard deviation is better for estimation than a large one.

Project Delivery Rates

Project delivery rates in the following tables are expressed in terms of hours per function point.

Table B-1: Project Delivery Rate by Industry Sector

	N	Min	P10	P25	Median	P75	P90	Max	Mean	Std Dev
Banking	80	0.7	3.0	4.0	7.9	22.1	31.2	55.1	13.4	12.1
Communication	426	0.8	3.6	6.5	11.5	19.4	30.0	78.7	14.9	11.7
Construction	12	2.8	3.1	3.5	4.3	6.3	8.7	9.1	5.0	2.2
Electronics & Computers	18	1.1	2.5	3.5	5.1	16.2	26.1	59.3	11.9	15.0
Financial	94	1.0	3.0	5.1	9.4	14.2	22.8	75.2	11.9	11.1
Government	153	1.2	4.9	7.7	11.7	19.8	36.2	61.8	16.3	13.0
Insurance	164	1.4	5.1	8.3	16.3	28.1	43.4	74.2	20.6	15.7
Manufacturing	101	0.6	1.6	2.6	5.4	13.0	29.2	52.5	10.4	12.0
Medical and Health Care	10	1.5	2.5	2.9	4.1	7.8	9.3	13.7	5.5	3.8
Professional Services	30	1.1	3.9	5.0	9.3	11.5	19.7	36.6	10.4	7.6
Service Industry	86	0.7	2.2	4.9	8.4	14.3	23.2	42.3	10.7	8.4
Wholesale & Retail	55	2.4	6.1	12.6	22.3	29.3	54.0	60.6	24.4	16.5

Table B-2: Project Delivery Rate by Organization Type

	N	Min	P10	P25	Median	P75	P90	Max	Mean	Std Dev
Banking	80	0.7	3.0	4.0	7.9	22.1	31.2	55.1	13.4	12.1
Billing	17	14.4	14.6	15.6	24.0	28.8	46.2	60.6	27.2	13.7
Communication	419	0.8	3.6	6.6	11.8	19.6	30.0	78.7	15.0	11.7
Community Services	22	0.7	5.5	7.8	13.9	17.5	22.7	24.4	13.0	6.9
Construction	12	2.8	3.1	3.5	4.3	6.3	8.7	9.1	5.0	2.2
Finance / Property / Business Services	90	1.0	3.0	5.2	10.0	14.3	23.0	75.2	12.2	11.2
Government	154	1.4	5.4	7.8	11.9	20.4	37.4	61.8	16.7	13.1
Insurance	164	1.4	5.1	8.3	16.3	28.1	43.4	74.2	20.6	15.7
Local	14	8.2	8.9	11.4	15.5	21.6	27.6	30.2	16.8	7.4
Manufacturing	90	0.6	1.6	3.0	5.6	15.0	29.5	52.5	11.0	12.4
Medical and Health Care	10	1.5	2.5	2.9	4.1	7.8	9.3	13.7	5.5	3.8
Ordering	23	5.6	10.0	17.0	28.6	41.5	54.7	60.4	30.4	17.3
Professional Services	12	3.2	4.7	7.2	8.8	9.3	9.3	9.9	7.8	2.2
Public Administration	20	1.2	1.9	4.7	10.1	14.5	18.3	29.6	10.5	7.9
Recreation / Personnel Services	12	1.7	2.0	4.5	6.4	8.7	12.9	23.9	7.7	6.1
Sales, Marketing	12	1.1	2.5	4.3	5.9	14.7	22.9	36.6	11.1	10.6
Transport & Storage	21	1.4	1.8	2.5	4.4	7.0	12.9	29.4	6.4	6.4
Voice Provisioning	15	12.3	24.6	27.3	53.5	62.1	64.9	69.7	46.4	18.6
Other	84	1.0	2.5	4.3	7.1	14.7	32.9	70.3	12.8	14.5

Table B-3: Project Delivery Rate by Business Area

	N	Min	P10	P25	Median	P75	P90	Max	Mean	Std Dev
Financial	10	1.2	6.7	8.0	9.3	9.9	37.1	55.1	15.4	16.5
Insurance	26	1.2	2.6	5.3	10.9	16.7	28.3	45.2	13.1	10.4
Manufacturing	17	0.6	0.9	1.3	2.4	4.2	8.0	20.8	4.2	4.9
Telecommunications	240	1.0	3.3	6.3	10.9	18.1	31.5	78.7	15.3	13.4
Other	22	0.8	2.3	6.2	10.0	18.5	28.7	31.6	12.9	9.4

Table B-4: Project Delivery Rate by Application Type

	N	Min	P10	P25	Median	P75	P90	Max	Mean	Std Dev
Billing	42	0.7	3.7	8.2	17.2	25.1	31.8	60.6	18.7	13.4
Catalogue of Things or Events	34	3.5	7.4	8.6	12.4	17.7	32.2	42.3	15.8	9.9
Document Management	26	3.5	4.9	8.2	16.2	32.7	42.3	59.4	20.7	15.2
Electronic Data Interchange	20	1.3	6.7	9.7	15.0	22.0	45.5	75.2	19.9	17.9
Executive Information System	14	1.2	3.3	6.6	12.7	17.6	30.6	61.8	16.1	15.7
Financial	102	3.1	5.0	5.8	7.1	9.2	11.6	14.3	7.7	2.5
Financial Transaction Process Accounting	311	0.7	3.0	5.4	11.2	21.8	34.6	74.2	15.5	14.0
Logistics	14	1.3	2.2	5.5	10.1	18.2	23.8	45.3	13.3	11.7
Management Info System	75	0.6	3.1	5.8	10.0	17.4	29.1	68.2	13.8	12.7
Ordering	51	0.8	2.4	5.3	12.6	28.1	42.0	60.4	18.3	16.8

Personnel	12	1.6	2.9	3.4	6.6	13.2	15.8	41.4	10.2	11.0
Real-Time System	35	1.4	3.3	5.1	10.6	17.1	29.0	70.2	14.0	13.4
Sales, Marketing	48	1.5	2.6	4.6	6.9	14.6	26.2	44.8	11.6	10.2
Telecommunications	26	0.8	3.3	5.6	9.1	15.1	23.9	52.1	12.6	11.9
Trading	22	1.1	3.4	4.1	8.4	14.6	23.0	36.6	10.9	9.1
Transaction / Production System	169	1.0	3.9	6.3	12.4	22.0	35.7	78.7	16.8	14.7
Web / E-Business	23	1.0	2.9	3.6	6.4	11.4	18.1	48.0	9.4	9.9
Other	176	1.4	3.4	5.5	10.2	22.1	48.6	70.3	17.2	17.3

Table B-5: Project Delivery Rate by Development Platform

	N	Min	P10	P25	Median	P75	P90	Max	Mean	Std Dev
Mainframe	452	0.6	3.6	7.2	14.0	25.6	40.0	79.7	18.7	15.6
Midrange	128	1.3	4.8	7.0	11.4	19.6	30.5	74.2	15.6	13.3
PC – Microcomputer	204	1.0	2.5	4.0	8.1	13.2	22.7	60.1	10.7	10.0
Multi	480	0.8	3.6	5.6	8.8	16.2	26.1	61.8	12.6	10.7

Table B-6: Project Delivery Rate by Development Type—All Platforms

	N	Min	P10	P25	Median	P75	P90	Max	Mean	Std Dev
Enhancement	1147	0.6	3.9	6.3	12.0	21.7	35.7	79.7	16.2	14.2
New development	512	0.6	2.4	4.5	7.9	14.7	27.5	76.5	12.0	11.9
Redevelopment	22	0.8	4.6	6.0	10.1	18.9	26.8	49.8	14.5	12.1

Table B-7: Project Delivery Rate by Development Type—Mainframe Platforms

	N	Min	P10	P25	Median	P75	P90	Max	Mean	Std Dev
Enhancement	366	0.6	3.9	7.4	13.7	25.6	40.0	79.7	18.6	15.5
New development	83	0.6	2.9	6.5	15.9	26.0	38.9	75.2	19.0	16.1

Table B-8: Project Delivery Rate by Development Type—Midrange Platforms

	N	Min	P10	P25	Median	P75	P90	Max	Mean	Std Dev
Enhancement	79	2.0	4.9	7.3	14.6	21.1	33.9	74.2	17.4	14.7
New development	49	1.3	4.8	7.0	9.2	13.5	26.3	49.6	12.6	10.0

Table B-9: Project Delivery Rate by Development Type—PC Platforms

	N	Min	P10	P25	Median	P75	P90	Max	Mean	Std Dev
Enhancement	78	1.0	2.5	3.8	8.8	14.8	22.7	60.1	11.4	10.9
New development	117	1.0	2.5	4.0	7.5	11.8	22.2	47.0	9.9	8.6

Table B-10: Project Delivery Rate by Development Type—Multiplatforms

	N	Min	P10	P25	Median	P75	P90	Max	Mean	Std Dev
Enhancement	296	1.1	4.4	6.1	9.8	18.8	27.0	61.8	13.8	10.7
New development	177	0.8	2.7	4.7	7.2	12.1	23.1	60.9	10.6	10.6

Table B-11: Project Delivery Rate by Language Type—All Platforms

	N	Min	P10	P25	Median	P75	P90	Max	Mean	Std Dev
2nd generation language	12	3.8	4.6	8.2	15.7	23.0	34.8	45.8	17.9	13.2
3rd generation language	1105	0.6	3.5	5.9	11.4	22.5	37.9	79.7	16.7	15.1
4th generation language	359	1.2	3.2	5.4	8.7	14.5	21.9	55.5	11.3	8.8
5th generation language	23	6.4	8.5	9.8	16.1	22.2	25.5	37.1	17.1	8.2
Application generator	17	4.7	5.6	8.2	10.8	16.1	26.9	48.3	14.7	11.3

Table B-12: Project Delivery Rate by Language Type—Mainframe Platforms

	N	Min	P10	P25	Median	P75	P90	Max	Mean	Std Dev
3rd generation language	365	0.6	3.7	7.8	15.3	27.5	42.2	79.7	19.9	16.3
4th generation language	41	1.2	3.2	4.6	7.3	17.5	29.2	52.5	12.0	10.9
Application generator	16	4.7	5.9	8.9	11.5	17.5	27.7	48.3	15.3	11.4

Table B-13: Project Delivery Rate by Language Type—Midrange Platforms

	N	Min	P10	P25	Median	P75	P90	Max	Mean	Std Dev
3rd generation language	71	1.3	4.4	7.0	10.8	20.8	33.8	74.2	16.2	15.0
4th generation language	47	2.0	5.5	7.8	13.2	19.9	28.8	55.5	16.0	11.4

Table B-14: Project Delivery Rate by Language Type—PC Platforms

	N	Min	P10	P25	Median	P75	P90	Max	Mean	Std Dev
3rd generation language	140	1.0	2.8	4.6	8.6	12.6	22.7	60.1	10.9	10.0
4th generation language	50	1.2	2.4	2.8	5.9	13.1	16.4	33.8	8.5	7.2

Table B-15: Project Delivery Rate by Language Type—Multiplatforms

	N	Min	P10	P25	Median	P75	P90	Max	Mean	Std Dev
3rd generation language	335	0.8	3.6	5.6	9.1	18.0	31.1	61.8	13.7	11.9
4th generation language	124	1.4	3.6	5.5	8.2	11.5	17.1	35.7	9.5	6.3
5th generation language	16	6.5	8.8	11.5	17.2	22.0	25.1	31.8	17.4	7.1

Table B-16: Project Delivery Rate by Language—All Platforms

	N	Min	P10	P25	Median	P75	P90	Max	Mean	Std Dev
ABAP	23	4.2	7.0	7.9	11.3	15.6	21.4	34.3	13.0	7.5
Access	10	1.6	2.4	2.7	7.1	8.7	13.0	14.5	6.8	4.5
ASP	22	1.8	2.6	3.6	6.7	9.9	15.6	30.6	8.6	7.0
Assembler	12	3.8	4.6	8.2	15.7	23.0	34.8	45.8	17.9	13.2

C	103	1.8	3.6	8.3	13.6	24.4	41.0	76.5	18.8	16.3
C++	80	1.0	4.9	8.2	14.8	31.3	54.2	78.7	23.1	20.0
C#	42	1.9	6.1	9.6	15.1	25.1	39.7	49.8	18.8	12.8
COBOL	199	0.8	4.2	6.7	15.3	28.1	48.6	79.7	21.1	18.4
Cool:gen	17	4.7	5.6	8.2	10.8	16.1	26.9	48.3	14.7	11.3
HTML	10	1.0	3.5	4.3	13.7	22.3	40.3	48.0	17.2	16.2
Java, J2EE	171	1.9	4.8	5.9	8.0	15.6	29.4	74.2	13.3	12.9
Lotus Notes	20	1.2	1.5	2.7	3.7	5.1	9.5	12.2	4.7	3.3
Natural	15	3.4	5.1	5.7	10.2	13.9	25.0	35.3	12.2	9.3
Oracle	86	1.2	3.0	4.7	8.2	15.7	23.8	33.8	11.2	8.4
PL/1	99	0.6	2.9	5.7	16.0	22.9	34.3	61.8	16.9	13.4
PL/SQL	18	0.8	1.3	1.7	4.6	9.7	26.4	42.1	9.4	12.0
Powerbuilder	19	4.2	5.0	6.4	9.3	14.1	18.6	23.6	10.9	5.6
Scripting language	26	1.4	3.7	5.1	7.6	13.2	22.5	61.8	11.7	12.4
SQL	60	2.4	3.9	6.2	11.4	16.7	27.2	55.5	13.5	10.7
Visual Basic	208	0.6	2.4	4.1	8.5	18.1	34.7	69.4	13.5	13.4
Other 3GL	95	4.0	6.7	10.2	14.2	22.5	30.1	43.1	16.8	9.1
Other 4GL	61	3.6	6.0	7.8	9.2	13.2	19.2	35.7	11.6	6.7
5GL	23	6.4	8.5	9.8	16.1	22.2	25.5	37.1	17.1	8.2
Other	125	0.7	2.5	5.3	8.6	15.0	24.1	59.3	11.6	10.2

Table B-17: Project Delivery Rate by Language—Mainframe Platforms

	N	Min	P10	P25	Median	P75	P90	Max	Mean	Std Dev
C	26	5.6	9.2	11.7	15.5	27.5	42.5	60.4	21.6	15.2
C++	14	5.8	10.7	17.1	32.2	49.6	53.3	75.2	34.3	20.2
COBOL	128	0.8	4.2	7.5	16.8	32.3	54.6	79.7	23.0	20.0
Cool:gen	16	4.7	5.9	8.9	11.5	17.5	27.7	48.3	15.3	11.4
Java	14	3.1	5.1	11.4	18.1	27.4	29.4	31.6	18.1	9.7
Oracle	19	1.2	2.9	4.3	6.6	18.5	29.7	31.7	12.1	10.2
PL/1	77	0.6	2.3	4.2	13.2	22.2	28.5	55.1	14.9	12.2
Scripting language	13	1.4	5.7	9.1	13.2	22.1	29.5	61.8	17.5	15.4
Visual Basic	19	0.6	3.6	18.4	27.4	30.3	38.9	54.6	24.7	13.9
Other 3GL	52	4.8	7.2	10.2	13.3	19.5	31.3	43.1	16.6	9.4
Other	74	0.7	2.9	6.4	10.7	16.0	31.5	52.5	13.9	11.6

Table B-18: Project Delivery Rate by Language—Midrange Platforms

	N	Min	P10	P25	Median	P75	P90	Max	Mean	Std Dev
C	14	3.6	8.4	13.1	15.1	22.4	29.5	34.2	17.6	8.8
C++	20	1.3	3.9	5.1	7.9	15.0	19.0	49.6	11.8	11.3
Java	22	4.2	4.5	7.3	9.3	20.9	60.1	74.2	19.0	21.5
Oracle	11	2.0	3.0	5.8	9.0	14.6	24.4	28.8	11.3	8.6
SQL	30	4.1	5.8	9.6	13.3	20.1	29.2	55.5	16.8	11.8
Other	31	3.5	5.3	7.1	10.5	20.8	33.8	42.1	15.1	10.9

Table B-19: Project Delivery Rate by Language—PC Platforms

	N	Min	P10	P25	Median	P75	P90	Max	Mean	Std Dev
ASP	11	2.2	2.6	2.7	5.9	7.8	9.5	14.3	6.0	3.8
C++	15	4.0	8.6	9.3	11.4	18.5	27.8	60.1	16.5	13.9
COBOL	18	2.8	4.2	5.2	10.4	19.7	24.0	35.1	12.7	9.4
Java	26	1.9	3.0	5.7	7.7	10.9	19.0	25.3	9.3	6.1
Oracle	16	1.2	2.3	3.7	9.0	13.5	19.8	33.8	10.6	8.8
Visual Basic	48	1.0	1.9	3.2	7.2	9.5	13.8	24.4	7.4	5.0
Other	59	1.0	2.2	3.6	7.3	14.6	25.6	49.8	11.2	11.5

Table B-20: Project Delivery Rate by Language—Multiplatforms

	N	Min	P10	P25	Median	P75	P90	Max	Mean	Std Dev
ABAP	18	4.2	6.5	7.8	9.6	14.6	20.3	34.3	12.1	7.3
C	11	1.8	1.9	2.2	3.9	10.1	13.0	31.3	7.7	8.9
COBOL	12	3.4	4.7	8.3	20.3	37.8	43.2	49.1	22.8	16.3
C#	34	1.9	5.7	8.0	13.7	22.8	32.2	48.8	16.7	11.1
Java	79	3.1	5.0	5.7	6.4	8.1	11.8	17.1	7.4	2.9
Lotus Notes	14	1.5	1.9	2.9	3.7	5.1	7.8	11.9	4.5	2.8
PL/1	20	8.0	12.5	15.6	20.8	26.8	46.8	61.8	24.9	15.1
PL/SQL	11	0.8	1.4	1.7	4.2	6.7	10.7	14.3	5.1	4.3
Visual Basic	115	0.9	2.5	4.2	8.6	18.6	36.8	60.9	14.1	13.9
Other 3GL	40	4.8	7.8	10.9	17.3	22.7	30.0	38.0	17.8	8.6
Other 4GL	56	3.6	6.0	7.8	8.7	12.5	19.2	35.7	11.3	6.5
5GL	16	6.5	8.8	11.5	17.2	22.0	25.1	31.8	17.4	7.1
Other	54	1.1	3.1	4.8	7.4	10.4	14.8	27.4	8.7	5.7

Table B-21: Project Delivery Rate by Architecture Type—All Platforms

	N	Min	P10	P25	Median	P75	P90	Max	Mean	Std Dev
Multitier	317	0.6	3.0	5.0	7.3	13.2	26.2	61.8	11.4	11.1
Client-server (not multitier)	321	1.1	4.5	7.5	12.8	20.3	30.2	75.2	15.5	11.4
Stand-alone	228	0.6	2.6	5.8	10.6	17.8	30.0	77.1	14.4	13.1

Table B-22: Project Delivery Rate by Architecture Type—Mainframe Platforms

	N	Min	P10	P25	Median	P75	P90	Max	Mean	Std Dev
Multitier	20	0.6	3.4	8.0	16.3	28.5	41.9	61.8	20.3	17.6
Client-server (not multitier)	20	3.8	4.5	7.8	22.4	30.0	35.7	75.2	21.7	17.1
Stand-alone	118	0.6	4.3	7.7	12.5	19.7	31.4	77.1	16.6	14.5

Table B-23: Project Delivery Rate by Architecture Type—Midrange Platforms

	N	Min	P10	P25	Median	P75	P90	Max	Mean	Std Dev
Client-server (not multitier)	30	1.3	6.6	10.9	17.0	23.5	42.4	55.5	19.7	13.2
Stand-alone	45	2.0	5.8	7.5	11.8	19.5	29.8	70.2	15.6	12.4

Table B-24: Project Delivery Rate by Architecture Type—PC Platforms

	N	Min	P10	P25	Median	P75	P90	Max	Mean	Std Dev
Client-server (not multitier)	45	1.2	3.2	5.5	9.5	15.3	36.1	49.8	13.4	11.9
Stand-alone	62	1.0	1.4	2.9	6.5	11.9	24.1	49.1	9.7	9.5

Table B-25: Project Delivery Rate by Architecture Type—Multiplatforms

	N	Min	P10	P25	Median	P75	P90	Max	Mean	Std Dev
Multitier	297	0.8	3.0	5.0	7.1	12.6	23.7	60.9	10.8	10.3
Client-server (not multitier)	164	1.1	5.3	8.1	13.2	21.6	29.3	61.8	16.0	10.9

Project Delivery Rate by Use of CASE Tools

Table B-26: Project Delivery Rate by Use of CASE Tools—All Platforms

	N	Min	P10	P25	Median	P75	P90	Max	Mean	Std Dev
CASE tools not used	515	0.7	2.7	5.1	9.5	21.6	35.5	77.1	15.3	14.5
CASE tools used	158	0.6	3.2	5.6	10.4	17.2	28.9	78.7	14.3	13.7

Table B-27: Project Delivery Rate by Use of CASE Tools—Mainframe Platforms

	N	Min	P10	P25	Median	P75	P90	Max	Mean	Std Dev
CASE tools not used	186	0.7	3.5	7.3	16.5	28.0	42.9	77.1	20.3	16.8
CASE tools used	41	0.6	3.1	4.4	10.2	17.4	29.6	44.8	13.5	11.3

Table B-28: Project Delivery Rate by Use of CASE Tools—Midrange Platforms

	N	Min	P10	P25	Median	P75	P90	Max	Mean	Std Dev
CASE tools not used	45	3.6	4.7	7.0	9.3	13.7	23.4	74.2	13.8	14.2
CASE tools used	20	4.1	6.0	7.6	17.0	25.3	46.3	70.2	21.4	17.6

Table B-29: Project Delivery Rate by Use of CASE Tools—PC Platforms

	N	Min	P10	P25	Median	P75	P90	Max	Mean	Std Dev
CASE tools not used	65	1.5	2.5	3.5	7.3	11.4	22.6	49.8	10.5	10.2
CASE tools used	38	1.0	2.5	4.1	10.4	14.4	22.8	60.1	11.8	10.9

Table B-30: Project Delivery Rate by Use of CASE Tools—Multiplatforms

	N	Min	P10	P25	Median	P75	P90	Max	Mean	Std Dev
CASE tools not used	216	0.8	2.4	4.4	7.7	15.8	34.3	60.9	12.7	12.4
CASE tools used	17	5.5	8.4	11.0	17.1	19.4	36.8	45.3	18.7	11.3

Project Delivery Rate by Use of Methodology

Table B-31: Project Delivery Rate by Use of Methodology—All Platforms

	N	Min	P10	P25	Median	P75	P90	Max	Mean	Std Dev
Methodology not used	37	1.0	3.4	5.3	9.2	15.7	28.8	36.7	12.2	9.5
Methodology used	968	0.6	4.5	7.1	12.1	21.8	35.6	78.7	16.6	14.0

Project Delivery Rate by Relationship Between Customer, Developers, Users

Table B-32: Project Delivery Rate by Inhouse/Outsourced Development

	N	Min	P10	P25	Median	P75	P90	Max	Mean	Std Dev
Inhouse development	93	0.8	2.9	5.6	11.0	19.8	36.6	75.2	16.5	15.1
Outsourced development	518	1.0	4.5	7.5	12.6	20.4	30.7	78.7	15.6	11.7

Table B-33: Project Delivery Rate by User Type

	N	Min	P10	P25	Median	P75	P90	Max	Mean	Std Dev
Internal users	441	0.8	4.1	7.3	12.5	20.9	31.7	78.7	15.9	12.4
External users	170	1.2	4.6	7.7	11.5	19.6	31.5	61.8	15.5	12.0

Table B-34: Project Delivery Rate by Relationship to Market

	N	Min	P10	P25	Median	P75	P90	Max	Mean	Std Dev
Inhouse for internal users	71	0.8	3.3	5.6	11.3	20.4	36.7	75.2	16.4	15.1
Inhouse for external users	22	1.2	3.0	7.5	10.9	17.7	34.1	59.3	16.5	15.2
Outsourced for internal users	370	1.0	4.4	7.5	12.8	20.9	30.3	78.7	15.7	11.8
Outsourced for external users	148	1.4	4.7	7.8	11.5	19.8	30.7	61.8	15.4	11.5

Breaking down Tables B-32 to B-34 by platform type provides no useful extra information.

Project Delivery Rate by Project Size

Table B-35: Project Delivery Rate by Project Size—All Platforms

	N	Min	P10	P25	Median	P75	P90	Max	Mean	Std Dev
0 to 200	912	1.0	4.4	6.6	12.4	22.6	38.3	79.7	17.4	15.2
201 to 400	399	0.6	2.8	5.5	10.3	18.4	29.7	75.2	14.0	11.7
401 to 600	138	0.6	2.6	4.0	7.2	13.2	21.9	52.9	10.1	9.4
601 to 800	80	1.0	2.8	4.4	7.9	15.3	27.4	54.6	11.4	9.9
801 to 1,000	32	1.9	3.2	5.6	7.8	13.3	19.5	29.4	10.0	6.8
Over 1,000	120	0.7	1.5	2.8	6.3	10.4	16.4	59.8	8.4	8.1

Table B-36: Project Delivery Rate by Project Size—Mainframe Platforms

	N	Min	P10	P25	Median	P75	P90	Max	Mean	Std Dev
0 to 200	284	1.2	5.3	8.9	15.9	28.5	45.1	79.7	20.9	16.5
201 to 400	109	0.6	2.4	5.5	13.3	22.9	31.0	75.2	16.0	13.4
401 to 600	24	0.6	2.4	3.8	7.2	15.1	16.8	52.9	10.5	10.9
601 to 800	16	2.0	2.7	7.1	13.9	28.9	34.0	54.6	19.0	15.2
801 to 1,000	6	3.1	–	5.1	11.1	18.6	–	29.4	13.1	10.2
Over 1,000	13	0.7	1.2	3.8	5.4	15.0	23.5	31.6	9.9	10.0

Table B-37: Project Delivery Rate by Project Size—Midrange Platforms

	N	Min	P10	P25	Median	P75	P90	Max	Mean	Std Dev
0 to 200	60	3.5	5.3	8.6	16.1	27.4	35.7	74.2	20.6	16.0
201 to 400	21	1.3	3.0	7.9	10.1	17.3	28.8	49.6	14.4	12.1
401 to 600	19	3.6	4.4	5.4	7.6	9.3	15.2	22.2	8.7	4.8
601 to 800	10	4.3	4.9	7.3	10.0	15.0	17.6	21.6	11.1	5.7
801 to 1,000	2	7.5	–	–	10.4	–	–	13.2	10.4	4.0
Over 1,000	16	4.4	5.7	6.8	8.2	11.4	14.7	29.0	10.2	5.9

Table B-38: Project Delivery Rate by Project Size—PC Platforms

	N	Min	P10	P25	Median	P75	P90	Max	Mean	Std Dev
0 to 200	79	1.0	2.9	5.1	10.1	15.6	23.6	60.1	12.5	11.0
201 to 400	51	1.0	2.6	3.3	7.2	10.6	24.4	49.8	10.4	11.3
401 to 600	28	1.2	2.7	5.3	9.0	15.3	25.4	39.9	11.9	9.7
601 to 800	14	1.0	2.5	3.8	5.0	8.8	11.3	16.3	6.4	4.2
801 to 1,000	7	4.5	–	5.7	8.2	12.1	–	13.4	8.8	3.7
Over 1,000	25	1.0	1.7	2.5	5.8	9.8	11.9	24.7	7.3	6.0

Table B-39: Project Delivery Rate by Project Size—Multiplatforms

	N	Min	P10	P25	Median	P75	P90	Max	Mean	Std Dev
0 to 200	222	1.7	4.7	6.0	8.9	17.0	27.3	61.8	13.2	11.1
201 to 400	138	1.4	4.4	6.8	11.9	18.4	32.6	49.1	14.8	10.9
401 to 600	42	0.8	2.3	3.5	5.6	11.0	20.2	43.4	8.8	8.3
601 to 800	28	1.9	3.7	6.0	8.4	13.1	23.4	34.2	11.1	8.5
801 to 1,000	12	1.9	2.3	6.2	8.1	11.9	21.1	26.3	10.2	7.4
Over 1,000	38	0.9	1.6	2.3	5.0	7.3	15.9	59.8	7.5	10.2

Project Delivery Rate by Maximum Team Size

Table B-40: Project Delivery Rate by Maximum Team Size—All Platforms

	N	Min	P10	P25	Median	P75	P90	Max	Mean	Std Dev
1 to 4	157	1.0	2.9	4.9	7.4	12.4	21.1	77.1	11.0	11.3
5 to 8	212	0.6	3.4	5.9	10.3	16.9	28.0	76.5	13.8	12.4
9 or more	215	0.6	4.2	8.8	16.5	26.9	40.0	78.7	20.0	15.2

Table B-41: Project Delivery Rate by Maximum Team Size—Mainframe Platforms

	N	Min	P10	P25	Median	P75	P90	Max	Mean	Std Dev
1 to 4	41	3.8	5.3	8.0	13.8	21.0	42.0	77.1	19.2	16.9
5 to 8	43	0.6	4.0	8.2	13.6	23.3	47.8	75.2	19.4	17.5
9 or more	45	0.6	2.1	7.5	18.4	27.2	35.3	68.2	20.1	16.1

Table B-42: Project Delivery Rate by Maximum Team Size—Midrange Platforms

	N	Min	P10	P25	Median	P75	P90	Max	Mean	Std Dev
1 to 4	6	2.0	—	5.8	6.0	7.4	—	12.4	6.7	3.4
5 to 8	25	3.0	5.1	9.0	11.6	16.8	31.1	45.3	15.3	10.6
9 or more	30	6.8	7.8	11.6	17.0	26.4	30.5	70.2	20.6	13.6

Table B-43: Project Delivery Rate by Maximum Team Size—PC Platforms

	N	Min	P10	P25	Median	P75	P90	Max	Mean	Std Dev
1 to 4	19	1.0	2.8	4.0	6.4	11.2	17.9	42.3	9.7	9.7
5 to 8	35	1.0	1.8	3.5	8.4	11.1	16.8	39.2	9.3	8.7
9 or more	29	1.2	4.2	7.5	9.8	17.6	32.9	49.8	15.0	13.1

Table B-44: Project Delivery Rate by Maximum Team Size—Multiplatforms

	N	Min	P10	P25	Median	P75	P90	Max	Mean	Std Dev
1 to 4	18	3.9	5.1	5.6	7.5	10.8	18.3	22.9	9.4	5.6
5 to 8	50	1.9	4.6	7.3	8.8	14.0	21.9	41.2	11.4	7.3
9 or more	57	1.1	4.3	10.1	16.6	25.2	38.1	61.8	20.1	13.6

The Impact of Maximum Team Size and Project Size on Project Delivery Rate

The preceding tables analyze each factor individually, without taking into account any interactions between them. Now we look at the effect of different factors, after allowing for the effect of other factors that have an important effect on PDR.

Platform and language are important factors for characterizing the environment in which a project is developed, and the primary language used to develop the project. PDR values for different combinations of platform and language are presented in Tables B-16–20.

Team size and project size are also known to be important factors that affect PDR (in fact, analysis of ISBSG data shows that these are the two most important factors).

Table B-45 summarizes the residual project delivery rates for different combinations of maximum team size and project size, *after* the effect of language and platform has been taken into account. (This table is based on analysis of 508 of the 1,681 projects analyzed in this appendix, for which language, platform, project size, and maximum team size are all known.)

The data analyzed here suggests that PDR gets worse as team sizes increase, but that PDR improves as functional size increases. While these factors are clearly not independent (larger projects tend to have larger teams), you can study Table B-45 to gain an understanding of each factor separately as well as together.

You can see that small teams do not develop large projects, as expected (Table B-45 does not present statistics for samples of fewer than five projects, because the sample is simply too small).

We can use Table B-45 to identify the average effect of maximum team size and project size. We do this by looking at the averages: both median and mean are worth considering.

For example, if we consider medians, Table B-45 shows that projects with a functional size of up to 200 UFP and a maximum team size of 1 to 4 have an average project delivery rate that is 6.7 hours per UFP lower than the overall average, once language and platform have been taken into account. If we consider means, the difference is 4.1 hours per FP, instead of 6.3 hours per UFP.

In other words, suppose you start with an estimate of project delivery rate for a given project, based on its platform and language (see Tables B-16–20). If its size is up to 200 UFP and you expect to use a development team of 1 to 4 people, you could lower your estimated project delivery rate value by 4 to 6 hours per UFP. For a similar functional size but with a team size of 9 or more, you could raise your estimated PDR value by 11 to 15 hours per UFP. Other combinations of functional size and team size have different effects, as shown in Table B-45.

Table B-45: Effect of Maximum Team Size and Project Size

Team Size	Project Size (UFP)	N	Min	P10	P25	Median	P75	P90	Max	Mean	Std Dev
1 to 4	3 to 200	99	–19.6	–14.1	–11.1	–6.7	–1.7	7.6	55.1	–4.1	12.2
1 to 4	201 to 400	25	–19.8	–14.2	–11.7	–5.1	–2.1	3.3	14.6	–5.3	7.8
1 to 4	401 to 600	5	–18.8	—	–10.3	–9.1	–7.4	—	–3.6	–9.8	5.6
1 to 4	601 to 800	–									
1 to 4	801 to 1,000	2									
1 to 4	More than 1,000	–									
5 to 8	3 to 200	91	–17.0	–10.7	–4.7	–0.2	5.2	19.3	59.5	2.1	12.8
5 to 8	201 to 400	53	–14.8	–12.0	–8.3	–5.4	0.2	6.3	54.5	–2.2	11.6
5 to 8	401 to 600	16	–15.9	–12.9	–12.1	–6.3	–3.6	–0.7	0.8	–7.3	5.3
5 to 8	601 to 800	14	–15.6	–12.2	–10.6	–8.1	–5.9	–4.3	–3.3	–8.5	–3.5
5 to 8	801 to 1,000	3									
5 to 8	More than 1,000	4									
9 or more	3 to 200	44	–5.0	–1.0	2.0	11.0	22.2	44.4	59.7	15.5	17.3
9 or more	201 to 400	67	–16.9	–9.8	–2.9	1.9	14.4	27.3	36.9	5.3	13.5
9 or more	401 to 600	23	–17.5	–12.9	–8.6	0.5	5.8	20.0	224.0	0.5	11.6
9 or more	601 to 800	22	–20.0	–13.2	–6.4	–0.5	0.7	5.2	17.7	–2.1	8.4
9 or more	801 to 1,000	9	–14.0	—	–6.1	–3.6	–3.2	—	9.8	–3.9	6.4
9 or more	More than 1,000	31	–17.9	–14.4	–7.9	–4.8	–0.9	1.6	13.6	–4.9	6.5

The variation increases as team size and project size increase. For example, for 80 percent of the projects with a functional size up to 200 UFP and a team size of 1 to 4, the residual PDR ranges from –14.1 to +7.6 hours per UFP (these are the P10 and P90 values). This is a spread of 21.7 hours per UFP. For teams of 5 to 8 the corresponding spread is 30.0 hours per UFP, and for teams of 9 or more the spread increases to 45.4 hours per UFP. Similar trends can be seen for other variations in team size and project size. The low end (the minimum and P10 values) changes less than the high end (P75 and P90) as team size increases, and the high end gets progressively worse as team size increases.

Broadly, as team size increases PDR deteriorates. As functional size increases PDR tends to improve. As both increase, individually and together, PDR becomes more variable.

APPENDIX C
Estimation Equations

In this appendix we provide equations that you can use to obtain indicative or ballpark estimates for:

- **Project Delivery Rates** Productivity expressed as hours per function point
- **Effort** Person hours for the development team only
- **Duration** Elapsed months
- **Speed of Delivery** Function points delivered per elapsed month for the project as a whole
- **Speed of Delivery per Person** Function points delivered per elapsed month per development team member

What Are These Estimates Based On?

Studies of the projects in the ISBSG Repository have shown that Size and Maximum Team Size are the most important drivers of effort and duration. Size is the most important. For this reason, two groups of equations are provided with the following independent variables:

- Equations that utilize Size (in function points) and Maximum Team Size
- Equations that utilize Size only

Within these two groups, equations are provided by:

- Platform (mainframe, midrange, PC, and multiplatform)
- Language type (3GL, 4GL)
- Development type (enhancement, new development)
- Combinations of platforms, language types, and development types

These are the main project characteristics that you are likely to know at the beginning of a project that are also most useful for ballpark estimates.

Which Equation(s) Should You Use?

You should choose the equation(s) that best suit your needs:

- If your specific combination of platform, language type, and development type is present in the tables at the end of this appendix, use the equation provided for that combination. You can be assured that the equation, and all its components, play a useful role for estimation (but pay attention to N, R2adj, and Median MRE—explained shortly—to understand how useful the equation is).
- If your exact combination of platform, language type, and development type is not given in the tables at the end of this appendix, you will have to step back to a more general equation that matches some of your platform/language type/development type, but not all of them.
  - A particular combination might be missing because the ISBSG does not have enough projects for a particular combination of platform, language type, and development type to derive a legitimate estimation equation.
  - Another possibility is that sometimes the analysis shows that a particular equation has no better than random chance in generating an estimate, or that one or more of the independent variables make no significant contribution to the estimate, or the equation has very little explanatory value. In such cases the equation is simply not presented in the table, since it has no value for you.
- Treat "re-development" as "new development" projects.
- Treat "Application generator" as 4GL projects.

Do These Equations Apply to My Project?

These equations have been produced from an analysis of 1,681 projects in the ISBSG Repository (Release 11).

- All of these projects provide data regarding Size (unadjusted function points) and Effort (person-hours for the development team).
- 584 provide data for Maximum Team Size, 1,311 provide Duration, and 561 provide both.

The ranges of project characteristics are as follows:

- All are sized with IFPUG function points, version 4 or later, or are new developments sized using the NESMA approach.
- All have high data quality rating (A or B).
- 25 <= Size (UFP) <= 4,200 FP.
- 80 <= Effort <= 61,500 hours.
- Maximum team size <= 52.
- 0.5 <= Duration < 34 months.
- 0.65 <= PDR <= 80 Hrs/FP.
- 4.5 <= Speed of delivery (for the entire project team) < 520 FP/month.
- 0.7 <= Speed of delivery (per project team member) < 45 FP/month/person.
- Project completion date is 1999 or later.
- (Normalized effort for development team / reported effort for development team) < 1.25.

It is reasonable to apply the equations tabulated later in this appendix if your project falls within these ranges. *These equations cannot be relied upon for projects that fall outside these ranges.*

What Do the Statistics Mean?

Be aware of the *N, R2(Adj),* and *Median MRE* columns. N is the number of projects. R2(Adj) and Median MRE have been provided to give some indication of reliability.

- N is important, because care must be taken not to draw unwarranted conclusions from small samples of projects.
- R2(Adj), or Adjusted Squared Multiple R, is a measure of how much of the variability between different projects is actually explained by the equation. The maximum value is 1.00, which would occur when every project agreed exactly with the equation. The closer the value is to 1, the better. Even low values here can be meaningful; something is being explained, but randomness or variation in other predictive factors may have diluted the predictive effect. Low values do not tell you much (equations with an R2(Adj) less than 0.25 are not even reported in these tables). High values, such as 0.80, are extremely encouraging (but are not necessarily conclusive).
- Median MRE is an indication of how accurate the regression equation is on average. The minimum value is 0.00, which would occur when every project agreed exactly with the

equation. The closer the value is to 0, the better. It shows the halfway point for accuracy of the estimates. For example, if Median MRE is 0.35, it means that the estimate from the regression equation is within 35 percent of the true value for half of the projects; for the other half the error is more than 35 percent. If Median MRE is 0.20, the estimate is within 20 percent of the true value for half of the projects.

Table C-1.0: Project Delivery Rate, estimated from software size and maximum team size

- Dependent (Y) = PDR (Project Delivery Rate, Hours per Function Point)
- Independent (X_1) = Size (Software Size in Function Points)
- Independent (X_2) = MaxTeam (Maximum Team Size)
- Equation: $\mathbf{PDR = C \times Size^{E1} \times MaxTeam^{E2}}$

Class	C	E_1	E_2	N	R2(Adj)	Median MRE
All	**57.39**	**–0.558**	**0.710**	584	0.33	0.37
Enhancement	**79.12**	**–0.616**	**0.692**	381	0.33	0.37
New development	**37.48**	**–0.496**	**0.759**	203	0.32	0.37
MR	**60.76**	**–0.664**	**0.960**	61	0.65	0.23
Multi	**34.49**	**–0.510**	**0.875**	125	0.46	0.30
3GL	**51.74**	**–0.526**	**0.693**	367	0.27	0.38
4GL	**32.90**	**–0.468**	**0.692**	141	0.42	0.30
New & MR	**35.09**	**–0.597**	**1.080**	16	0.57	0.24
New & Multi	**37.41**	**–0.463**	**0.736**	47	0.36	0.30
Enh & MR	**115.90**	**–0.759**	**0.872**	45	0.73	0.19
Enh & Multi	**38.97**	**–0.566**	**0.951**	78	0.50	0.31
New & 3GL	**39.40**	**–0.489**	**0.762**	127	0.33	0.38
Enh & 4GL	**64.10**	**–0.605**	**0.728**	98	0.60	0.27
MR & 3GL	**42.94**	**–0.605**	**0.994**	27	0.61	0.28
MR & 4GL	**56.86**	**–0.664**	**0.967**	30	0.66	0.18
Multi & 3GL	**36.44**	**–0.491**	**0.832**	91	0.43	0.30
Multi & 4GL	**9.35**	**–0.282**	**0.801**	32	0.39	0.23
Enh & MR & 3GL	**81.76**	**–0.647**	**0.785**	19	0.68	0.24
Enh & MR & 4GL	**162.70**	**–0.865**	**0.963**	25	0.76	0.19
New & Multi & 3GL	**72.34**	**–0.530**	**0.666**	30	0.38	0.43
New & Multi & 4GL	**6.72**	**–0.228**	**0.839**	16	0.33	0.16
Enh & Multi & 3GL	**25.63**	**–0.462**	**0.909**	61	0.46	0.30
Enh & Multi & 4GL	**13.98**	**–0.372**	**0.829**	16	0.42	0.21

Table C-1.1: Project Work Effort, estimated from software size and maximum team size

- Dependent (Y) = PWE (Normalized Project Work Effort for development team, Hours)
- Independent (X_1) = Size (Software Size in Function Points)
- Independent (X_2) = MaxTeam (Maximum Team Size)
- Equation: **PWE = C × Size^{E1} × MaxTeam^{E2}**

Class	C	E_1	E_2	N	R2(Adj)	Median MRE
All	**57.39**	**0.442**	**0.710**	584	0.57	0.37
Enhancement	**79.12**	**0.384**	**0.692**	381	0.53	0.37
New development	**37.48**	**0.504**	**0.759**	203	0.61	0.37
MR	**60.76**	**0.336**	**0.960**	61	0.81	0.23
PC	**23.67**	**0.570**	**0.678**	83	0.53	0.42
Multi	**34.49**	**0.490**	**0.876**	125	0.67	0.30
3GL	**51.74**	**0.474**	**0.693**	367	0.55	0.38
4GL	**32.90**	**0.532**	**0.692**	141	0.73	0.30
New & MR	**35.09**	**0.403**	**1.080**	16	0.86	0.24
New & PC	**11.06**	**0.723**	**0.634**	50	0.54	0.42
New & Multi	**37.41**	**0.537**	**0.736**	47	0.68	0.30
Enh & MR	**115.90**	**0.241**	**0.872**	45	0.76	0.19
Enh & Multi	**38.97**	**0.434**	**0.951**	78	0.64	0.31
New & 3GL	**39.40**	**0.511**	**0.762**	127	0.63	0.38
New & 4GL	**6.53**	**0.833**	**0.585**	43	0.70	0.37
Enh & 3GL	**70.85**	**0.413**	**0.673**	240	0.48	0.39
Enh & 4GL	**64.10**	**0.395**	**0.728**	98	0.78	0.27
MR & 3GL	**42.94**	**0.395**	**0.994**	27	0.67	0.28
MR & 4GL	**56.86**	**0.336**	**0.967**	30	0.87	0.18
PC & 3GL	**28.66**	**0.501**	**0.780**	65	0.56	0.42
Multi & 3GL	**36.44**	**0.509**	**0.833**	91	0.68	0.30
Multi & 4GL	**9.35**	**0.718**	**0.801**	32	0.82	0.23
Enh & MR & 3GL	**81.76**	**0.353**	**0.786**	19	0.63	0.24
New & PC & 3GL	**14.24**	**0.656**	**0.724**	37	0.57	0.42
New & Multi & 3GL	**72.34**	**0.470**	**0.666**	30	0.65	0.43
New & Multi & 4GL	**6.72**	**0.772**	**0.839**	16	0.82	0.16
Enh & Multi & 3GL	**25.63**	**0.538**	**0.909**	61	0.66	0.30
Enh & Multi & 4GL	**13.98**	**0.628**	**0.829**	16	0.81	0.21

Table C-1.2: Project Duration, estimated from software size and maximum team size

- Dependent (Y) = Duration (Elapsed Time – Inactive Time, Months)
- Independent (X_1) = Size (Software Size in Function Points)
- Independent (X_2) = MaxTeam (Maximum Team Size)
- Equation: **Duration = C × Size^{E1} × MaxTeam^{E2}**

Not one suitable equation can be used. In most cases, the reason is that the maximum team size does not make a significant contribution to the equation. There is only one equation in which C, E1, and E2 all contribute significantly, and the R2(Adj) value for that equation is so low (0.18) that the equation is not useful.

Table C-1.3: Speed of Delivery for Whole Project, estimated from software size and maximum team size

- Dependent (Y) = Speed of Delivery (Function Points per Elapsed Month)
- Independent (X_1) = Size (Software Size in Function Points)
- Independent (X_2) = MaxTeam (Maximum Team Size)
- Equation: **Speed for project = C × Size^{E1} × MaxTeam^{E2}**

Class	C	E_1	E_2	N	R2(Adj)	Median MRE
Enh & Multi	**0.44**	**0.852**	**–0.228**	78	0.59	0.28

Table C-1.4: Speed of Delivery per Person, estimated from software size and maximum team size

- Dependent (Y) = Speed of Delivery per Person (Function Points per Elapsed Month per Person)
- Independent (X_1) = Size (Software Size in Function Points)
- Independent (X_2) = MaxTeam (Maximum Team Size)
- Equation: **Speed per person = C × Size^{E1} × MaxTeam^{E2}**

Class	C	E_1	E_2	N	R2(Adj)	Median MRE
All	**0.778**	**0.696**	**–1.011**	561	0.61	0.36
Enhancement	**0.643**	**0.729**	**–1.005**	369	0.62	0.36
New & PC	**3.373**	**0.465**	**–1.007**	46	0.58	0.43
Enh & Multi	**0.436**	**0.851**	**–1.228**	78	0.70	0.28
New & 4GL	**3.677**	**0.393**	**–0.872**	42	0.44	0.39
Enh & 3GL	**0.667**	**0.724**	**–1.022**	231	0.59	0.37
Multi & 3GL	**0.479**	**0.793**	**–1.116**	89	0.64	0.29
New & PC & 3GL	**4.464**	**0.431**	**–1.059**	34	0.49	0.43

Table C-2.0: Project Delivery Rate, estimated from software size only

- Dependent (Y) = PDR (Project Delivery Rate, Hours per Function Point)
- Independent (X_1) = Size (Software Size in Function Points)
- Equation: **PDR = C × Size^{E1}**

No equation is useful. Several are "statistically significant"—they pick up a genuine relationship between size and PDR—but the relationship is so weak that it never explains more than 15 percent of the variation in PDR.

Table C-2.1: Project Work Effort, estimated from software size only

- Dependent (Y) = PWE (Normalized Project Work Effort for development team, Hours)
- Independent (X_1) = Size (Software Size in Function Points)
- Equation: **PWE = C × Size^{E1}**

Class	C	E_1	N	R2(Adj)	Median MRE
All	**33.37**	**0.770**	1681	0.46	0.55
Enhancement	**31.16**	**0.793**	1147	0.43	0.55
New development	**23.25**	**0.814**	534	0.45	0.55
MF	**44.03**	**0.749**	452	0.38	0.56
MR	**35.43**	**0.783**	128	0.60	0.43
PC	**17.35**	**0.844**	204	0.50	0.51
Multi	**2.86**	**0.830**	480	0.54	0.52
3GL	**39.56**	**0.754**	1105	0.42	0.57
4GL	**20.06**	**0.832**	359	0.58	0.46
New & MF	**34.49**	**0.809**	86	0.33	0.58
New & MR	**19.08**	**0.883**	49	0.59	0.42
New & PC	**13.83**	**0.884**	126	0.50	0.53
New & Multi	**22.48**	**0.809**	184	0.50	0.45
Enh & MF	**50.10**	**0.718**	366	0.35	0.55
Enh & MR	**45.90**	**0.734**	79	0.52	0.44
Enh & PC	**23.10**	**0.789**	78	0.47	0.54
Enh & Multi	**16.35**	**0.912**	296	0.56	0.52
New & 3GL	**29.16**	**0.790**	351	0.44	0.55
New & 4GL	**5.28**	**1.032**	112	0.60	0.49

Class	C	E_1	N	R2(Adj)	Median MRE
Enh & 3GL	**37.64**	**0.774**	754	0.39	0.57
Enh & 4GL	**22.83**	**0.819**	247	0.55	0.43
MF & 3GL	**51.34**	**0.730**	365	0.37	0.56
MF & 4GL	**18.39**	**0.838**	41	0.44	0.51
MR & 3GL	**43.17**	**0.742**	71	0.53	0.45
MR & 4GL	**29.07**	**0.830**	47	0.65	0.40
PC & 3GL	**13.83**	**0.889**	140	0.56	0.51
PC & 4GL	**31.05**	**0.710**	50	0.36	0.57
Multi & 3GL	**23.96**	**0.831**	335	0.52	0.58
Multi & 4GL	**15.86**	**0.867**	124	0.63	0.34
New & MF & 3GL	**34.38**	**0.823**	64	0.33	0.58
New & MF & 4GL	**18.14**	**0.846**	15	0.37	0.50
Enh & MF & 3GL	**60.52**	**0.692**	301	0.34	0.56
Enh & MF & 4GL	**22.66**	**0.787**	26	0.27	0.51
New & MR & 3GL	**42.48**	**0.744**	31	0.35	0.45
Enh & MR & 3GL	**42.47**	**0.747**	40	0.54	0.45
Enh & MR & 4GL	**62.27**	**0.685**	37	0.45	0.39
New & PC & 3GL	**13.57**	**0.898**	85	0.55	0.49
New & PC & 4GL	**13.21**	**0.844**	30	0.46	0.53
Enh & PC & 3GL	**14.83**	**0.868**	55	0.55	0.51
New & Multi & 3GL	**33.67**	**0.754**	132	0.49	0.46
New & Multi & 4GL	**4.06**	**1.071**	49	0.58	0.46
Enh & Multi & 3GL	**13.49**	**0.957**	203	0.54	0.57
Enh & Multi & 4GL	**17.59**	**0.869**	75	0.70	0.33

Note that R2(Adj) values tend to be quite a lot lower here than in Table C-1.1, where the estimate was based on size and team size, not just size alone; and Median MRE tends to be quite a lot higher. This means that estimates based on both size and team size are probably more accurate than estimates based on size alone. This is no surprise—you would expect to get better estimates when more information is available.

If a size estimate and the team size are both available to you, and your particular combination of platform, language, and development type is present in Table C-1.1, you should use Table C-1.1 instead of Table C-2.1.

Table C-2.2: Project Duration, estimated from software size only

- Dependent (Y) = Duration (Elapsed Time – Inactive Time, Months)
- Independent (X_1) = Size (Software Size in Function Points)
- Equation: **Duration = C × Size^{E1}**

Class	C	E_1	N	R2(Adj)	Median MRE
New development	**0.543**	**0.408**	494	0.30	0.41
PC	**0.507**	**0.418**	191	0.33	0.39
Multi	**0.589**	**0.394**	394	0.28	0.44
4GL	**0.507**	**0.429**	304	0.36	0.37
New & PC	**0.297**	**0.505**	115	0.42	0.42
New & Multi	**0.423**	**0.440**	179	0.33	0.41
New & 3GL	**0.645**	**0.378**	327	0.27	0.42
New & 4GL	**0.239**	**0.538**	108	0.40	0.43
Enh & 4GL	**0.540**	**0.428**	196	0.34	0.36
PC & 3GL	**0.468**	**0.436**	132	0.36	0.40
Multi & 4GL	**0.201**	**0.599**	98	0.46	0.40
New & PC & 3GL	**0.284**	**0.523**	78	0.43	0.42
New & PC & 4GL	**0.324**	**0.459**	29	0.41	0.32
New & Multi & 3GL	**0.558**	**0.392**	128	0.33	0.37
New & Multi & 4GL	**0.107**	**0.679**	48	0.38	0.52
Enh & Multi & 4GL	**0.174**	**0.656**	50	0.63	0.22

These results show that it is rarely possible to estimate duration with any confidence using a regression equation. So what can you do if your project does not fit into any class in Table C-2.2?

1. Estimate effort, using Tables C-1.1 and C-2.1.
2. Use the effort estimate as the base for estimating duration:
   a. If you know your planned team size, effort divided by that team size gives an estimate of the number of hours per staff member for the project. Dividing that number by the number of hours worked by a staff member per month gives an estimate of duration in months.
   b. If you do not know your planned team size, you can use the estimation equation (derived from the entire data set) **Months = 0.370 × Effort$^{0.328}$**. R2(Adj) for this equation is 0.35, and Median MRE is 0.36.

Table C-2.3: Speed of Delivery for Whole Project Team, estimated from software size only

- Dependent (Y) = Speed of Delivery (Function Points per Elapsed Month)
- Independent (X_1) = Size (Software Size in Function Points)
- Equation: **Speed for project = C × Size^{E1}**

Class	C	E_1	N	R2(Adj)	Median MRE
All	**1.183**	**0.661**	1311	0.55	0.42
New development	**1.842**	**0.592**	494	0.48	0.40
PC	**1.972**	**0.582**	191	0.49	0.42
Multi	**1.698**	**0.606**	394	0.48	0.42
4GL	**1.974**	**0.571**	304	0.50	0.40
New & PC	**3.370**	**0.495**	115	0.41	0.39
New & Multi	**2.367**	**0.560**	179	0.44	0.40
Enh & Multi	**1.536**	**0.615**	215	0.46	0.44
New & 3GL	**1.550**	**0.622**	327	0.50	0.42
New & 4GL	**4.181**	**0.462**	108	0.33	0.43
Enh & 4GL	**1.853**	**0.572**	196	0.48	0.36
MR & 3GL	**0.464**	**0.846**	70	0.74	0.34
PC & 3GL	**2.138**	**0.564**	132	0.49	0.43
Multi & 4GL	**4.982**	**0.401**	98	0.27	0.42
New & PC & 3GL	**3.520**	**0.477**	78	0.39	0.42
New & PC & 4GL	**3.082**	**0.541**	29	0.49	0.32
New & Multi & 3GL	**1.792**	**0.608**	128	0.55	0.34
Enh & Multi & 4GL	**5.744**	**0.343**	50	0.31	0.28

Table C-2.4: Speed of Delivery per Person, estimated from software size only

- Dependent (Y) = Speed of Delivery per Person (Function Points per Elapsed Month per Person)
- Independent (X_1) = Size (Software Size in Function Points)
- Equation: **Speed per person = C × Size^{E1}**

There is no useful equation. There is no evidence here that speed of delivery per person can be estimated directly from project size.

APPENDIX D

Project Sample Demographics Used in Chapter 3

Details of the group of projects used for the analysis contained in Chapter 3 are as follows. In each case, percentages are related to the number of projects for which data was provided for that attribute. For example, the percentages for architecture are based on the 651 projects for which this is known (not on the 861 projects that form the entire data set).

- The projects come from 24 different countries, with the greatest representation from Australia, Brazil, Canada, China, Denmark, India, Italy, Japan, the Netherlands, the United Kingdom, and the United States.
- Over 83 percent of the projects were completed in 2000 or later, and 50 percent in 2004 or later.
- **Organization type** The main types of organization represented are banking, communications, computers/software/IT, insurance, government/public administration, insurance, and manufacturing. Each has at least 45 projects, and together these provide 76 percent of the projects.
- **Application type** The projects are dominated by transaction/production systems (41 percent), management information systems (16 percent), e-business/EDI (15 percent), document management (9 percent), real time (8 percent), and communications (7 percent).
- **User base** 61 percent of projects are for use by a single business group and/or single location; 25 percent are for six or more business groups and six or more locations.

- **Development type** 46 percent are new developments, 49 percent are enhancements, and 5 percent are redevelopments.
- **Architecture** 53 percent of projects use a client/server architecture, 7 percent use a multitier architecture, 40 percent are stand-alone systems.
- **Platform** 30 percent run on mainframes, 7 percent on midrange computers, 41 percent on PCs, and 22 percent on multiple platforms.
- **Language** 74 percent use 3GLs, 21 percent use 4GLs, 5 percent use application generators, 1 percent use 2GLs. ABAP, ASP, Access, C, C++, C#, COBOL, Cool:Gen, Java, Oracle, PL/I, SQL, and Visual Basic each have at least 18 projects, and together they account for 85 percent of projects.
- **CASE tools** These are used in 32 percent of projects.
- **Software development methodologies** A methodology is used in 85 percent of projects. In-house methodologies dominate (48 percent in-house, 38 percent purchased and/or adapted, 15 percent no methodology).
- **Relationship to market** 47 percent of projects are developed internally, 53 percent are outsourced. 46 percent are developed for internal users, 54 percent for external users.
- **Team size** Small teams (1 to 4 developers) account for 19 percent of projects, 38 percent have teams of 5 to 8, and 43 percent have teams of 9 or more developers.

Size and other key project indicators:

- **Software size** Size ranges from 14 to 10,000 unadjusted function points. The median is 280 FP. If adjusted function points are used as the size measure, the range is from 14 to 20,000 AFP, and the median is 335 AFP. (Note: The UFP and AFP maximums are for different project sets.)
- **Effort** For just the development team, the effort ranges from 17 to 134,000 hours; the median is about 2,640 hours. For the entire project effort (including support staff and user effort), the range is from 17 to 267,000 hours; the median is about 3,000 hours. These numbers refer to actual reported effort. Normalized effort for the entire project team ranges from 26 to 267,000 hours, with a median of 3,430 hours.
- **Duration** Projects range from 1 to 84 months. The median is 7 months.

- **Project delivery rate (normalized effort for the development team only, per unadjusted function point)** PDR varies from less than 1 to over 300 hours per function point. The median is about 10 hours per function point.
- **Function points per elapsed month per team member** This ranges from 1 to 250; the median is 4.4 function points per month per team member.

APPENDIX E

The Benefits of Submitting Projects to the ISBSG Repository

When you submit a project or projects for inclusion in the ISBSG Repository, you will receive a free Project Benchmark Report that will provide you with a comparison of the project submitted to a group of similar projects already in the repository.

How to Submit a Project

The ISBSG will accept data submissions a number of ways:

- On the Word form that can be downloaded from the ISBSG web site (see following)
- On an Excel spreadsheet (use the Word form for guidance on data requirements and data descriptions)
- Via the ISBSG XML facility

To submit a project for inclusion in the ISBSG Repository using the Word form:

1. Download the appropriate submission forms from the web site.
2. Enter all the information that you have about your project onto the form.

3. E-mail your submission to the ISBSG Administrator (contact details can be found at www.isbsg.org/isbsgnew.nsf/webpages/~GBL~Contact).

All submissions are kept strictly confidential and will remain anonymous. On receipt of a submission, the ISBSG administrator removes the identification information from the submission, replacing this with a unique identification code. The submission is then sent to the repository manager who rates it, adds it to the repository, and produces a benchmark report, which is returned to the administrator to be forwarded to you. You can use the code(s) that you have been issued with to identify your projects on the ISBSG Data Suite. No one else can identify your projects.

A Description of the Project Benchmark Report

When you submit a project to be included in the repository, a Project Benchmark Report will be returned by e-mail. This report can be used to assist in effort and cost estimation in the future. The report also provides valuable benchmarking of your organization's productivity. It provides a graphic comparison of the submitted project against similar projects in the repository. You can use it as the base from which to launch process improvement.

For example, assuming your project has the following characteristics:

- Development Platform = Midrange
- Methodology = Developed in-house
- Language Type = 4GL
- Maximum Team Size > 8

Your project delivery rate (PDR) was 10.0 hours per function point.

The following is a sample extract from the report you will receive when you submit a project. Your PDR is shown in bold type:

Influencing Factor	N	P10 %	P25 %	Median		P75 %		P90 %
Development Platform: Midrange	152	2.4	6.7	8.9	**10**	11.8		12.4
Language Type: 4GL	201	2.7	5.3	7.2		9.9	**10**	14.3
Team Size: >8	112	4.5	7.6	9.1	**10**	19.3		23.4

For the two factors with the most significant impact on productivity, Development Platform and Language Type, the following sample chart shows how your project delivery rate compares to projects with the same Development Platform and Language Type:

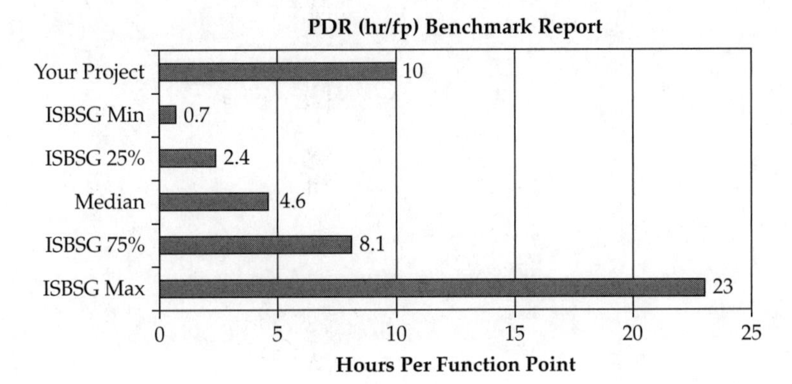

APPENDIX F

ISBSG Member Organizations

Australia
QESP (Quantitative Enterprise Software Performance)
Julian Day or Pam Morris
E: info@qesp.org.au or pam.morris@totalmetrics.com
W: www.qesp.org.au

China
CESI (China Electronic Standardization Institute)
Ms. Li Yunqin
P: +86 10 82825888
F: +86 10 82825777
E: rhymelee@126.com or liyq@cesi.ac.cn
W: www.en.cesi.cn

Finland
FiSMA (Finnish Software Measurement Association)
Mr. Pekka Forselius
P: +35 8505 160416
F: +35 8934 42771
E: pekka.forselius@4sumpartners.com
W: www.fisma.fi

Germany
DASMA (Deutschsprachige Anwendergruppe fur Software Metrik and Aufwandschatzung)
Mr. Stavros Pechlivanidis
P: +49 172 715 4326
F: +49 211 5426 9771
E: isbsg@dasma.org
W: www.dasma.de

India
NASSCOM (National Association of Software & Service Companies)
Bidhan Kankate
P: +91 40 5536 6111, 6222
M: +98 493 37650
F: +91 40 5536 6333
E: bidhan@nasscom.in
W: www.nasscom.in

Italy
GUFPI-ISMA (Gruppo Utenti Function Point Italia—Italian Software Metrics Association)
Luca Santillo
P: +39 339 7933980
E: luca.santillo@gmail.com
W: www.gufpi-isma.org

Japan
JFPUG (Japan Function Point User Group)
Shigeru Nishiyama (Adviser and technical officer for internationalization)
P: +81 25 2262401
F: +81 25 2271021
E: s02.nishiyama@city.niigata.lg.jp
W: www.jfpug.gr.jp

Netherlands
NESMA (Nederlandse Software Metrieken Gebruikers Associatie)
Ton Dekkers (Vice President)
P: +31 30 6961464
E: office@nesma.nl or tdekkers@galorath.com
W: www.nesma.nl

Spain
AEMES (Asociacion Espanola de Metricas de Software)
Jose Carrillo Verdun
P: +34 91 3366921
F: +34 91 3367412
E: jcarrillo@fi.upm.es or admon@aemes.org
W: www.aemes.org

Switzerland
SwissICT
Thomas Fehlmann
P: +41 44 253 1306
F: +41 86079 332 7056
E: thomas.fehlmann@e-p-o.com
W: www.swisma.ch, www.swissICT.ch

USA
SSCI (Systems and Software Consortium, Inc.)
Cheryl Parker
P: +1 703 742 7310
F: +1 703 742 7350
E: parker@systemsandsoftware.org
W: www.systemsandsoftware.org

USA (International)
IFPUG (International Function Point Users Group)
Dan Bradley
IFPUG Office
P: +1 609 799 4900
F: +1 609 799 7032
E: ifpug@ifpug.org
W: www.ifpug.org

Glossary

When the International Software Benchmarking Standards Group (ISBSG) was formed in 1994, one of the objectives written into the original charter was:

> "To develop the profession of software measurement by establishing a common vocabulary and understanding of terms."

Consistent with this objective, the ISBSG has defined terms and metrics for the purposes of:

- Assisting in the collection of project data into the repository
- Standardizing the way the collected data is analyzed and reported

What follows is a consolidated list of ISBSG definitions and terms used. We hope this will help us to meet our charter. We would appreciate any comments you may have to assist us in meeting this objective.

This glossary is divided into two parts—Terms and Metrics—and provides definitions of terms used in ISBSG documents. This includes project data collection forms, publications, and data releases. Some of these terms refer to items no longer collected by the ISBSG but which may be found in documents or analysis of earlier data.

Where appropriate, these definitions have been adjusted to align with international standards.

Terms

Adjusted function points (AFPs) A software size based on the functional size multiplied by the technical complexity adjustment. The resultant adjusted size is reported in adjusted function points (AFPs) and applies to IFPUG. Each of the following functional size measurement methods has its own mechanisms for moving from its equivalent of UFPs to its equivalent of AFPs, and each uses its own terminology (FiSMA, NESMA, and MARK II).

Application type How the application is meeting the business area requirements. Classification of an application as a type is according to its primary intended use. The following is a list of common application types:

- 3D modeling or automation
- Artificial intelligence
- Catalog/register of things or events
- Customer billing/relationship management
- Decision support
- Device or interface driver
- Document management
- Electronic data interchange
- Executive information system
- Fault tolerance
- Financial transaction process/accounting
- Geographic or spatial information system
- Graphics and publishing tools or system
- Image, video, or sound processing
- Embedded software for machine control
- Job, case, incident, project management
- Logistic or supply planning and control
- Management information system (MIS)
- Management or performance reporting
- Mathematical modeling (finance or engineering)
- Network management
- Office information system
- Online analysis and reporting
- Operating system or software utility
- Personal productivity (for example, spreadsheet)
- Process control
- Software development tool
- Stock control and order processing
- Trading
- Transaction/production system
- Workflow support and management

Architecture The organizational structure of a system and its implementation guidelines. This derived attribute for the project indicates if the application is stand-alone, multitier, client-server, or multitier with web public interface.

Business area type The business area within the organization that the application will be supporting.

CASE (Computer Aided Software Engineering) The use of computer software to assist in completing tasks defined within a system's development life cycle methodology.

CASE may be used across the entire project life cycle or used to assist with specific parts of the cycle. The three categories are

- **Upper CASE** Environment independent and generally used to perform analysis tasks, for example, logical data modeling, process modeling, data flow diagramming, and so on.
- **Lower CASE** Environment dependent and generally used to assist in physical design and construction tasks, for example, physical data base design, code generation, and so on.
- **Integrated CASE** Fully integrating Upper and Lower CASE, for example, logical models are converted to physical models, which in turn generate database tables and code.

Client roles The roles performed by the computers that provide the interface to the software's external users.

Client-server Client-server computing or networking is a distributed application architecture that partitions tasks or workloads between service providers (servers) and service requesters, called "clients."

Client-server description A description of the architecture of the client/server software application or product.

Cost The price paid (either through money, time, labor, and so on) to acquire, produce, accomplish, or maintain the product. The following methods of collecting COST are believed to be the most common:

- **Cost recorded** The daily recording of all *cost* incurred by each person on project-related tasks.
- **Cost derived** It is possible to derive the *cost* where it has not been collected on a daily basis as in *cost recorded.*

Count approach A description of the method used to size the project software. For most projects in the ISBSG Repository, this is the functional size measurement method (FSM method) used to measure the functional size (for example, IFPUG, MARK II, NESMA, COSMIC, and so on). For projects using other size measures (for example, LOC, and so on) this is a short name for that method, and in data releases the size data is not included with sizes measured by an FSM method but rather is in a section "Size Other than FSM."

Data quality rating This field contains an ISBSG rating code of A, B, C, or D applied to the project data by the ISBSG quality reviewers to denote the following:

A = The data submitted was assessed as being sound with nothing being identified that might affect its integrity.

B = The submission appears fundamentally sound, but there are some factors that could affect the integrity of the submitted data.

C = Due to significant data not being provided, it was not possible to assess the integrity of the submitted data.

D = Due to one factor or a combination of factors, little credibility should be given to the submitted data.

Defect A problem, which if not corrected, could cause an application to either fail or to produce incorrect results. There can be three categories:

- **Minor defect** A minor defect does not make the application unusable in any way (for example, a modification is required to a screen field or report).
- **Major defect** A major defect causes part of the application to become unusable.
- **Extreme defect** A failure of some part of an application that causes the application to become totally unusable.

The following information has been collected in relation to application defects both within the project duration (defects and hours per project phase) and after implementation (defects found within the first month of use of the software). Of the following, only defect found, repair hours, and rework hours per project phase are currently collected:

- **Defect found** The number of defects detected in the process in that particular effort breakdown or found within the first month of use of the software after implementation.

- **Defect originating** The number of defects put into the process in that particular effort breakdown only.
- **Defect removed** The number of defects removed from the process in that particular effort breakdown.
- **Repair hours** The effort in hours taken to correct defects detected in that particular effort breakdown.
- **Rework hours** The effort in hours taken in that particular effort breakdown after correction of defects, to return the project to the point reached before defect detection.

Degree of confidence An expression of the confidence the organization has in the data provided, expressed in a range 1–4:

1 = Not confident

2 = Slightly confident

3 = Confident

4 = Very confident

Degree of customization How much customization was involved if the project was based on a packaged software customization.

Development platform Defines the primary software development platform (as determined by the operating system used). Each project is classified as PC, midrange, mainframe, or multiplatform.

Development type

- **New development** Full analysis of the application area is performed, followed by the complete development life cycle planning/feasibility, analysis, design, construction, testing and implementation). Examples are
  - A project that delivers new function to the business or client. The project addresses an area of business (or provides a new utility) that has not been addressed before.
  - Total replacement of an existing system with inclusion of new functionality.
- **Enhancement** Changes made to an existing application where new functionality has been added, or existing functionality has been changed or deleted. This would include adding a module to an existing application, irrespective of whether any of the existing functionality is changed or deleted.
- **Redevelopment** The redevelopment of an existing application. The functional requirements of the application are known and will require minimum or no change.

Redevelopment may involve a change to either the hardware or software platform. Automated tools may be used to generate the application.

- This includes a project to restructure or reengineer an application to improve efficiency on the same hardware or software platform. For redevelopment, normally only technical analysis is required.

Functional size A size of the software derived by quantifying the functional user requirements (that is, what functions the software must support). This excludes quality and technical requirements. This may be reported in different units depending on the functional size measurement method (for example, UFP for IFPUG and NESMA, CFP for COSMIC, and so on).

Functional size measurement (FSM) The process of measuring functional size. Internationally recognized functional sizing methods include IFPUG, NESMA, COSMIC, FiSMA, and MARK II.

Functional size unit (FSU) The unit of measure of size used by a functional size measurement method (for example, function points).

Functional sizing technique The technology used to support the functional sizing process. Certain technologies used in function point counting can affect the count's potential accuracy.

Implementation date The actual date of implementation of the project outcome.

Intended market Describes the relationship between the project's customer, end users, and development team.

Language type Defines the language type used for the project: for example, 3GL, 4GL, application generator, and so on.

Life cycle phases Used in the context of the time at which functional sizing is carried out (*see also* "project effort breakdown").

- **Early life cycle** Up to the completion of the system requirements definition.
- **Mid life cycle** From requirements definition to completion of the technical design.
- **Late life cycle** From technical design specification until after implementation.

Maximum team size The maximum number of people during each component of the work breakdown who are simultaneously assigned to work full-time on the project for at least 1 elapsed month.

Methodology acquisition Describes whether the development methodology (if used) was purchased or developed in-house, or a combination of these.

Methodology used Whether a development methodology was used by the development team to build the software.

Normalized work effort For projects covering less than a full software development life cycle, this value is an estimate of the full development life cycle effort. For projects covering the full development life cycle, and projects where development life cycle coverage is not known, this value is the same as summary work effort.

Organization type A standard classification for the business within which the organization as a whole operates. *The organization is that for which the project has been developed.*

Packaged software customization Where a decision is made to acquire an existing product to provide the major component of the required functionality. *Count only the functionality required by the client.*

Primary programming language The primary language used for the software development: Java, C++, PL/1, Natural, COBOL, and so on.

Productivity The ratio of work product to work effort. In ISBSG documents and products this is given by project delivery rate (*see* entry in "Metrics" section).

Project A collection of work tasks with a time frame and a work product to be delivered. In ISBSG documents and products the work product delivered is software and its documentation.

- **Project start** A client/management decision is made formally/informally to involve information technology personnel in the development. This point is commonly known as the commencement of the "survey," "feasibility study," or "project initiation phase" of the system development life cycle.
- **Project end** The date when the work product is delivered (that is, the project software is placed in production, or the project deliverable is delivered).

Project activity scope Synonymous with the project effort breakdown.

Project effort breakdown Project effort is subdivided in two ways: by project phase and by role of the groups of people involved. For the breakdown by person role, *see* "work effort breakdown." *See also* "life cycle phases." The following table shows the major activities making up each phase:

Project Phase	Possible Phase Components
Plan	Preliminary Investigations Overall Project Planning Feasibility Study Cost Benefit Study Project Initiation Report Terms of Reference
Specify	Systems Analysis Requirements Specification Review & Rework Requirements Spec. Architecture Design/Specification Review & Rework Architecture Spec
Design	Functional/External Design Create Physical/Internal Design(s) Review and Rework Design(s)
Build	Package Selection Construct Code & Program Software Review or Inspect & Rework Code Package Customization/Interfaces Unit Test Integrate Software
Test	Plan System or Performance Testing System Testing Performance Testing Create & Run Automated Tests Acceptance Testing
Implement	Prepare Releases for Delivery Install Software Releases for Users Prepare User Documentation Prepare & Deliver User Training Provide User Support

The following table is provided as a guide for those organizations that use the ISO 12207 standard.

	ISO 12207 Project Steps (Steps in ISO 12207 – Software Engineering Lifecycle Processes)	ISBSG Effort Phase
1	Requirements Elicitation	Specify
2	System Requirements Analysis	Specify
3	System Architecture Design	Specify
4	Software Requirements Analysis	Specify
5	Software Design	Design
6	Software Construct (Code & Unit Test)	Build
7	Software Integration	Build
8	Software Testing	Test
9	System Integration	Test
10	System Testing	Test
11	Software Installation	Implement
12	User Support	Implement

Project elapsed time The calendar period in months between the project start and end including any period of inactivity (that is, end date minus start date).

Project ID A primary key for identifying projects. (These identification numbers have been "randomized" to remove any chance of identifying a company.)

Project inactive time Total time (rounded to whole months) during the project elapsed time, in which no project activity took place. This time, subtracted from project elapsed time, derives the actual time spent working on the project.

Project life cycle A collection of generally sequential project phases whose name and number are determined by the control needs of the organization or organizations involved in the project. A life cycle can be documented with a methodology. (*See also* "project effort breakdown.")

Project work effort All personnel effort that is directed toward the completion of a particular project including out-of-hours effort, whether paid or unpaid. It includes the effort of client representatives in addition to that of information technology personnel.

A good test as to whether an activity constitutes project work effort is to ask the question:

"Would the activity be undertaken if there was no project?"

It excludes nonproject activities such as:

Public holidays
Annual leave
Sick leave
Training (nonproject)

It is measured in whole hours.

Rating *See* entries for "data quality rating" and for "unadjusted function point rating."

Server roles The services provided by the host/server computer(s) to the software application or product.

Software size In general, synonymous with functional size, but the units of software size can be other than that derived by a functional size measurement method, for example, lines of code.

Staged development A decision was made during project planning to develop and implement the application as discrete functional units. This may apply to any development type, but must be preplanned. When an application is developed in total, but implemented over a period of time at a number of locations, it is not a staged development.

Note that where a stage of a staged development changes any functionality delivered in a previous stage, the project should be defined and treated as an enhancement.

- **1st stage** The 1st stage comprises a high-level analysis of the overall application (hence defining the scope of each of the stages and possibly some overall design) and full software development cycle of the 1st stage.
- **Subsequent stage** Subsequent stages of the software development will concentrate on detailed analysis and implementation of another logical part of the overall application.

Summary work effort *See* "project work effort."

Target platform Categorizes the implementation platform, to describe the target environment. Determined primarily by the device the software is implemented into. A project may be classified as:

- Device embedded (DE)
- PC
- Midrange
- Mainframe
- Multiplatform

Time recording methods The following methods of collecting *work effort* are believed to be the most common:

- **Staff hours (recorded)** The daily recording of all of the *work effort* expended by each person on project-related tasks. As an example, a person who works on a specific project from 8 A.M. until 5 P.M. with a 1-hour lunch break will record 8 hours of *work effort*.
- **Staff hours (derived)** It is possible to derive the *work effort* where it has not been collected on a daily basis as in Staff hours (recorded) above. It may have only been recorded in weeks, months, or years.
- **"Productive" time only (recorded)** The daily recording of only the "productive" effort (including overtime) expended by a person on project-related tasks. Using the same example as just used in staff hours (recorded), when the "nonproductive" tasks have been removed (coffee, liaise with other teams, administration, read magazine, and so on), only 5.5 hours may be recorded.

Type of server A description of the server to the software application or product.

Unadjusted function point rating This field contains an ISBSG rating code of A, B, C, or D applied to the functional size (unadjusted function point count) data by the ISBSG quality reviewers to denote the following:

A = The unadjusted function point count was assessed as being sound with nothing being identified that might affect its integrity.

B = The unadjusted function point count appears sound, but integrity cannot be assured as a single figure was provided.

C = Due to unadjusted function point or count breakdown data not being provided, it was not possible to provide the unadjusted function point data.

D = Due to one factor or a combination of factors, little credibility should be given to the unadjusted function point data.

Unphased effort Where phase breakdown of effort is provided, and the sum of that breakdown does not equal the summary work effort, the difference is the unphased effort. Where no phase breakdown is provided, this is the same value as the summary work effort.

User base Data collected about the extent of usage of the system produced by the project. The following classifications are used:

- **User base—business units** Number of business units (or project business stakeholders) serviced by the software application.
- **User base—concurrent users** Number of users using the system concurrently.
- **User base—locations** Number of physical locations being serviced/supported by the installed software application.

Value adjustment factor (VAF) The adjustment to the IFPUG functional size, which takes into account various technical and quality characteristics. The VAF is calculated based on an assessment of the 14 general systems characteristics (GSCs) for an application, and when multiplied by functional size gives the adjusted size.

Web development A derived indicator of whether the project data includes any comment that it is a web development.

Work effort breakdown Data collected about the people whose time is included in the project work effort. *See* also "project effort breakdown." Three levels are identified in the project data collection package.[1] For example, if Level 2 is specified, this means that the data submitted includes the development team and the development team support personnel effort. For the process of collecting and reporting project work effort, the following classifications are used:

- **Level 1—Development Team** Those responsible for the delivery of the application under development. The team or organization, which specifies, designs, and/or builds the

[1] It should be noted that this Glossary reflects the data collection package introduced in 2002. The previous data collection package had four levels of work effort.

software. It typically also performs testing and implementation activities. It comprises
Project Team
Project Management
Project Administration
Any member of IT Operations specifically allocated to the project

- **Level 2—Development Team Support/IT Operations** Those who operate the IT systems that support the end users and are responsible for providing specialist services to the Development Team (but not allocated to that team). Support comprises
Database Administration
Data Administration
Quality Assurance
Data Security
Standards Support
Audit & Control
Technical Support
Software Support
Hardware Support
Information Center Support
- **Level 3—Customers/End Users** Those responsible for defining the requirements of the applications and sponsoring/championing the development of the application. Also the software's end users. The relationship between the project customer and the software's end users can vary, as can their involvement in a software project. It comprises
Application Clients
Application Users
User Liaison
User Training

Metrics

Defect density Measures the quality of software in terms of defects delivered in unit size of software. It is defined as the number of defects per 1,000 functional size units of delivered software, in the first month of use of the software. It is expressed as *Defects per 1,000 functional size units.*

Project delivery rate (PDR) Measures the rate at which a project delivers software functionality to the end user as a factor of the effort required to do so. In ISBSG documents and products it is defined as project work effort (measured in hours) over functional size of the delivered software (measured in functional size units). It is expressed as *hours per functional size unit.*

Project delivery rate is used regardless of how the software is produced because it may:

- Comprise all new software
- Be a modification of existing software
- Use packaged software in part or as the total solution

Speed of delivery Measures the speed achieved by the project team in delivering a quantity of software over a period of time. It is defined as the functional size of the delivered software (measured in functional size units) over the project elapsed time (measured in months) multiplied by the number of people in the project team. It is expressed as *functional size units per person per elapsed month.*

References

Introduction

- "CHAOS Summary 2009," Standish Group, www1.standishgroup.com/newsroom/chaos_2009.php.

Chapter 1

- Dekkers, Carol. "Demystifying Function Points—Clarifying Common Terminology" (IT Metrics Strategies, March 2001). Cutter Consortium, www.cutter.com.
- ISO/IEC 14143-1:2007 Information technology—Software measurement—Functional size measurement—Part 1: Definition of concepts, www.jtc1-sc7.org/.
- IFPUG. *IFPUG Function Point Counting Practices Manual Release 4.3,* Glossary (IFPUG, September 2009), www.ifpug.org.
- Dekkers, Carol. "Navigating the Minefield: Estimating Before Requirements," 2004 Proceedings of EuroSPI conference, November 2004, Trondheim, Norway, www.EuroSPI.net.
- Dekkers, Carol. "Requirements are (the Size of) the Problem" (IT Metrics Strategies, March 1998), www.cutter.com.
- Bundschuh, Manfred and Carol Dekkers. *The IT Measurement Compendium—Estimating and Benchmarking Success with Functional Size Measurement* (Springer, 2008).
- Project Management Institute. *Project Management Body of Knowledge (PMBOK®) Version 4* (Project Management Institute, 2008).

Chapter 2

- Boehm, Barry et al. *Software cost estimation with COCOMO II* (Prentice Hall, 2000).
- ISO/IEC 20926 Information Technology—*Function Point Counting Practices Manual* (ISO/IEC, 2003).

- Finnish Software Measurement Association, FiSMA ry. "FiSMA Specification for ND21," available at: www.fisma.fi/in-english/methods.

Chapter 3

No references

Chapter 4

- ISO/IEC 14143-1:2007 Software engineering—Software measurement—Functional size measurement—Definition of concepts.
- ISO14143-6 Information technology—Software measurement—Functional size measurement—Part 6: Guide for use of ISO/IEC 14143 series and related international standards.
- Morris, Pam. "Levels of Function Point Counting–Version 1.3" (Total Metrics, 2004), www.Totalmetrics.com.

Chapter 5

- "Proposals for project collection and classification from the analysis of the ISBSG Benchmark 8," GUFPI-ISMA SBC (Natale, Santillo, Della Noce, Lelli, Lombardi, Moretto, Ortona), in Procs. International Workshop on Software Measurement, Berlin, 2004.
- Santillo, Conte, Meli. "Early & Quick Function Point: Sizing More with Less," Procs. METRICS 2005, 11th IEEE International Software Metrics Symposium, Como, Italy, 2005.

Chapter 6

No references

Chapter 7

No references

Chapter 8

No references

Chapter 9

- ESTOR (Mukhopadhyay et al., 1992) and ANGEL (Shepperd et al., 1996).

Chapter 10

- PMBOK 2008, Chapter 6.3.2 (Estimate Activity Resources: Tools & Techniques).
- Thomsett, Rob. *Third Wave Project Management* (Yourdon Press, 1989).

- PMBOK 2008, Chapter 6.4.2 (Estimate Activity Durations: Tools & Techniques) Three-Point Estimates.

Chapter 11
No references

Chapter 12
No references

Chapter 13
No references

Chapter 14

- Cockburn, A. *Crystal Clear* (Addison-Wesley, 2005).
- Cohn, M. *Agile Estimation and Planning* (Prentice Hall, 2004).
- Beck, K. and M. Fowler. *Planning Extreme Programming* (Addison-Wesley, 2001).
- International Function Point Users Group (IFPUG). *Function Point Counting Practices Manual: Release 4.3* (IFPUG, 2009).

Chapter 15
No references

Chapter 16
No references

Chapter 17

- ISO14143-6 Information technology—Software measurement—Functional size measurement—Part 6: Guide for use of ISO/IEC 14143 series and related international standards.

Chapter 18
Software Metrics Associations Supporting Functional Size Measurement Method(s):

- International Function Point Users Group (IFPUG): Supports and maintains the IFPUG method (current release 4.3): www.ifpug.org.
- UK Software Metrics Association: Supports and maintains the Mark II method: www.uksma.co.uk.
- Netherlands Software Users Metrics Association: Supports and maintains the NESMA method: www.nesma.nl.
- COSMIC Consortium: Supports and maintains the COSMIC-FFP method: www.cosmicon.com.
- Finnish Software Measurement Association (FiSMA): Supports and maintains the FISMA method: www.fisma.fi.

- ISO/IEC Standardized Functional Size Measurement Methods (FSMM).
- ISO/IEC Functional Size Measurement Framework Standards.

All standards are accessible at www.jtc1-sc7.org/.

Chapter 19
No references

Chapter 20
No references

Chapter 21
No references

Chapter 22
No references

Index

E

F

Q

R

S